PRAISE FOR *A DOCT*

'The word "awesome" has been mu(
in *A Doctor's Sword* fully deserves t
Dr Aidan MacCarthy will take h
Irish Ex

C000200022

'Incident packed ... a gripping saga'
The Irish Times ★★★★

'Wonderful stuff'
Entertainment.ie ★★★★

'Stirring story of endurance and survival'
Irish Independent

'A fantastic story of shocking suffering and extraordinary endurance
and bravery'
Sunday Independent

PRAISE FOR *A DOCTOR'S WAR* BY AIDAN MACCARTHY

'Jaw-dropping account of life as an RAF doctor during the Second
World War' Pete McCarthy, author of *McCarthy's Bar*

'A stranglehold of a book'
Ireland on Sunday

'Quite unlike any other war memoir'
Sunday Tribune

'Riveting, sometimes harrowing tale'
The Village

'An engrossing and uplifting read'
The Irish Times

'A gripping read'
Evening Echo

'Reads like the screenplay of an Oscar winner.'
Irish Independent

Dr Aidan MacCarthy, shortly after joining the RAF.

A DOCTOR'S SWORD

HOW AN IRISH DOCTOR SURVIVED WAR, CAPTIVITY AND THE ATOMIC BOMB

A DOCTOR'S SWORD

HOW AN IRISH DOCTOR SURVIVED WAR, CAPTIVITY AND THE ATOMIC BOMB

BOB JACKSON

The Collins Press

PUBLISHED IN 2017 BY
The Collins Press
West Link Park
Doughcloyne
Wilton
Cork
T12 N5EF
Ireland

First published in hardback 2016
Reprinted 2017, 2018

Photographs courtesy MacCarthy family archives unless otherwise credited.
Maps courtesy Gambit Pictures Ltd and Ronan Coyle.

A CIP record for this book is available from the British Library.

Paperback ISBN: 978-1-84889-320-7

Typesetting by Carrigboy Typesetting Services
Typeset in 13pt/15pt BemboMTStd and Remingtoned
Cover design by Artmark

Printed in Poland by Białostockie Zakłady Graficzne SA

Cover photographs
Front: (clockwise from top) the military sword of 2nd Lieutenant Isao Kusuno (Barry
Murphy); Dr Aidan MacCarthy soon after he joined the RAF; 2nd Lieutenant Isao
Kusuno; (background): Torii gate of Sanno Shrine, Nagasaki (Yamahata); *Back*:
(clockwise from top left): POWs at Camp 26, August 1945; POW officers at Keisen,
August 1945; post-bomb Nagasaki (Wikicommons). *Inside front*: mushroom cloud over
Nagasaki (Wikicommons); *inside back*: ruins of Urakami Catherdral, Nagasaki (Getty).

For Stephanie

Contents

Prologue

In early January 1944, a steam train slowly dragged a line of rusting metal goods wagons north-west through Java towards its destination, Batavia (now Jakarta). Its human cargo of emaciated prisoners of war had been crammed by their Japanese guards into the wagons in the stifling heat. This was two years into their captivity. Starvation, brutality, disease and death had dominated their lives since they became prisoners of the Imperial Japanese Army in March 1942.

Inside the wagons the prisoners gasped for air amid the stink and filth of human waste. They were given no water or food. Eventually the train arrived at Batavia – the doors of the wagons were opened and the prisoners spilled out. The first thing that hit them was the unbearable heat and humidity; their previous camp had been in the mountains where the temperatures were cooler and the humidity less severe.

The prisoners were pushed, beaten and screamed at, counted, made to stand to attention, then counted again. Then they were marched to their destination: Cycle Camp, a former Dutch Army barracks with a terrifying reputation. This was mostly due to its commandant, Lieutenant Kenichi Sonei, who was waiting for the prisoners at the gates, eager to make a lasting impression on the new arrivals. To demonstrate his willingness to use violence, he beat and screamed orders and abuse at guards as well as prisoners. Among them was Aidan

MacCarthy, a young Irish doctor. Many years later, he recalled Sonei's welcome to the prisoners with dread:

> This is a hard place – and you will be treated hard. Any breach of discipline will be punished by a beating. Any attempt at escape will be punished by death.[1]

They were marched through the gates and barbed-wire fences into the camp, lined up under the full glare of the tropical sun, then beaten and counted again. Ordered to stand to attention without moving, they were denied water, use of toilets and rest. Anyone who moved was beaten. After two long hours Sonei, obviously enjoying the power he had over his captives, screamed:

> You are all criminals and you deserve nothing. You are criminals because you are allied to the American bastards who are trying to destroy our glorious empire. In this camp we shall show you the error of your ways. In this camp you will learn how strong and invincible the Japanese people are.[2]

MacCarthy's heart sank. Sonei's body language and pronouncements made it clear that he was insane. All MacCarthy could do was pray for the strength to endure what lay ahead as his life was now in the hands of a maniac. He was a million miles from home.

1

Home

Home for Aidan MacCarthy was Castletownbere, a small fishing town on the Beara Peninsula in west Cork. The peninsula is one of five that extend out into the Atlantic Ocean from the south-west coast of Ireland. Castletownbere lies on the northern shore of Bantry Bay. Its sheltered harbour is protected from the open seas and wild Atlantic storms by the hills of Bere Island, which lies about a mile off the mainland. The scenery is dramatic and the weather erratic. The rugged hills of the Caha Mountains are mostly bare sandstone, dotted with patches of bog. Lower down towards the sea, small fields and clusters of forestry compete for the scarce fertile soil. The climate is mild and temperate due to the effects of the Gulf Stream and during the summer it can seem almost tropical with patches of evergreen trees right down to the shore. But during winter, this jagged coastline on the edge of Europe is battered with numbing regularity by ferocious Atlantic storms.

The MacCarthys lived in an apartment above the family business, MacCarthy's Bar and Grocer on the Square in the centre of the town.

In 1860, Aidan's grandfather Michael began the business when he was thirty-three years old. He was bright, athletic and resourceful. He had decided it was time to take the plunge and open his grocery store on the main square of the town. Over

MacCarthy's Bar in Castletownbere today. BOB JACKSON

time, Michael built up his trade as a general merchant and later began supplying the Royal Navy base in the harbour. Britain had kept a permanent naval presence at Fort Berehaven in Bantry Bay since the failed French invasion attempt in 1796. Michael bought fish locally, which he salted and sold to feed the crews of the large ships that were stationed in the harbour. He later expanded his interests, importing anything that was in demand, including coal and salt. Michael's reputation as a businessman with a sharp mind made him a prominent figure in what was quickly becoming a thriving port in the latter half of the nineteenth century.

At the time, the only places selling alcohol in the town were shebeens – illegal, unlicensed drinking houses serving poitín (bootleg alcohol distilled from potatoes and wheat). One day, a representative from a brewery in Dublin arrived in the town to court businessmen interested in obtaining a licence to sell beer, wine and spirits. He entered McCarthy's General Supply Store and Michael was naturally interested. When his wife, Eileen, a devoutly religious woman, overheard the conversation taking place in the shop she was horrified. This was the era of the pious temperance movement in Ireland and she was not willing to tolerate the sale of alcohol on the premises.[1] She intervened, but Michael had already made up his mind. He barked at her to go back into the kitchen and look after her side of the business so that he could look after his.[2] Soon after, McCarthy's General Supply Store became one of the first licensed premises in the town.

Two years later, Michael's eldest son, Timothy, was born, followed by John D. and Denis Florence (or D.F., as he became known). Like their father, the three brothers were athletic and bright. They nurtured what became a family tradition, which would be continued by future generations: they wrote poetry. Timothy went on to study engineering, emigrated and later became New York City Engineer. John D. studied law, practised as a solicitor and was appointed sheriff of County Carlow. The youngest brother, D.F., stayed at home in Castletownbere, working hard to help his father to run the family businesses.

Eventually D.F. took over from his father and his stature in the town grew with his success, as the business expanded. As the shipping agent of North German Lloyd Liners he was given the title 'Lord High Admiral of Berehaven'.[3]

Early in 1903, D.F. was selected by the town council to give the welcoming speech for the visit of King Edward VII, who was due to arrive later that year at the Royal Navy base, a few miles east of the town.[4] D.F. had to buy a top hat and tails for the occasion. The committee rehearsed the welcome, daily, for weeks before the visit. The event passed off successfully and about a month after the king left Ireland D.F. was offered a knighthood. He declined the offer. The exact reasons for his refusal are unknown, but his now-elderly father, Michael, had lived through the Great Famine, which had decimated the country and particularly the Beara Peninsula in the 1840s. In his old age Michael was known for his ability to recall those dark days with vivid memory. It may have been the attitude of King Edward's mother, Queen Victoria, towards Ireland, at that time, and the fact that D.F.'s father was still alive, which prompted D.F. to decline the knighthood.

As well as developing the family businesses, D.F. also continued to nurture his poetry and had a few of his poems published, including one in the local *Southern Star* newspaper titled 'My Darling Ju'. It was written for Julia Murphy, the daughter of another local businessman. D.F. had fallen in love with her. They married on 4 January 1904, when Julia was twenty-four years old. A year later, they celebrated the birth of the first of ten children, when Eileen was born.

As the town grew, the local clergy decided that a new church was needed. Work began in 1907 and it officially opened in 1911. Craftsmen were brought from as far away as Italy to tile the floors and carve the ornate stone decorations and wood fittings. D.F. saw an opportunity to make use of the skills of the visiting craftsmen, who frequented his bar. He employed them to use the materials left over from their work in the church to renovate his business premises. The Italians tiled the floor, carved new shelves for the bar fixture and crafted a mosaic inscription of 'D.F. McCarthy' on the threshold of the door to the bar.[5] These features can still be seen today.

The MacCarthys had a neighbour, Thomas McCarthy, who was not a relation. To avoid confusion between the two families, D.F. changed the spelling of the family name from 'McCarthy' to 'MacCarthy'. The mosaic on the threshold of

The wedding photograph of Aidan MacCarthy's parents, D.F. McCarthy and Julia Murphy, 4 January 1904.

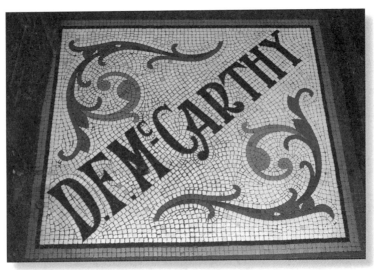

The shopfront and mosaic floor of MacCarthy's Bar. BOB JACKSON.

the pub confirms that up until at least 1911 the family name was 'Mc' instead of 'Mac'.

D.F. was bright, meticulous and hard working. He was also a man of his word and expected the same of others. If someone borrowed something from him he would make a note of it in his ledger and make sure it was returned at the agreed time.[6]

Julia, his wife, was a warm, kind woman and was also a driving force behind the various businesses.[7] They were a popular couple, known for their generosity and for extending credit to their customers. They treated their staff well and their housekeeper, Nora O'Shea, was regarded as one of the family. She was originally from Allihies, 10 miles west of Castletownbere. Every day she cooked for all the staff working for the MacCarthys as well as the family. In her old age, they looked after her until her death.[8]

Like his wife, D.F. was also religious, but his poaching of the Italian craftsmen hired by the Church to renovate his public house may have irked the local clergy. A year after the new church opened, D.F.'s 86-year-old father, Michael, was gravely ill in bed in the apartment above the family business. When it was clear that he was close to death, the local priest was called. The priest arrived but paused at the door, and then he announced that he would not enter because alcohol was sold on the premises. D.F. was outraged. He had no choice but to administer the last rites himself to his dying father. The fact that Michael, a devoutly religious man his entire life, was denied the last rites by the pettiness of the priest had a profound effect on D.F.. He refused to go to Mass for years afterwards and this caused a lot of tension with Julia. After his father's death, D.F. moved his young family into the apartment above the bar and grocer. A year later, Joseph Aidan MacCarthy was born in the family home on the

Ellen Mary (Eileen)
Born Sunday 28th May 1905
at 10.30 a.m.
Sponsors Mrs. O'Shea Aunt, and
Mr. MacCarthy Grandfather

Mary Born Saturday
8th September 1906 at 9 o'clock
Sponsors (Katie & Frank) Proxies
for Meg & Jim MacCarthy Uncle
Died 18th February 1909.

Michael Patrick born.
Sunday 9th February 1908.
at 12.0 midday
Sponsors F Murphy Grandfather
and Mrs. L Sullivan Aunt

James Dermot. Born Sept.
5th 1909. Sunday at 3 a.m.
Sponsors Birdie O'Shea Cousin
and Bernard. Murphy. Uncle.

Sheila Mary (Sheila). Born.
May 12th 1911. Friday 1.30 a.m.
Sponsors Miss Murphy aunt
and Mr. D. Harrington godparents
(the day of the thunderstorm, the
worst we had for years)

The first of ours to be baptised
in the New Church by Fr J O'Connor
(Church opened Xmas 1910)
(Dedicated 30th July Sunday 1911)

Joseph Aidan Born Wednesday
19th March 1913 St Josephs Feast
at 11.30 p.m. 1913
Eugene Sullivan & Eileen Sponcers
Fr Crown baptised him

Finbarr Denis (Barry) Born 12th June 1914
Friday 2.30 a.m.
Sponcers Miss Birdie Harrington
Mr. Dan McCarthy
baptised by Fr Charles Dower.

Aine Maura born 18th Feby 1917
11.30 Sunday night
Frank & Maude Harrington Sponcers
Baptised by Canon McDonnell
Died 24th Nov 1918.

Ita Mary Brigid born 5th November 1918
Tuesday about 3 p.m.
Sponcers Maggie O'Neill &
John Houlahan parish clerk
proxy for Dr Jim Murphy
Baptised by Canon McDonnell

Bernard Humphrey born 20th Aug 20
Friday 3 P.M.
Sponcers Meg & Bernard (uncle aunt)
Baptised by Fr Jn Gilmore

Pages from Julia MacCarthy's notebook showing the dates of birth of her children, including 'Joseph Aidan born Wednesday 19th March 1913', and (*right*) some home remedies.

Recipes

For Bronchitis
Beaten up whites of eggs and a few drops of Brandy.
If the child is very young a little hot water through it
Also Whisky punch about 1 glass to ½pt boiling water + lump sugar —

For Cough on Chest
Equal parts Glycerine and lemon juice, or glycerine and Whisky.

For constipation in Children
Liquid Magnesia or Syrup of Figs.

For Thrush in infants. Wash the mouth with warm water + borax. (or) + Bread Soda, a small pinch dissolved in warm water, to wash the mouth out with.

Breadsoda is very good for burns if not Skinned wet with cold water + apply. If skin is off apply olive oil.

Bread Soda is good for toothache also

A cloth wrung out of [...] water + pat round the [...] relieves croup
The white of an egg [...]

Feast of St Joseph at 11.30 p.m., on 19 March 1913. Like all of their children, D.F. and Julia's sixth child was born at home, delivered by the local doctor.

Julia was a devoted mother who kept a notebook in which she meticulously recorded the details of her children's births and progress through life. Their christenings, holy communions, graduations and other events are also noted in her delicate handwriting. It is clear from her notebook that these sacraments and rites of passage played a central role in the MacCarthy family.

Her notebook details remedies she made, using everyday household ingredients. These were traditional cures that she used when her children were sick. By mixing quantities of bread soda, lemon juice, glycerine, alcohol, fig syrup, egg whites or milk, she could cure anything from bronchitis, coughs and constipation to burns and toothaches. Similar to other mothers in the area, she had no choice but to be resourceful, as there were no pharmacies on the peninsula. These traits may have later had an influence on one of her children pursuing a career in medicine and another in dentistry. Julia's example and influence would serve her son well in later years.

In June 1914, Aidan's brother Barry was born and a month later the Great War began. Castletownbere became a boomtown virtually overnight. Huge battle squadrons began to arrive and filled the sheltered bay between Bere Island and the town. This was naval shipping on a scale the harbour had never seen previously. MacCarthy later recalled that at times the many warships were packed so closely together that you could almost walk across to Bere Island – covering the mile across the harbour – by stepping from one deck to the next. The ships needed vast amounts of supplies – salted fish, bread, meat and coal. Some of the huge vessels burned 2,000 tons of coal in a week and their crews were larger than the population of the town itself. When sailors went on shore leave, anyone selling anything from alcohol to food to rides in jaunting cars could make a small fortune.[9]

D.F. recognised the increased level of demand for bread, so he set up his own bakery. The price of salted fish went up, so he expanded his fish-processing business. When a schooner arrived with its cargo of coal, he employed locals to unload it. The schooner then needed ballast to replace the weight of the coal, so he employed the same men to collect scrap, sold it to the captain and arranged for it to be loaded on board.[10] D.F. was fast becoming one of the biggest employers in the town, with people working in the bar, the grocery, the bakery, on his farms and in the coal and salt stores. He sourced fish from nearby fishing villages, preserved it in salt, and exported as far away as America.[11]

The boom times got even better when America joined the war in 1917. Huge squadrons of American destroyers, battleships and submarines, including the USS *Utah* and USS *Oklahoma*, began to arrive in the harbour. Their mission was to protect Allied ships transporting supplies, as well as over a million American troops across the Atlantic to the battlefields of Europe. The US Navy Bantry Bay Squadron also patrolled the waters between Cork harbour and Bantry Bay.[12] This included the stretch of coast where, in 1915, the RMS *Lusitania* was sunk by a German U-boat, just 11 miles off the Old Head of Kinsale.

Each morning, the crews from the multitude of ships would arrive in the town, placing large baskets in front of the stores and butchers, leaving lists of how much bread, milk, meat and other supplies they needed.

The local Castletownbere steamships *Princess Beara* and *Lady Elsie* were hard pressed, travelling daily from the railhead in Bantry town picking up flour and meal, to meet the unprecedented level of demand in the isolated town.

While the US Navy was based in Castletownbere harbour, Aidan's uncle Timothy McCarthy returned on a visit from New York. He climbed Hungry Hill, a few miles east of the town, and took in the spectacular view across Bantry Bay. As he looked down on the water from a height of over 2,000 feet, he noticed that it was possible to see the American submarines moving through the bay. At sea level, the same submarines were invisible. This led him to devise a system for detecting submarines, which was adopted by the US Navy. (He used a balloon, with an observer, attached to the ship to keep watch for submarines under the water. From the vantage point above the ship the observer could signal when a submarine was spotted.)

During the Great War, Ireland was very much a part of the British Empire. Over 200,000 Irishmen fought in the war and most families had at least one relative in uniform. Almost 50,000 were killed. There was a military convalescent hospital on Bere Island for wounded soldiers and this brought home the horror of what millions were enduring on the front, just a few hundred miles away. When the war ended, with Armistice Day in November 1918, the town erupted in celebration. It lasted for days and MacCarthy recalled seeing drunken sailors falling from boats into the water. In many cases nobody missed them and three sailors drowned during the celebrations.[13]

During the war, Castletownbere had become one of the richest towns of its size in the United Kingdom. For the merchants and businessmen of the town, the jubilation would have been muted.[14] D.F. had prospered, saved his money and added an extra storey to the family home, to accommodate his growing family.[15] But the US Navy would soon be leaving and the Royal Navy presence would return to pre-war levels.

Less than a fortnight after the war ended, tragedy struck, from which prosperity was unable to shield them: D.F. and Julia's daughter Aine died of Spanish flu on 24 November.[16] She was Julia's 'angel' and just a few months short of her second birthday.

By the time the Great War broke out, Julia had given birth to seven children: Eileen, Mary, Michael, James, Sheila, Aidan and Barry. Aine was born in 1917, followed by Ita, and then their youngest, Bernard. Mary also died in childhood, shortly before her third birthday.

As life in Castletownbere returned to its pre-war rhythm, the only sources of income, apart from supplying the navy, were fishing and farming. Access to the rest of the country was only possible via a dirt road or by sea and in this uncertain environment, the fortunes of the area began to wane.

These were turbulent times in Ireland. The general election of December 1918 saw a rise in support for nationalist political parties seeking to create an independent republic. Sinn Féin, the more radical nationalist party, won most of the seats and, within a few months, the War of Independence was under way.

The young Aidan would not have been concerned by the events unfolding around him as he made his first holy communion in 1919. In September of the following year, at the age of seven, he began attending the Dominican Convent boarding school in Cabra, Dublin. He travelled with his sister Sheila who was just two years older than him. At the time, this was an epic journey through what was becoming an increasingly violent period. They boarded the *Princess Beara* steamship at the pier in Castletownbere, which took them to Bantry. From there, they travelled on the West Cork Railway to Cork city, where they transferred to the Dublin train. They were met by a taxi on arrival in Dublin, which took them to the school in Cabra.

The MacCarthy children in 1917 (l–r): Michael, Eileen (holding baby), Sheila and Aidan (aged four).

(L–r): Jim, Eileen (holding baby), Michael, Sheila and Aidan. Barry is seated in front.

The MacCarthy brothers (l–r): Barry, Michael (seated), Jim (standing) and Aidan (aged six).

It was a long and precarious journey, as many of the bridges had been blown up and roads sabotaged. The journey to or from school in Dublin could sometimes take two to three days. In addition, they had to travel through west Cork where the fighting was the most intense outside of Dublin. On one occasion, in February 1921, the West Cork Railway was ambushed at Upton and eight civilians, as well as a number of British soldiers, were killed.[17] Such was the level of danger that Aidan and Sheila would often stay with their uncle John D. in Carlow to avoid the long and, potentially fatal, journey home to Castletownbere.

In December 1921, the War of Independence concluded with the signing of the Treaty that established the Irish Free State. Castletownbere was one of the three Treaty Ports where the Royal Navy were allowed to maintain a presence while all other British forces left the Free State. The signing of the treaty led to the shorter Civil War (1922–23) fought between Free State and Anti-Treaty Republican forces, who regarded the terms of the treaty a betrayal of the Irish Republic proclaimed during the Easter Rising of 1916.

During the Civil War, travelling in west Cork was made more complicated by the level of anti-treaty activity in the area. MacCarthy described travelling by road from Castletowbere by car: Free State officials in the town would issue the driver with a travel pass. By the time the car had driven 10 miles east along the peninsula to Adrigole there was usually an armed Republican checkpoint. The Republicans would tear up the Free State pass and issue a new one. When the driver got to Bantry, the same process was repeated in reverse and Free State soldiers issued a new pass. This was repeated the entire way to Cork and there was still no guarantee that the journey would be completed, because the roads and bridges were usually sabotaged.

Meanwhile, the nuns at the Dominican Convent had their own conflict to deal with when trying to discipline their unruly boarder from west Cork. Aidan was constantly getting in trouble, so it came as a relief to them when he was transferred to the prestigious Clongowes Wood College in County Kildare in September 1923. He was ten years old and later described his new school as the Irish Catholic equivalent of Eton. Unusually for an Irish school at the time, but much to Aidan's delight, Clongowes had a swimming pool.

Shortly after he had left the Dominican Convent, his younger sister Ita arrived in Cabra as a boarder. Unsure of herself in the unfamiliar surroundings, she got a frosty reception from the nuns. There was one who had a particular dislike of her older brother. Ita was immediately asked 'are you related to that boy Aidan MacCarthy?'[18] Knowing full well that the nuns read every letter and message that was sent in and out of the convent, Aidan wrote to his sister from his dormitory in Clongowes. He deliberately did not seal the envelope just to make sure it would be read. The letter enquired 'is that bitch of a Reverend Mother, Sister _____ still there?' When the nun in question read the letter, she demanded an apology.

Aidan inherited his father's stubborn streak. He was a strong-willed child and regularly got into trouble with his parents. On one occasion, when he was eight and at home in Castletownbere on holidays, he had an argument with his father. D.F. shouted at him, telling him to behave himself. Aidan felt that he had been wronged and went into a rage. Marching out of the house onto the square, he rolled up his sleeves and screamed for his father to come out 'and fight me like a man'. A crowd soon gathered in the square to see what all the commotion was about. The sight of the rowdy young son of such a pillar of the community as D.F. MacCarthy was a scandal in the rural town. Aidan's

Aidan MacCarthy, aged twelve.

reputation as an independent-minded, rebellious youngster was beginning to grow.

D.F. and Julia were well liked in the town and were regarded as a decent, generous family. Christmas was always a huge event in the MacCarthy household. The table was extended, with up to twenty guests sitting around the dinner table. The food was prepared in the kitchens downstairs and brought upstairs to be carved and served on the huge dining table. They would invite local people who had no family to share Christmas with them.

Their success in business was won through hard, honest work and D.F. and Julia instilled these values in their children. Later in life, their daughter Eileen was known for supporting families all over the peninsula with food, money and clothing.

For Julia and D.F., there were two reasons for sending their children to boarding school. It meant the children were well educated and it also allowed them to focus on running the family businesses. Their aim was not to make money for its own sake but to pay for their children's education and provide for their future. As a result, the children only experienced home life during their holidays.

In later years, MacCarthy described life on the peninsula during the 1920s and 1930s as 'difficult'. It was 'an isolated community … we had a hard existence; we had to fight'. Electricity did not arrive in the town until 1952. Up until then, the only source of lighting was gas or paraffin oil lamps. The roads of the peninsula were not tarmacked until the mid 1950s and the town square was full of potholes. After fair day, when traders and local farmers arrived to sell their goods and animals, the streets, footpaths and even the shop windows were so covered in mud and cow dung that they had to be washed down. Travel by land was difficult and the only real contact with the outside world was by sea: 'it was that or face an awful thirty mile road on horseback … you could never get radio into this part of the world because of the mountain ranges. Nothing came through.'[19] As a result, the main source of entertainment during the long bleak winters was playing cards so from the age of five, the MacCarthy children gathered in the lounge upstairs above the bar where they learned to play cards. There was always a prize of some sort to be won. MacCarthy later realised that, considering his own upbringing, it was no surprise that Irish people had such a reputation for gambling.

Growing up in a harbour town, he had learned to swim at an early age and was always hanging around the pier. On one occasion, a local fisherman who was short of money knocked the young Aidan off the pier, picked him out of the water and brought him home. When he presented the child he had saved from certain drowning to D.F., he was thanked and rewarded with a few drinks on the house. When this occurred on a more regular basis, D.F. became suspicious and the dunkings came to an end.

As MacCarthy grew up, he developed a reputation as one of the most powerful swimmers in west Cork. He got the chance to demonstrate his prowess in front of a home crowd at the annual regatta – one of the highlights of the year in Castletownbere. It takes place every August bank holiday Monday. Huge crowds gather, many returning from abroad to meet up with friends and family and soak up the atmosphere. It is not as genteel a festival as the name suggests, with more trawler races than yacht races, and pints of stout rather than the G&Ts expected at a yachting regatta.

The MacCarthy family all got involved: D.F. was on the committee and the children competed in the various events. A local newspaper account of the 1926 regatta describes D.F. firing the starting gun for the boat races. Sheila beat her eldest sister, Eileen, in the rowing competition, while the thirteen-year-old Aidan won the hundred-yard swimming race. Ita recalled that when he was swimming, all you could see was water splashing everywhere: no apparent style or technique, just raw strength and determination.[20] Over time it became a foregone conclusion that he would win any race in which he competed. Informal betting was always a feature of the regatta competitions and Aidan managed to make money by backing himself as the winner. He would even go so far as to give his opponents a few yards' head start to lengthen the odds and, on occasion, he would slow up to narrow the winning margin.[21]

He recalled in later years that it was always the prayer of the committee that the day would be pleasant enough to get the events started on the water, while the prayer of the publicans was that the rain would fall to keep the people in the pubs a little longer. Either way, things worked out well for D.F.[22] But with the excitement, celebrations and alcohol, the regatta often turned raucous. At times the gardaí would lock up local troublemakers early in the day to save themselves the bother of doing so later on, when the revellers had a few drinks on board.

When he returned home for the summer holidays from boarding school, Aidan, along with his brothers and friends, organised two local water polo teams. They bought a ball, made floating goalposts and travelled to compete at other regattas in Bantry, Kilmacillogue, Kenmare, Baltimore and elsewhere in west Cork and Kerry. The owners of the pubs grew to hate them because, as soon as it was announced that the match was about to start, the pubs would empty out as the crowd rushed to the pier to place bets and get a good view of the game.[23] Little did MacCarthy know how much this experience in cold water and, in particular, his strong sprint which gave him an edge over competitors, would stand to him later in life.

Another major influence on his youth was the religious faith that Julia instilled in all her children from an early age. This stayed with MacCarthy all his life. Like his brothers, Aidan served as an altar boy at the nearby Church of the

Sacred Heart on the main street. But with so little time at home they wanted to be outdoors during their holidays and would always leave it as late as possible before making their way to the church. Once they heard the bells ring they would race along the laneway behind the house to get there just in time.

Although faith was important to MacCarthy, he was not afraid to challenge the orthodoxy of the Church. One morning, during summer holidays as a teenager, he saw a crowd gathering for a wedding at the Protestant church on Main Street. At the time, the Catholic Church forbade its members from entering a Protestant church. Out of curiosity and mischief, MacCarthy sneaked in and sat at the back of the congregation. After the ceremony, he accompanied the guests to the reception, enjoying the food and hospitality and remaining enigmatic about his invitation. When he arrived back in MacCarthys, he announced where he had been and gave a full report about the ceremony to his siblings and the customers in the bar. Julia adored her son but when she found out that he had disobeyed the Church 'there was war'.[24] MacCarthy disappeared and petitioned his aunt Kit to sound out his mother. Julia was furious and wanted him go to the priest and explain what he had done, knowing full well that the priest would find out sooner or later. But he refused. This was typical behaviour for the young Aidan who was 'always in trouble'.[25]

While studying at Clongowes he began playing rugby and was also a member of the debating team. He was obviously very bright and found time to keep up the tradition of his father and uncles by spending a lot of his spare time writing. This was mainly prose but at the age of sixteen wrote his first poem:

Gold

The yellow illustrious metal
That has turned the brains of man,
Has wrought more desolation
Than the devil ever can.

Men have toiled and men have suffered,
Bartered health and life and grace,
For this cold enticing magnet,
With hell's glitter on its face.

Towns were emptied, homes abandoned
When it's 'panned' from river sand.
Then the rush of men to dig it
From without a frozen land!

It has lured men from God's service
Who ne'er counted cost nor pain
And has made the slaves of Mammon,
And his dross of earthly gain.

They have passed into the shadow,
And in lonely graves lie cold,
They gave up their lives and heaven,
For a metal men call gold.

This poem shows an incredible level of maturity and awareness at such an early age and seems to reference the plight of the many from the Beara Peninsula who travelled to Butte, Montana and on to the Klondike gold rush after the copper mines closed in nearby Allihies during the late 1800s.

ABOVE Clongowes' graduation class of 1930. Aidan MacCarthy is seated, centre front.
BELOW Aidan MacCarthy's UCC registration card for 1935.

SESS.
1935-36.

Name (in full) — Joseph Aidan Mac Carthy
Date and Place of Birth — 19th March 1913 Castletown Berehaven
Faculty and Year (1, 2, 3, etc.) — Medicine IV year.
Name and Date of last Univ. Exam. passed — II medical March 1935
(Matric or First Med...etc.) — Expect III in Dec.
School or College last attended before University — Presentation College Cork
Name of Father (if dead, say so) — Denis F. Mac Carthy
Home Address — The Square - Castletown Berehaven
Cork Address — 33 South Mall
12 St. Patrick's Terrace, Magazine Rd.
Name and Address of Guardian (if any) —
Date — 4th October 1935   Religion — Catholic

MICKEY & BYRNE

25

In June 1930 he left Clongowes at the end of fifth year – a year before completing his secondary education.[26] He transferred to Presentation Brothers College in Cork city before attempting the university matriculation examination. This would allow him to study medicine at University College Cork (UCC). He stayed with his sister Sheila in Cork city, partly because his parents believed that, under her watchful eye, he had a better chance of passing the Irish language exam. This was a prerequisite for entering most universities at the time but there may also have been another reason for his change of schools. The MacCarthy family finances had taken a further hit in the years following the economic crash of 1929. Shipping, trade and exports were down and Castletownbere was not the busy harbour it had once been.

To make matters worse, D.F. was landed with a huge tax bill from Revenue. Julia calmly took control and sent D.F. to America for a year to visit his brother Timothy in New York. This gave her power of attorney over the family businesses and allowed her to sort out the family's affairs.

MacCarthy was now closer to home, staying in Sheila's apartment at 33 South Mall in the centre of the city. She was a domestic science teacher and her apartment was just a short walk from her brother's new school on the Mardyke. When enrolling he was asked two questions: 'are you prepared to work hard?' and 'do you play rugby?' He answered 'yes' to both, was accepted and spent the following year preparing for the matriculation exams. When he entered the oral Irish test he had learned off a series of phrases about the public transport system in Cork city. No matter what question he was asked in Irish, he was going to repeat what he had learned. As the examiner began the conversation MacCarthy butted in and rattled off his phrases. Somehow, he managed to pass the exam and was accepted into first year at the medical faculty at UCC.

A few months later, in October 1931, he began his studies to become a doctor.[27] He obviously made an impression as a strong swimmer during his first year at university because the following year, he was selected as a member of the Munster relay team that took on a Welsh team on Thursday 8 September. The visiting team was renowned and included international and Olympic swimmers. The venue was the Municipal Baths on the banks of the River Lee, close to the university. MacCarthy, nineteen years old at the time, was the last of four to compete. His opponent was the 26-year-old Olympian P. Currie.[28] MacCarthy finished just a foot behind his competitor and the race set a new record for the venue.[29]

A week later, University College Dublin (UCD) visited the same venue to compete in an annual intervarsity competition. A huge crowd gathered to see the main event, a relay race between four-man teams from UCC and UCD. The race was one of the most competitive and exciting 'squad' races ever witnessed at the Baths. In the final leg MacCarthy took on UCD's star sprinter H.P. Dockrell. On the return sprint they were level but MacCarthy managed to touch the finishing bar a fraction of a second before his competitor. He won the race for UCC and beat the record set the week before.[30]

One summer when he was home on holidays from university, Aidan, his mother, aunt, a family friend and a number of children went out into the harbour in the family's wooden motorboat. They were on their way to have a picnic near Dunboy Castle when, a few hundred yards from the shore, the boat's engine caught fire and stopped working. The boat was slowing to a halt and would soon sink as the fire began to spread. MacCarthy quickly grabbed the rope used to tie the boat to the pier, secured it round his waist and jumped into the water. He swam as fast as he could towards the shore dragging the burning boat behind him. Eventually, he felt the rocks under his feet, secured his footing and pulled frantically on the rope, dragging the boat closer to the shore. At the moment the boat touched the rocks, the engine suddenly dropped out of the back of the boat, leaving a gaping hole. The engine had burnt through the wood. Water surged in and the smouldering boat lay on the shore, half sunk in the water.

Had he hesitated or not made the right decision, it was generally accepted that there would have been a number of drownings that afternoon. He was already showing several of the characteristics that would stand to him in later life – the ability to make the right decision in a crisis, the confidence to act quickly and the physical strength to pull it off.

This story added to his popularity in the town, which was mostly due to his personality, attitude and willingness to help people. On another occasion when he was home on holidays, one of the locals approached MacCarthy and asked him if he would 'stand' for him as best man at his wedding the following morning. He had not expected to be asked but was happy to oblige. Word went out around the town to find a waistcoat for him. But because of his barrel chest it was impossible at such short notice to find one to fit. Someone came up with a solution – they cut the back of a waistcoat and laced it up like a corset. While MacCarthy was standing on the altar the following morning, he could feel the laces unravelling as he wriggled around trying to keep them in place. He managed to get through to the end of the ceremony without too many people noticing his discomfort.

He played rugby throughout his time at UCC and was blind-side flanker on one of the most successful teams the university

The formal team photo of the 1936 UCC team. Aidan MacCarthy is third from left in the back row. UNIVERSITY ARCHIVES, UCC, IMAGE © TOMÁS TYNER

Standing: T.K. Murphy (Hon.sec), P. Coffey M.E. (Hon.treas.), A. McCarthy, D. Herlihy, D. O'Loughlin, D. Tierney, Dr McGrath (President), J. Russell, J. Reade, J. Buckner, Dr. D. Barry (Vice Pres.), J. Downey, B. Comm. (Vice Pres.). *Seated*: C. Dillon, C. Clohessy, B. McKenna, C. Moloney, D. Bergin, B. O'Brien (Captain), D. Lane, J. Laycock, B. Collins, J. McDermott, D. O'Riordan. *On Ground*: R. O'Driscoll. B. McClement. *Cups*: Munster Senior League Shield, Munster Senior Cup, Bateman (Ireland) Cup, Cork Charity Cup and Musgrave Cup. *Insets*: W. O'Sullivan, J. O'Connor.

Aidan MacCarthy's UCC
Rugby cap 1932–33

Munster Cup final, 1936: UCC RFC versus Cork Constitution.
Aidan MacCarthy is third from right. UNIVERSITY ARCHIVES, UCC,
IMAGE © TOMÁS TYNER

ever produced. They won the Munster Senior Cup in 1935 and retained it the following year. Also in 1936 they beat University College Galway by seventeen points to nil to win the prestigious Bateman Cup for the first time. In the same year they won the Munster Senior League Shield, the Cork Charity Cup and the Musgrave Cup. In 1937 they won the Munster Senior Cup for a third time in succession.

With so much going on between swimming, rugby and socialising MacCarthy was not regarded as the most diligent student, especially by his siblings. Somehow he managed to find the time to become a prominent member of the Cork Little Theatre Society.[31] His studies suffered and each year he usually had to repeat a number of exams. When he was home on holidays, his parents would send him to a small room on the flat roof of the house to study. It had been built for his brother Jim who had contracted tuberculosis around 1925, at the age of sixteen. Jim had been sent to South Africa for a year and when he returned home he lived on the roof as the fresh air would help his recovery. When MacCarthy used it as a study, he took every opportunity he could to slip off the roof, out the back lane and down to the water.

MacCarthy completed his medical training at the North and South Infirmaries in Cork city. His sister Ita recalled how, at one stage, he wrote to his parents asking them to send him more money. He told them that his training required that he 'entertain the nurses' as it was 'part of becoming a doctor'.[32] She had followed her brother to UCC in 1935, where she also stayed with their older sister Sheila. She was one of just two women studying dentistry at the university that year, an indication of how progressive D.F. and Julia were. A few years later, when Ita qualified, she was one of the first female dentists in the country.[33]

The UCC medicine graduation class, 17 January 1939. Aidan MacCarthy is in the front row, far right.

In December 1938, MacCarthy finally completed his medical exams; it had taken him seven years to complete his studies. It should have taken him six but he had to repeat his final year.[14] He was twenty-five years of age and would be conferred a few weeks later. His parents were hugely proud that their son had completed his studies but were unable to congratulate him because he disappeared in Cork for days, celebrating. The parents became anxious, so D.F. sent his eldest son, Michael, on the train to bring the young doctor home. Several days passed and there was still no word from either of them so, exasperated at this stage, D.F. sent his other son, Jim, to bring the pair home to Castletownbere. MacCarthy got on very well with his parents in general, but at times he tested their patience.

As he graduated he was making the final transition to adult life. The innocent days of his youth were coming to an end. This was at the same time that Europe was also coming to the dreadful realisation that war was again on the horizon. The dark clouds of conflict, on a scale that had not been seen for a generation, were gathering. Fascism was on the rise. In March 1938, Nazi Germany annexed Austria.

In Ireland, the Free State government was anxious to secure the return of the Treaty Ports. In the looming conflict these would be of huge strategic importance in a war that the new state was anxious to avoid being dragged into. In September 1938, the forts and batteries in Fort Berehaven were handed over to the Irish Free State. As the Royal Navy sailed out of the harbour for the last time, the sound of their hooters was a death knell for the isolated town. For many in Castletownbere, including D.F., this was a dark day: with the loss of business, the town faced decades of decline.

When the Free State took over Fort Berehaven, the huge steel oil-storage tanks, which had been built when the ships had changed from coal- to oil-powered engines, were no longer needed. These were immediately sold as scrap metal, which was bought by the Japanese government. They sent engineers to cut down the steel tanks, which were then shipped to Japan from Furious Pier.[35] At the time, Japan was busy scouring the world for steel for its arms industries and within a few short years the reasons for this demand would become apparent. MacCarthy later joked ruefully that this was the same steel that was fired at him as bullets in the jungles of Java and Sumatra.

In October 1938, while MacCarthy was studying for his final medical exams, German tanks rolled across the border into the Sudetenland in Czechoslovakia and by March the following year the rest of the country had been taken over.

Aidan MacCarthy's graduation photograph, 17 January 1939, when he was aged twenty-five.

Now that MacCarthy had completed his education, the fledgling doctor needed to gain experience in medical practice. The problem was that his family were west Cork merchants and had no connections in the closed shop of Irish medical practice. Nepotism was a way of life in a profession where positions in surgeries were passed from father to son – 'the dispensaries were all spoken-for'.[36] With no prospects for employment at home, around 50 to 60 per cent of newly qualified Irish doctors had to take the boat to England to earn money and gain experience.[37] Having spent Christmas 1938 at home MacCarthy was packing his bags early in the new year. He was conferred on 17 January 1939, from which time he would be known as Dr Aidan MacCarthy.[38] He set off for London two weeks later.

War in Europe

When Aidan MacCarthy arrived in London, a sprawling city of over 8 million people, he was immediately drawn to the energy and excitement of the place. At the time, the population of the Irish Free State was just under 3 million. For a young man from a rural fishing town in the west of Ireland, London could not have been more of a contrast. He had enrolled in a post-graduate course at Hammersmith Hospital but was enjoying himself so much that it was not long before his money ran out, so he applied for locum work in south Wales.[1] He travelled to the mining valleys where he treated patients in communities that had been decimated during the decade following the Great Depression. He was appalled by the general poverty, and after his many years of study, was shocked at the amount of work he had to do for very little pay.[2] He decided to return to London and started working at a 'shilling surgery' in East London. These were surgeries set up to provide cheap healthcare for the poorest of the poor. The patients he treated were so filthy that after their five-minute consultation, they dropped the shilling fee directly into a bowl of antiseptic liquid to avoid transmitting skin diseases.

As the months wore on, MacCarthy came to the realisation that he was drifting. More ominously, war was the topic of every conversation. It was on the radio and in the newspapers.

By March 1939 Germany had taken over all of Czechoslovakia and it was obvious that Poland was next. British Prime Minister Neville Chamberlain had announced a guarantee to the House of Commons that Britain would stand by Poland in the event of a German invasion. Throughout the summer, the tension grew. The summer had started cooler than usual but, perhaps reflecting the political atmosphere, thunderstorms began to gather as August came to a close.

MacCarthy followed the developing political situation with interest. He was twenty-six and, like many men his age, he felt that the looming war offered the possibility of excitement and adventure. On Friday 1 September Hitler's forces invaded Poland. Nature seemed to mirror the turbulent historical events that were unfolding and thunderstorms were heard again over London throughout the following day. At 11.15 a.m. on the morning of Sunday 3 September, Chamberlain declared war on Germany. Later that day MacCarthy bumped into two Cork doctors with whom he had studied at UCC. They were in a similar situation: between locum jobs and becoming disillusioned with the banal reality of general practice. Although the dangers were obvious, the fervour of war offered an outlet for the pent-up frustration of a generation of young men. They sat in the garden at the centre of Leicester Square and argued the pros and cons of joining the services. They decided to go for a drink. The conversation continued around the bars of the West End until they ended up in a nightclub in the early hours of the morning. By that stage they had made up their minds that they were going to join the services but had not yet decided which one.[3] First they eliminated the army. The choice, then, was between the navy and the air force. MacCarthy was unsure which to choose. He was a good swimmer but he really wanted to fly. Eventually they asked one of the hostesses to toss a coin

Two photographs of
Dr Aidan MacCarthy,
taken soon after he
joined the RAF.

and it came down on the side of the Royal Air Force (RAF). The outcome of this simple coin toss would reverberate through the rest of his life. Had it fallen on the side of the navy, who knows what might have happened? MacCarthy perhaps might not have survived or maybe he would have avoided what was to come.

The following morning three very hung-over young doctors presented themselves to the Air Ministry 'to make enquiries'. The officials were so glad to see them that they were interviewed, medically examined and accepted in time for them to have the first drink in the pubs when they opened at half past eleven.[4] On 4 September 1939 MacCarthy began his career with the RAF as a Flying Officer on a Short Service Commission for three years.[5] His first posting was to a training wing on the south coast of England where they were preparing incoming pilots for progression to the elementary flying school. Because war had just broken out, the RAF was desperate to train vast numbers of pilots and navigators as quickly as possible.

France had also declared war on Germany, and was followed by Australia and New Zealand. A week later both South Africa and Canada joined what was now becoming a world war. The fate of Europe and the world was sealed, as was MacCarthy's. The next six years would define the rest of his life.

Britain went on a war footing and, initially, a blackout was imposed in the country (to protect against enemy bombers, no lights were allowed at night). The public expected heavy bombing but when this did not materialise, the conflict entered a strange period known as the 'Phoney War'. Almost immediately after the declaration of war, thousands of British soldiers began crossing the Channel with the British Expeditionary Force. They took up positions in France but there were no major clashes with German forces until December.[6] During the first few months, the war at sea intensified while the war on land and in the air seemed to languish.[7] As time dragged on, MacCarthy, stuck on an RAF base on the south coast of England, was desperate to escape the 'woolly confines of seaside suburbia' and become involved in the struggle overseas.[8] At that time he had a feeling, which he would later rue: he was actually looking forward to the war.

In December 1939 he was delighted to receive his first overseas posting when he was allocated as Senior Medical Officer to No. 14 Group in northern France. It says something about the shortage of experienced personnel at the early stages of the war that just a few months after joining the RAF MacCarthy had become a Senior Medical Officer. Perhaps more telling is the fact that when he arrived in France he could not find No. 14 Group. Nobody could tell him where it was based. He spent the next two weeks wandering around northern France by train until eventually he bumped into officers from No. 14 Group by chance at a hotel in Arras. They brought him to their headquarters and bombarded him with questions about where he had been, to which he 'remained tactfully enigmatic'.[9]

At that time, the Allied forces in northern France were distributed from west to east, alternating between British and French zones. The French troops in No. 14 Group's area did not inspire much confidence, being comprised mainly of reservist veterans of the First World War.

To make matters worse for MacCarthy and his medical staff, at the outset of the war the French army had ordered 80 per cent of their civilian doctors to join the services. This left huge areas of rural France, including villages and small towns, with no medical cover apart from a few nurses.[10] As a result MacCarthy had to act as general practitioner for entire villages as well as providing medical cover for his own troops.

The language barrier was his main difficulty and a lack of maternity cover made a bad situation almost impossible.

Whenever he was called to deliver a baby he rushed into a situation where the woman had usually already gone into labour. With no knowledge of the mother's medical history or the baby's position in the womb, MacCarthy had no choice but do his best to deliver the infant. His assistant midwife was his medical sergeant who was trained to treat battle wounds and, prior to serving in France, had never even seen a baby being born. MacCarthy was very proud of the fact that, in spite of the circumstances, they delivered twenty healthy French babies without losing a single mother or child. He was also delighted to participate in the local tradition of lavishing gifts of food and wine on the delivery team and opening a bottle of champagne immediately after the birth. On one occasion they were given a horse, which they kept tethered outside their makeshift surgery. But the practicalities of feeding and stabling the animal under the circumstances soon forced MacCarthy and his midwife to sell it.

Bored by the constant waiting, the thousands of young men posted in France occupied themselves with drinking and the company of prostitutes. MacCarthy had the unenviable task of making weekly visits to the local brothels in the cold light of day to examine the prostitutes in order to limit the spread of venereal diseases. He hated the depressing atmosphere of these houses, with the overpowering smell of stale booze, cigarettes and cheap perfume. The madam of the house was always terrified that he would find an infected case and close down her business so he was always met at the door with a bottle of champagne to mollify his medical opinion.

Still the Phoney War dragged on and on. An unusually heavy snow began to fall during late December. Far away in Castletownbere the Christmas table was set for the usual sitting of as many as twenty people, but there was no place for Aidan. It was the first Christmas he spent away from home.

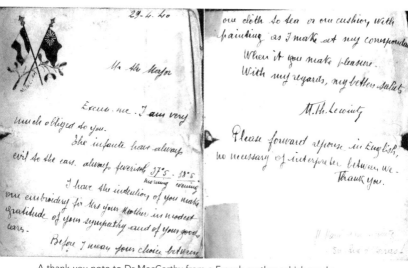

A thank-you note to Dr MacCarthy from a French mother, which reads:

29 April 1940

Mr Dr Major,

Excuse me, I am very obliged to you.
The infante have always evil to the ears. Always feverish. 37°5 C (morning),
38°5 C (evening).
I have the intention of you make one embroidery for Mrs your mother in
modest gratitude of your sympathy and of your good cares.
Before I mean your choice between one cloth to tea or one cushion, with
painting as I make out my correspondence.
When if you make pleasure,
with my regards, my betters saluts,
M.th. Lecoiutz

Please forward response in English, no necessary of interpreter between
we. Thank you.

M. Marie Thérèse Lecouitz
50 Rue D'Arras

The snowfall continued early into the New Year. Roads were blocked throughout northern France and troops were confined to their barracks and mess halls. MacCarthy described this two-week period as one of intense boredom. He passed the time playing cards, reading books, writing letters, smoking, and being constantly drunk on champagne and cognac.[11] He discovered that one of the uncomfortable side effects of drinking copious amounts of champagne was bad piles. This left a lasting impression and it took him many years to develop a taste for it again.

The snow eventually melted but still the Germans waited on their side of the border. The war continued in this surreal state as MacCarthy celebrated his twenty-seventh birthday near Arras on 19 March 1940.

With the arrival of spring, the weather began to improve and the diesel engines of the Nazi war machine were heard again in the distance. In April, Denmark and Norway fell to Hitler's forces. All along the western borders of Germany, Allied forces braced themselves for the impending onslaught. Security in northern France became more of a concern because of increased activity by Nazi saboteurs and sympathisers operating in the area. Occasionally the drinking water of Allied troops was poisoned. Fountain pens were often found around their accommodation. These 'souvenirs' would explode when unscrewed, causing loss of fingers and even hands.[12] MacCarthy described one occasion where a pilot on an airfield near Lille noticed that a nearby windmill moved its sails whenever planes took off. When French military police searched the windmill they discovered two men and a woman. They were dragged out and shot on the spot.

The Phoney War had by now dragged on for eight months. MacCarthy and his comrades were desperate to see some action.

On 8 May, the Germans obliged with air attacks. This was the initial 'softening up' by air before their blitzkrieg or 'lightning war' was unleashed.

Two days later Hitler made his move. German tanks rolled simultaneously into Holland, Belgium, Luxembourg and France in a carefully coordinated plan by Hitler's generals to make it seem as though their main focus was on Holland and Belgium. It was intended to draw the British and French forces north from their positions on the Franco-Belgian border. The Germans then planned to attack into northern France. Their fast-moving tanks would rush westwards along the Somme valley to the Channel coast. Once they reached the coast, the British and French forces would be trapped, cut off from the rest of France and with their backs to the sea.

MacCarthy and his comrades were unaware of the giant trap into which they were being led by the nose. The scale of the German attack caused complete confusion in the Allied ranks and was typified by a lack of coordination between the various nationalities. Soon, all effective communication had collapsed. While the British were desperate to secure serviceable airfields in Belgium for the RAF, Belgian forces were busy destroying the same airfields. MacCarthy ruefully recalled the French Air Force's love of pomp as they lined their aircraft in neat symmetrical rows in front of the hangars. Low-flying German pilots gleefully bombed and strafed the French planes to pieces before they even had a chance to get off the ground.[13]

A week after the attack began, No. 14 Group was ordered to relocate to Belgium. MacCarthy and his unit packed up and made their way across the border, exactly as the Germans had planned.

Almost immediately after they had unloaded their supplies in Belgium they were ordered to return to France. Soon after they arrived back at their base near Arras, they were told that all future British and French Air Force operations would be carried out from across the English Channel – from bases in the UK. MacCarthy felt like they were useless pawns on a vast chessboard being moved about by a highly incompetent chess player.[14]

Complete chaos was unfolding across the front. The next order MacCarthy received was that his unit would be flown back to the UK from the city of Boulogne on the coast, 80 miles to the north-west. He was instructed to take the ground staff of around 150 servicemen there. He assembled a convoy of about fifteen vehicles, including an ambulance, a water carrier, a fuel truck, troop carriers and five motorcycle outriders. As they headed west towards the town of Saint-Pol-sur-Ternoise they passed nervously through an ammunition park with stacks of bombs, shells, ammunition and petrol drums every 20 yards on either side of the road. He expected to be bombed at any moment by the enemy planes that seemed to be constantly overhead. The town was in pandemonium: the streets were choked with refugees, and businesses were being looted by drunken French soldiers. As MacCarthy's convoy struggled through the clogged streets, the mayor begged them for food. MacCarthy gave him a full day's rations for 300 men on condition that he clear a route through the town.

Since the outbreak of the war French civilians had been restricted to their local area and required a transit pass to leave. With the sudden German advance, panic-stricken French civilians were ignoring these orders and fleeing before the advancing enemy in their thousands. As they flooded south they blocked roads, causing bedlam for the French and British forces as they attempted to move in the opposite direction to engage the enemy. The Germans were quick to exploit the confusion. They infiltrated soldiers amongst the refugees to engage in

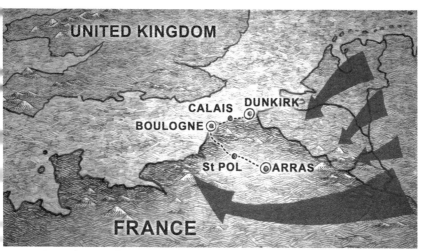

Map of France showing the route of MacCarthy's convoy to Dunkirk, with arrows indicating the German advance.

sabotage and reconnaissance. MacCarthy heard of bizarre incidents, including one where a 'nun' was seen urinating in a standing position. When challenged, 'she' was found to have a sub-machine gun under her habit and was shot.[15]

As MacCarthy's convoy pushed on towards Boulogne and the hope of escape, they approached the small town of Montreuil. Suddenly one of his motorcycle outriders came racing back with terrifying news: they were travelling parallel to a German tank column which was moving west. The Germans were just a mile or two south of their position. This was a battalion from the Austrian 2nd Panzer Division. MacCarthy and his unarmed motley convoy of medical staff and ground crew could not have encountered a more mobile and lethal enemy.

With the enemy already to the south and rapidly moving west, the trap laid for the British and French forces was closing.

MacCarthy ordered his column to swing north, heading for the coast by the shortest possible route. On the way they diverted to an airfield in the hope of flying back to the UK, but the squadrons had long since gone and the remaining RAF personnel were busy destroying every abandoned plane and piece of equipment. In a bizarre example of the lack of coordination between the two allies, a French Air Force ground crew was fitting an engine to a bomber at the opposite end of the same airfield. MacCarthy ordered his men to hurry further up the coast to Boulogne. They found the town defended by battalions of Irish and Welsh Guards who had been landed to defend the port. The convoy arrived at the docks, desperately hoping to get back to England by sea but every ship had already left. As medical staff, fitters and riggers, they were not going to be much use in defending the town so the Guards regarded them as 'unwanted mouths' and told them to move on to Calais, some 20 miles further up the coast. Shortly after leaving Boulogne they learned that the road they had just travelled was cut off by tanks from the 2nd Panzer Division as the first German divisions reached the coast. The trap had closed and they were now cut off from the rest of France.

As they struggled north, their progress was again slowed by crowds of refugees streaming south from Calais. The refugees were unaware that they were fleeing into the arms of the Germans. The scenes of chaos were exploited by Luftwaffe pilots, who machine-gunned and dive-bombed the crowded roads. MacCarthy decided not to stop and try to provide first aid: 'there were too many casualties to be dealt with and we were desperately short of medical supplies'.[16] His main concern at that stage of the war was with saving himself and the 150 men under his command.

Eventually they reached Calais where they were met by a captain from a British tank regiment who told them that the town was being prepared for a siege. He requested that anyone in their convoy with a rifle to 'please step forward and be ready to defend the town'.[17] MacCarthy, anxious to get to Dunkirk just 25 miles away, argued with the captain that his men were technical airmen who were not trained for combat. Unfortunately, some of the men had picked up rifles during their escape and now found themselves desperately trying to get rid of their 'souvenirs'. Luckily, the captain was distracted, lost interest and waved them on. They hurried off as quickly as they could towards Dunkirk and possible escape.

The German planes relentlessly dive-bombed the road and soon it became impassable. It was badly damaged by bomb craters and as the fighting increased in ferocity, the tide of refugees began to swell. MacCarthy had no choice but to order most of the vehicles to be abandoned except for the ambulances and the water carrier. His group continued on foot and eventually reached the beach at Gravelines where they collapsed, exhausted, and fell asleep. Being just a few miles from Dunkirk, they set off early the following morning and soon arrived at the western edge of the town. It was 'a burning shambles in which thousands of French and British troops and civilians wandered in a daze'.[18] MacCarthy reported to a temporary HQ to offer his medical services but was told the nearby hospital was fully staffed. Soon afterwards he was ordered to take his men to a designated spot on the beach. He was appalled by the lack of organisation and discipline there. The main harbour had been blocked by ships sunk in an air attack the previous day, which was slowing the evacuation. His men were ordered by an RAF officer to dig individual foxholes in the sand. This would be their only protection from the bombing and machine-gun strafing of the German planes. A direct hit would kill them instantly. It was there that MacCarthy learned the truth of the saying, 'there are no agnostics in foxholes.'[19] The petrified men chain-smoked, cried, sang and prayed while others sat in numb silence as they waited for the next attack. Every now and again, a man driven mad by fear would try to make a break for it and get away before his unit was called for evacuation. A military policeman would shoot him dead on the spot.[20]

MacCarthy's unit waited there for three long days and two terrifying nights before receiving orders to move. The fact that RAF personnel were being evacuated infuriated the nearby British Army soldiers because it seemed there were no RAF fighters protecting the beaches from the German planes. RAF fighter squadrons were, in fact, engaging the Germans further inland, slowing their advance, but the soldiers did not know that.

As RAF personnel were being evacuated from the beach, their British Army comrades randomly opened fire on them and MacCarthy was lucky not to have been shot by his own side. Due to the shallow nature of the beach, the group under MacCarthy's command filed along a long jetty that brought them to deeper waters where they waded out till the water was chest-high and got on small boats which took them to larger destroyers.[21] The destroyers then transferred them to passenger ferries waiting further out at sea. They boarded a former Larne-to-Stranraer ferry, shattered but relieved. When they were about 2 miles off Dunkirk there was panic among the evacuees when they heard a loud explosion below decks.[22] They scrambled to the side where a gaping hole was visible on the waterline: the ship had been torpedoed by a German submarine. The quick-thinking ferry captain ordered everyone on the ship to move over to the opposite side, which tilted the ferry at an angle that kept the hole clear of the water. Luckily, the weather was calm as the ship limped its way back across the English Channel.[23]

MacCarthy quickly set up a surgery on board, converting the dining room into an operating theatre. The tables which were fixed to the floors were used as operating units. As he began treating wounds he was initially surprised to discover British .303 bullets from Lee Enfield rifles in many of the wounded. He had expected to treat shrapnel wounds from German bombs. This confirmed that British troops on the beaches of Dunkirk had fired on their own soldiers and airmen either in panic, out of jealousy or possibly rage at the fact that they themselves were not being evacuated.[24]

Discipline on the beach in Dunkirk was eventually established and roughly 338,000 were evacuated, but were forced to leave most of their equipment and weapons on the beach.[25] It became known as the 'Miracle of Dunkirk'.

3

Bomber Command

The evacuees arrived back at Dover, demoralised and worn out. They were confined to barracks for a number of weeks and cross-examined about their experiences in France. Some got into serious trouble for deserting their units in the final chaotic days of the evacuation.

In June 1940 news from the war front could not have been worse. On 25 June, France formally surrendered and was added to the growing list of countries that were now part of Hitler's Third Reich. This included Austria, Czechoslovakia, Poland, Denmark, Norway, Holland, Belgium and Luxembourg. Mussolini saw an opportunity to be on the winning side and declared war against Britain and France on 10 June. The Soviet Union and the United States would not declare war for at least another year. In Europe, Britain stood alone against a German war machine that seemed unstoppable. It was expected to be the next to fall.

In July, MacCarthy was assigned as Squadron Leader at RAF Honington, a Bomber Command station on the Norfolk/ Suffolk border. Many of the Bomber Command stations were located in this area because it was closer to Germany and on the same longitude as Berlin. The shorter distance reduced the amount of fuel required, which meant more bombs could be carried on board.

The base at Honington operated Wellington bombers, which flew night raids over German cities. Bomber Command staff were divided between aircrew, who flew the bombing missions, and ground crew who stayed at the base. Medical staff were ground crew and did not fly on bombing raids. Instead, they worked through the night, waiting for the aircrews to return so they could treat the wounded. Their lives were far removed from the media spotlight on the dashing heroics of the Spitfire and Hurricane aces of RAF Fighter Command.

Life for medical staff and ground crew was safe and routine when compared with aircrew who ran a gauntlet few could expect to survive. The odds were stacked against airmen and most were dead before completing their 'tour' of thirty missions. Just 30 per cent of aircrew could expect to survive their first tour of duty. Of those who volunteered for a second tour of duty, only 10 per cent would survive. It was impossible for a pilot to calculate the odds because so much depended on chance, rather than skill. As crew became more experienced they avoided some problems, but the evidence also shows that many became psychiatric casualties after doing a number of missions because the stress on mind and body was so great.[1]

They faced enemy fighter aircraft, engine failure, bombs dropped by their own squadron from higher altitudes and flak shells launched by anti-aircraft defences. These burst into thousands of razor-sharp metal shards that ripped through aircraft, destroying engines, fuel tanks and crew.

It was rare for a crew to complete a mission unscathed. The average age of Bomber Command airmen was twenty-two. They could expect to survive their new career for just a matter of weeks. Casualties among Bomber Command were among the highest of any Allied fighting force: over 55,500 lost their lives.

Aidan MacCarthy (*third from right, back row*) with ground crew at RAF Bomber Command, Honington.

As damaged aircraft limped home, MacCarthy's task was to treat the crew injured by flak, burns, bullets, hypothermia and crash landings.[2] Crews were often so badly wounded that their blood and remains had to be hosed out of the fuselage.

When a plane was lost on a mission, the entire crew would most likely never be seen again. The crew of another bomber might witness what happened but often the missing plane would simply disappear. There was little room for sentimentality and funerals were rare because bodies were usually not recovered.

MacCarthy spent the following year at Honington. The war situation continued to deteriorate as Germany added Yugoslavia and Greece to its tally of conquered European countries in April 1941.

The following month an incident occurred at Honington that MacCarthy would never forget. One night in early May he was keeping up his familiar vigil in the control tower, waiting to be alerted if any of the returning planes were in trouble. At about 2 a.m. on a dark cloudy night a Wellington bomber was returning to base from a night raid on Germany with a young pilot on his first mission as captain. At this stage of the war all the bomber airfields in the area had grass runways. A blackout was in operation so ground crew would light flares known as 'chance lights' in sequence and the pilot landed over these. The flares were put out as soon as the plane had passed.[3] In order to get six aircrew and the plane safely home a pilot essentially had to land the plane in the dark with very little visual aid. This placed immense stress on the pilot. On this night everything went wrong for the normally efficient but inexperienced young airman.[4]

In the control tower, MacCarthy heard the pilot's voice crackle over the radio. He was frantically communicating that both the red and green indicator lights on the instrument panel were on. This meant that his landing gear was down but he did not know whether it was locked or not. He was afraid the undercarriage would collapse on landing. A full emergency procedure was set in motion and the fire engine went into action. MacCarthy rushed to the ambulance. As it sped to where the plane was expected to crash land, he prayed aloud whilst clinging to the rails.

The control tower staff instructed the pilot to approach at a faster speed than usual and to be prepared to take off again if the landing gear showed signs of collapsing. Suddenly a German fighter plane was spotted on the pilot's tail. The control tower warned him not to turn on his lights as he prepared to descend. This was a familiar tactic – German night-fighter planes would follow bombers back to base and shoot at them when they turned on their lights for landing. The German pilot realised he had been seen, knew the game was up and veered away but the panicked young pilot's confidence and sense of timing were already shattered. He came in over the boundary fence too fast, made a half-hearted attempt to land and then opened up the engines in a desperate effort to gain speed and take off again. As MacCarthy watched from the ambulance, he saw the plane bank to the right. The wing clipped the top of a bomb dump at the end of the runway, tearing the top from it. The plane cartwheeled. The cockpit was sheared off and burst into flames. The burning plane landed on top of the bombs, which did not explode, initially.[5]

In his account of the events MacCarthy displays genuine self-effacing modesty, describing himself as having the 'good luck' to be awarded a medal for what happened next.[6] The reality was far more terrifying and his actions far braver than the credit he allows himself. RAF records describe the event with more detail.[7]

There was a delay in getting the fire tender to the crash site because of the barbed-wire entanglements around the bomb dump. When the rest of the rescue team (who had been issued with fireproof asbestos suits) saw the burning plane lying on a bed of hundreds of 500 lb bombs, they fled. Without hesitating, MacCarthy and the driver of the fire tender, Group Captain John Astley Gray, climbed into the burning aircraft (without asbestos suits) and started pulling out the crew trapped inside.[8] By the time they managed to drag the first man to safety, the fire had spread from the starboard tanks to the cabin and on to the port tanks.[9] They managed to pull three of the crew out alive but the bullets, incendiaries and flares were beginning to ignite due to the flames. Then the fuel tanks erupted in flames. In spite of this they climbed back in and attempted to rescue the pilot who was trapped at the end of the fuselage. They dragged him as far as they could but his harness still held him to the burning aircraft. Before they could release him another petrol tank burst into flames. They had to give up. When they finally staggered clear of the burning plane, MacCarthy recalled that 'only a heaven-sent miracle had preserved us'.[10] By this stage the bomber station was being evacuated in case the bomb dump exploded. This eventually happened but, as MacCarthy described, 'the top bombs blew the others away so there wasn't a massive explosion'.[11] John Gray had suffered severe burns to his head and uniform. MacCarthy also received burns to the head. Despite the injuries and stress he had endured, MacCarthy refused to rest until everything possible had been done for the wounded. When he was asked later if he thought about what he was doing he said:

> I don't think I'd have done it if I had really appreciated what was going on ... you did it automatically, I think that you get beyond the stage of being scared to being terrified and when you're really terrified I don't think you can really think.[12]

For this action, both men were awarded the George Medal, the highest award for bravery in the British services for non-combat personnel. The medal was presented to MacCarthy by King George VI at Buckingham Palace in November 1941. MacCarthy was the first person from the Irish state to receive the award. On the night before the presentation his commanding officer made him responsible for three young bomber pilots

10th Sept 1941.

Sir,

On behalf of the Sergeants Mess, R.A.F. Station,
Honington, we should like to convey the congratulations
of all to you on the very well deserved award of
the George Medal. We are very proud and gratified
to hear of this award, which proves once more the
splendid spirit of the personnel at Honington.

I am, Sir,

Yours respectfully,

E Hawkridge   W/O.

Chairman Mess Committee.
Sergeants' Mess.

Squadron Leader J.A.McCarthy,
R.A.F. Station,
HONINGTON.

A letter of congratulation, dated 10 September 1941, from the Honington
staff to Aidan MacCarthy on being awarded the George medal.

who were being awarded Distinguished Flying Crosses. He was
given instructions to 'get them to the Palace – sober – properly
dressed – and on time'.[13] Unsurprisingly, the group had a night
of celebrations when they arrived in London but MacCarthy
managed to get the last one to bed around 3 a.m. The following
morning he rounded them up after a few hours' sleep and

as instructed, he got them sobered up, dressed and to the palace.[14] They joined a large group of policemen and policewomen, as well as others waiting to be awarded various decorations. The large conferring room was packed with relatives and friends waiting for the royal summons to begin. There were no toilets and after the celebrations of the night before the four RAF men desperately needed to relieve themselves. The call of nature became more insistent but they were told that if they left the room they would not be allowed back in under any circumstances. Nature, however, could not be denied so they edged their way to one of the enormous windows overlooking the palace gardens. They drew aside the red velvet curtains, raised the lower part of the window and watered the royal flowerbeds below.[15]

MacCarthy's heroics made an impression in the RAF and, after being awarded his medal, he was told to go to the War Office in London where he received orders to join a special overseas mission as Senior Medical Officer. He

GEORGE MEDAL FOR CORKMAN

An aircraft which tried to land at an aerodrome, with the under-carriage retracted, crashed into the main bomb dump and burst into flames.

Group Captain John Astley Gray, D.F.C., and Dr. Joseph A. MacCarthy entered the blazing 'plane and extricated two members of the crew who were trapped.

By this time the fire had spread, and ammunition, incendiaries and flares were burning in the wreckage, while numerous explosions erupted from the tanks. Despite this an attempt was made to rescue the pilot, who was dragged clear, but his harness still held him to the burning aircraft. Another petrol tank burst, and flames spread to such an extent that any further rescue attempts were impossible.

Gray and MacCarthy were assisted by two other officers, who both displayed great courage. Gray received severe head burns and his uniform was destroyed, but he continued until overcome by fumes. MacCarthy suffered facial burns.

Last night's *London Gazette* announces the award of the George Medal to the two heroes.

Group Captain Gray was born in [?]9, at Maiden Newton, Dorchester. [?] home is at Saxmundham, Suffolk. [?]erved in France in the R.N.A.S. [?]e last war, and won the D.F.C. [?]aliland in 1920.

[?]MacCarthy was born in 1913 at [?]en. County Cork, where his

The report of Aidan MacCarthy's heroism at Honington, which appeared in *The Irish Times* on 10 September 1941.

was delighted because after spending over a year at Honington, he would finally have the opportunity to see some real action overseas. On 8 December 1941 he joined 266 Wing and boarded HMS *Warwick Castle* at Gourock on the west coast of Scotland. They were carrying almost a squadron and a half of

Spitfires and Hurricanes in the holds, and were accompanied by an aircraft carrier that was carrying an active squadron of Spitfires.[16] 266 Wing was a fully independent fighter wing with mobile airfields, medical, administration and repair staff as well as aircrew. They were initially tasked to work in cooperation with the Free French forces in North Africa. Their mission was to protect the channel between Sicily and North Africa and keep the supply routes open to Malta, Crete and the North African coast.[17] German aircraft stationed in Sicily as well as German and Italian naval forces were attacking British convoys operating in the Mediterranean as Britain desperately held on in Egypt.[18] The British needed to maintain control of the Suez Canal because, if lost, it would have cut Britain off from its territories in India, the Pacific and Australasia. The Germans at the time were poised to gain the upper hand in North Africa as the famous General Erwin Rommel had arrived in early 1941. He was beginning to develop his reputation as the 'Desert Fox', inflicting heavy losses on British forces in Libya and Egypt.

As the convoy left the Clyde estuary, MacCarthy was unaware that around the world the war was moving into a new phase and he was about to take his place in its tragic story. The previous day, Imperial Japanese forces had launched simultaneous surprise attacks on the US Pacific Fleet based in Pearl Harbor, invaded the Malay Peninsula, attacked Hong Kong and began bombing Singapore. The Japanese onslaught suddenly changed the war from a conflict centred in Europe to a world war.

The United States declared war on Japan on 8 December 1941 and, in response, Hitler declared war on the United States three days later. In the frozen vastness of Russia, Soviet forces were at that time beginning to push back the German army from the outskirts of Moscow. Germany had invaded the Soviet Union in June that year and the fighting had quickly descended into a race war of unspeakable savagery.[19] By December, the German advance had been halted and would never again penetrate as deep into the Soviet Union.[20] History would later record that the tide of the conflict had finally begun to turn against Germany and its allies, but this would not be clear for some time.

In one of the many coincidences of MacCarthy's story, two of the US Navy battleships sunk by the Japanese at Pearl Harbor were the USS *Utah* and USS *Oklahoma*, which had both been stationed in Castletownbere as part of the Bantry Bay Squadron during the First World War.[21] D.F. would have done regular business with the crews of these huge ships and their custom helped pay for the upper floor of the MacCarthy family home.

Another event that week would later play a part in MacCarthy's story: the US had just begun secretly researching the atomic bomb. The Manhattan Project was given the green light on 6 December 1941.[22] As he braced himself against the cold December winds of the Irish Sea on the deck of HMS *Warwick Castle*, MacCarthy was unaware that he was setting out on a four-year journey that would take him, time and time again, to the brink of starvation, despair and death.

The convoy sailed towards North Africa but as the Japanese blitzkrieg in Asia gained momentum they were redirected down the west coast of Africa. MacCarthy spent Christmas Day 1941 sweating in Freetown harbour in Sierra Leone before the convoy was sent first to Cape Town and then to Singapore. They were to assist in the frantic attempt by the Allies to stem the advance of the Japanese sweeping down the Malay Peninsula towards Singapore. The British and their allies were rattled at that stage. The Japanese advance showed no sign of slowing. If anything, they were becoming more emboldened and every effort to stop them so far had failed. It was inconceivable that the island fortress of Singapore could fall. However, the bastion of British imperialism in Asia had been left vulnerable through a combination of arrogance and complacency. Its giant 15-inch diameter guns all pointed out to sea; there were hardly any fortifications covering the northern side of the island, which faced the Malay Peninsula.[23] This was precisely the reason the Japanese had chosen to attack the island state from the landward side. The British were aware that, if the 'Pearl of the Orient' fell, it would mean the end of their Empire.

4

War in the East

In order to appreciate what MacCarthy and his comrades were about to face, it is important to understand the context in which the war in Asia had arisen and how a very specific cultural perspective on surrender had evolved.

According to Japan's Shinto religion, Emperor Hirohito was a direct descendant of the sun goddess Amaterasu and his lineage dated back over 2,600 years, making the Empire of Japan the oldest nation state in existence.[1] This, combined with the mythology that its people were also of divine origin, led to the belief that Japan had a divine mission to rule the world.[2]

When the Emperor Meiji was restored to power in 1868, this brought to an end the era of the shogunate (a hereditary military dictatorship), which had maintained an isolated feudal society for more than two centuries. With the Meiji Restoration Japan went through a rapid process of modernisation in the latter half of the nineteenth and early twentieth centuries. The population exploded and Japan eyed the technology and industry of Western powers as a means to develop its own military prestige and influence.

Shinto was adopted as the state religion and creation myths were used to develop an emperor cult. A year after the restoration, the Yasukuni Shrine was founded in Tokyo by the Emperor Meiji as a place where the soul of anyone who died in the service of the Empire of Japan would be enshrined and worshipped as a god.

In 1882, Emperor Meiji issued a holy order or 'Rescript' to Japanese soldiers and sailors demanding absolute loyalty and discouraging participation or interest in politics. The code of Bushido, which literally translates as 'the way of the warrior', was incorporated as the moral basis of the army and navy. This was a set of principles which Samurai warriors had been expected to observe since the Middle Ages.[3] This indoctrination of Japanese soldiers was part of their basic training and on the surface seemed noble in its exaltation of bravery, loyalty and sincerity. But it also instilled unquestioning obedience and taught them that the greatest honour was to die for the Emperor and that to choose surrender over death would bring eternal shame upon them, their parents and wider families.[4]

The 'way of the warrior' encouraged soldiers to look on death as something to be embraced; 'duty is weightier than a mountain, while death is lighter than a feather.'[5] If a Japanese soldier allowed himself to be captured, then he and his family would be disgraced forever.

Vast numbers of willing and able subjects would be needed to fulfil Japan's destiny to rule. The military took control over the compulsory education system and began a process of reform. This brought the Bushido code into the classroom in a relentlessly martial environment where children were moulded into future soldiers through saluting, marching, drills, dress code and rifle training. Teacher education was militarised to such an extent that a visiting Irish academic, Lefcadio Hearn, observed in 1890 that a graduating teacher 'leaves the college a trained soldier'.[6] The Imperial Rescript on Education, issued in the same year, exhorted all Japanese students to be ready to devote themselves to the national interest, should the need arise.

Conformity was absolute and individualism was suppressed; generations of Japanese were bred to believe they were destined to serve not just the state, but their divine emperor. Military training of schoolchildren then progressed seamlessly into adulthood through conscription and the development of a network of reservist organisations throughout the country.[7] The overall aim of the Meiji government had been to militarise the population – and it worked. Discipline in the army was maintained through beatings, cultivating the celebration of extreme brutality in its soldiers and imbuing violence with sacred significance.[8] The late nineteenth and early twentieth centuries in Japan were defined by a rise in ultranationalism and militarism with a symbiotic link to the state religion of Shintoism.

Japanese soldiers were under the command of their god, the Emperor. They were the Soldiers of God, the Knights of Bushido of the Order of the Rising Sun.[9] Another innovation of the Meiji restoration was that the army rank and file began to be recruited from all classes of society.[10] The bearing of arms had previously been the preserve of the samurai, a powerful military caste, but now every Japanese could become a samurai. Military service – embodied by the powerful symbol of the sword – could be attained by anyone if they were willing to die for the Emperor. Then they would be worshipped as a god at the Yasukuni shrine.

Throughout this period the military were constantly in the ascendancy, they manipulated imperial rescripts to suit their agenda and eventually silenced any opposition by the Cabinet, Diet (national assembly) or the Emperor's advisers.[11] A law, introduced in 1900, decreed that the army minister would be a serving army officer. This gave the military control over the Japanese government because it could bring down the government by declining to nominate a minister.[12]

Japan began the twentieth century with an unexpected military triumph over Russia in 1905.[13] During the previous half-century, the country's population had been growing at a rate of 400,000 per year and had almost doubled to 58 million. The rate was increasing to such an extent that the year 1917 saw a record-breaking population increase of 800,000.[14]

Japan had few natural resources and was struggling to support its people. On its doorstep, other 'inferior' Asian nations were wealthy by comparison: to the south, Malaya produced most of the world's rubber and tin, while Sumatra and Java had rich oilfields. Japan's military leaders envied the prestige of European powers in the region and regarded their template of colonial expansion as a natural progression. The British and the Dutch had been the dominant colonial powers in East Asia for centuries. America had more recently joined this enterprise, exploiting people, resources and land under the guise of progress and stability. This inevitably led to resentment and gave rise to nationalist movements throughout the region, from Burma to Hong Kong. Japan sought to harness this resentment under the banner of the 'Greater East-Asia Co-Prosperity Sphere'. They presented themselves as the liberators of Asian peoples from their European masters. The reality would prove to be quite different as the resources coveted by the European powers were sought by the Japanese for exactly the same reasons, and the methods used by the Japanese were far more violent.

In 1926 Emperor Hirohito ascended to the throne as the 126th Emperor of Japan, becoming head of the oldest hereditary monarchy in the world, a lineage dating back to 660 BC. He rarely acted independently and relied on the advice of government and court officials.[15] The militarists used this as a justification for what they claimed as their duty – to protect the Emperor from advisers who sought to mislead him. In 1936, a group of officers led a revolt and killed a number of government ministers, arguing that they had been motivated by concern for their Emperor and country.[16] Hirohito was furious. His military officers had effectively mutinied against his authority and all of his trusted retainers were dead. The militarists had eliminated several key proponents of constitutional monarchy and demonstrated their ruthlessness against those who would challenge them. Direct and indirect opposition ended and the militarists had effective control over Japan from February 1936.[17]

The belief that it was Japan's divine right to rule over Asia became government policy. Japan had annexed Korea in 1910 and began its expansion into China in 1931 with the invasion of Manchuria where it set up a puppet state. In 1937 China was again invaded to expand Japanese influence and secure resources, resulting in the brutal Second Sino-Japanese war that cost millions of lives in an orgy of violence that is well documented.[18] Japanese officers were 'blooded' and had to pass 'trials of courage' where they were inducted into the respect of their peers by participating in barbaric acts of cruelty and violence.

In 1940 a Japanese politician said that as 'the sole superior race in the world' it was the nation's duty to 'lead and enlighten' its inferior Asian neighbours.[19] The military had been preparing to fulfil this destiny for decades. With expertise borrowed from Western powers, it had patiently developed a strong, technologically advanced military, which was now bearing fruit. By the time Japan unleashed its power against Western interests in December 1941 the national psyche had been harnessed towards this destiny. A lethal combination of military control over government and education, a living god as a head of state and a complicit state religion created a fertile ground for legitimising the coming expansion of the conflict. War was presented to the population as an inevitable response to the aggression perpetrated against Japan by its enemies. There could be no greater honour for a Japanese soldier than to die for his Emperor. In the years that followed, this honour was bestowed on an entire generation of Japanese who firmly believed that what they were doing was a justified and divine course of action against a demonised enemy.

Less than a year before Japanese soldiers began their takeover of South-East Asia, they were again explicitly instructed to commit suicide rather than surrender. This was made clear in a handbook of field service ethics, the *Senjinkun*, issued to Japanese soldiers on 8 January 1941. This ordered them to:

> meet the expectations of your family and home community by making effort upon effort, always mindful of the honour to your name. If alive, do not suffer the disgrace of becoming a prisoner; in death, do not leave behind a name soiled by misdeeds.[20]

As the Japanese attacks began on Pearl Harbor, the Malay Peninsula, Hong Kong, Singapore and elsewhere, Emperor Hirohito issued another divine Imperial Rescript on 8 December 1941. In it he professed Japan's desire 'to cultivate friendship among nations and to enjoy prosperity in common with all nations' (disregarding the reality in China and elsewhere) and accused Britain and America of obstructing by every means Japan's 'peaceful commerce':

> The situation being such as it is, Our Empire, for its existence and self-defence has no other recourse but to appeal to arms and to crush every obstacle in its path.[21]

Japanese troops landing on the Malay Peninsula were given a pamphlet titled 'Read This Alone – and the War Can be Won'.

It was a handbook on jungle warfare and tactics that also provided guidance on how their enemy should be regarded (in no less racist and derogatory language than similar Allied training manuals). It urged the reader to regard himself 'as an avenger come at last face to face with his father's murderer … Here at last is the man whose death will lighten your heart of its brooding anger. If you fail to destroy him utterly you can never rest in peace.'[22]

* * *

As they sailed across the Indian Ocean and along the equator on board HMS *Warwick Castle*, MacCarthy's excitement grew. The heat became more and more intense and at last, he thought, he and the rest of his unit would finally see some *real action*. Temperatures below deck were unbearable so they brought their mattresses on deck and slept in the open.[23]

They approached the Sunda Strait between Sumatra and Java. It was becoming clear they would be too late to unload at Singapore, assemble their planes and become an effective fighting force. Japanese artillery was already bearing down on the city, firing across the causeway as the island was being prepared for a siege. The convoy was diverted to the port of Batavia (now Jakarta) in Java where they disembarked, unloaded their supplies and assembled the planes.[24] It was now that they realised the planes had not been fitted with tropical cooling systems as they were originally destined for North Africa. They improvised with a locally produced cooling system but the speed and agility of the planes was reduced.[25]

Indonesia was known at that time as the Dutch East Indies, and was a target for the Japanese because they needed oil.[26] In particular, the Sumatran oilfields produced high-octane fuel, which was ideal for aviation.[27] An embargo had been placed on

67

Japan by America, the Netherlands and Britain in 1941 with the intention of curtailing its military expansion. This meant that Japan's oil supply was running out. Capturing Java and Sumatra would provide access to the fuel required for further expansion. With Dutch East Indies secured, a surprise invasion of Australia was possible. The Allies were aware of this and frantic efforts were being made to bring Australian forces to the north of the country to defend against what, at that time, seemed like an imminent invasion.

Now that they were back on dry land in Java after a journey that took almost two months, MacCarthy was delighted to be able to stretch his legs again and sample some of the pleasures of Dutch colonial life. One of the highlights of this was the Harmony Clubs, which offered accommodation, bars, restaurants, billiards, bowling greens and baths.[28] The facilities were open twenty-four hours a day and some even had swimming pools. As he swam in tropical luxury he was far removed from the murky river water of Cork Municipal Baths or the cold salt water of west Cork where he had honed his competitive swimming skills.

The exotic atmosphere was soured by the news that Singapore was about to fall. But being one to make the most of a bad situation, MacCarthy enjoyed the local hospitality on offer. Years later he would recall the taste of Dutch gin mixed with crushed ice and fresh lime juice, and the colonial feast of 'riz tafel' with a multitude of plates of meat, fish, vegetables, curries with steamed rice, all washed down with locally brewed Dutch draught beer.

This sojourn did not last long and soon 266 Wing was ordered across the Sunda Strait to Palembang in Sumatra. The ground crew travelled by boat and rail as aircrew flew the fighter planes across. On the boat, MacCarthy asked one of the men what

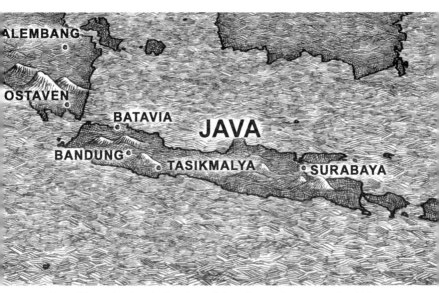

ALEMBANG

OSTAVEN

BATAVIA

JAVA

BANDUNG

TASIKMALYA

SURABAYA

Map of Java, showing the locations of the prisoner-of-war camps in which Aidan MacCarthy was held.

he knew about Sumatra. They both concluded that their only point of reference was the 1932 film *Bring 'Em Back Alive*, about an American animal trapper in the Malayan jungle.[29] On arrival they were brought to a rubber plantation to stay overnight and were amazed by the wildlife; lizards, spiders, flying foxes, snakes, tigers and crocodiles. They then travelled by train to Palembang, the colonial city at the centre of the large Dutch oil industry.

On 13 February thirty planes appeared over Palembang airfield. They were Hudson bombers with Royal Australian Air Force markings and there was general elation with the thought of their bombing force being strengthened. Suddenly the sky was dotted with parachutes as tiny figures tumbled out of the planes. The air raid sirens began to wail and chaos ensued: the paratroopers were Japanese. It later emerged that the planes had been captured intact during the Japanese advance through Malaya.[30] The objective of this initial Japanese invasion force was to secure the airfield at Palembang in order to land troops and supplies for the main invasion. MacCarthy was finally getting the 'action' he had craved. Japanese paratroopers floated into the jungle surrounding the airfield and opened fire with rifles and machine guns from cover.[31] Seven RAF airmen were injured. MacCarthy administered first aid and loaded them into an ambulance. He hopped in and the ambulance raced off towards Palembang city.

Soon after leaving the airfield the ambulance suddenly jolted to a halt. The rear doors swung open and three Japanese paratroopers pointed their rifles shouting '*kura kura*!' He guessed this meant 'get out' and replied with the only Japanese he knew – '*isha*' (doctor) and kept repeating the word, pointing frantically at his Red Cross armband. He climbed out and the paratroopers peered in, inspected the wounded and gestured to him to get back in. They slammed the doors and, to his amazement, told the driver to carry on. They sped to the Medical Centre in Palembang where word quickly spread about their encounter with the Japanese. On their return to the airfield they were not stopped. The outnumbered Japanese paratroopers had been wiped out, mainly by Dutch Ambonese soldiers – tough, stocky Indonesian islanders who were experienced in jungle warfare and armed with specially made rifles and short, sharp traditional swords. The Japanese were no match for them and the islanders used their traditional swords to cut off their heads. They would gather up five or six heads at a time like bunches of bananas and bring them back to a shocked MacCarthy and the other officers to show how proud they were of their handiwork.[32]

Soon after, the Japanese launched their main attack on Sumatra. The vastly outnumbered and ill-prepared British, Dutch, Indonesian and Australian forces were ordered to evacuate south. Spitfires and Hurricanes covered their retreat and attacked the barges being used by the Japanese to ferry invading troops deeper into Sumatra by river. Without anti-aircraft defences to protect the invasion force, the Allied pilots were able to sink the barges with ease, slowing the Japanese advance. Japanese soldiers trying to reach the riverbank were either caught by the fast moving current or attacked by crocodiles and poisonous water snakes.[33]

To have any chance of escaping to Java, the Allied forces beat a retreat down the jungle road to Oosthaven port 250 miles away on the southern coast of Sumatra island. As they set out, MacCarthy must have felt *déjà vu* after his experiences in northern France two years previously. MacCarthy described the journey in his 1979 memoir:

> The jungle road had a surprisingly good surface, but our main concern was the condition of the many river bridges on our way: we feared that these might have been blown up by demolition squads, but thankfully our fears were groundless. We had to make numerous stops *en route,* mainly to answer calls of nature, and to tend the wounded with dressing changes, drinks and medicines. Our original intention had been to select large tree-covered openings by the jungle road, with the idea of keeping in the shade and, more importantly, being camouflaged from Japanese planes. But our first stop in one of these clearings was soon interrupted by a horde of screeching monkeys who showered coconuts on the entire helpless convoy. The noise and coconut missiles created panic amongst the troops, who opened up with rifle fire,

fearing they were being attacked by the enemy. The convoy was hurriedly evacuated from this spot and we drove on to the next clearing, which seemed calm and peaceful. However, the Dutch soldier who was acting as a guide and interpreter suddenly noticed that a group of our men were playing with some large kittens they had found. He calmly pointed out that these were tiger cubs, and it would only be a matter of time before their irate mother came looking for her offspring. Once again a hasty evacuation was organised.

Our next stop was near a bridge over the river. Abandoning all thoughts of keeping under cover, we rushed towards the water for a cooling sluice down. But as we approached the whole bank seemed to move. Without further ado we fled back to the road, leaving behind hundreds of snorting crocodiles whose siesta we had rudely interrupted. As our rest periods were proving somewhat unrestful, we decided to continue straight on to Oosthaven.[34]

When they eventually arrived at Oosthaven, it was in chaos: oil-storage tanks were on fire and columns of smoke towered over the city and the frightened populace. The weary evacuees were relieved to find three KLM ferries waiting to take them back across the Sunda Strait to Java.[35]

Once back in Java they found a familiar scene: the country was in a state of frenzied activity, with frantic preparations being made for the imminent invasion. All key personnel – aircrew, radar and wireless operators, electronic and instrument fitters – were being evacuated to Australia and India on any suitable vessel available. Many escaped, but a huge number of vessels were sunk by the Japanese, with usually no time for lifeboats to be launched. It was standard practice for Japanese ships to pluck two or three officers from among the survivors as trophy prisoners, allowing the rest to drown.

On the morning of 19 February, four days after the fall of Singapore, the city of Darwin in northern Australia experienced its first aerial bombing by the Japanese. Aside from the psycho-logical impact of the first enemy attacks on mainland Australia, the raid destroyed most of the cargo shipping available to resupply the defence of Java.

When the last ship had sailed from Java, the Allied military authorities took stock of their forces there. MacCarthy found himself acting as Principal Medical Officer and was shocked that most of the army doctors had abandoned their posts, leaving 5,000 soldiers with just three of their own doctors. MacCarthy had to distribute twenty-five of his RAF doctors among the remaining forces.

There were now between 12,000 and 14,000 army, navy and air force troops in Java, many of who had been evacuated from Singapore.[36] There were not enough weapons to arm them all and in any case most of the skilled RAF and navy personnel had no training in the use of rifles or machine guns. The force was split in two, with the unarmed and untrained half surrendering to the Japanese while the remainder went to the mountains near Garut in south-west Java. MacCarthy went with the group heading to the mountains to make a final stand. Their objective was to put up a limited resistance in order to delay the inevitable capture of the entire island. British Prime Minister Winston Churchill made a broadcast directed to the forces in Java urging them to hold out as long as possible. This was to allow the Australians time to move defending forces up to the Darwin area. The force heading to the mountains was acutely aware of how serious the situation was.

As they made their way towards the mountains, MacCarthy recalled being given wads of Dutch guilders and British pounds in order to prevent the money falling into enemy hands. He and two other officers decided the money was not going to be much use to them so they collected £1,000 and put it all into a tin box and, after sealing it thoroughly, climbed up to the top of a school and wedged it into the corner of a roof beam. Years later, after the war ended, one of officers returned to the school to find the tin box still hidden with the seals intact. However, ants had found their way in and eaten the money, enjoying an expensive meal as they turned the cash into confetti.[37]

On 28 February, the invasion of Java began shortly after midnight with landings at four different locations. This confused Allied defence efforts and the Japanese met minimal resistance. The outcome was inevitable.

The defending forces reached the mountains and began setting up perimeter defence points and firing zones. They were joined by an Australian regiment, named Blackforce (after their commander, Brigadier Blackburn), as well as an American field gun company from Texas that had the distinction of being the first American combat troops to cross the equator on active service. MacCarthy wrote in his memoir:

> In our mountain retreat everything was quiet for a few days. Nevertheless, we were all on edge and our nerves were beginning to fray. Even the enemy aeroplanes kept their distance, and the lack of action made the tension unbearable. Diseases such as malaria and dysentery (amoebic and bacillary) began to appear amongst the troops, and a number of cases of venereal disease flared up. Gloomily I knew that we were not medically equipped for a long siege – nor would we be able to withstand any prolonged

attack. But our period of waiting was soon to end. On the fifth day, as the sun climbed into the azure sky, the Japanese suddenly appeared on our rear flank. Soon they were walking amongst us, without a shot being fired. It seemed more like a dream – than reality.[38]

The Japanese soldiers now in their midst had been indoctrinated in the Bushido tradition since childhood and believed that those who chose surrender over death were beyond contempt. They were under divine Imperial instruction to defend their Empire and avenge the injustices of the white colonials. As the Japanese soldiers corralled their European, American, Indonesian and Australian prisoners at bayonet point, many were surprised that their captives would even want their names to be reported to their families.[39]

5

The Shadow of the
Rising Sun

MacCarthy and his fellow prisoners later pieced together what had happened. The Japanese had made broadcasts and distributed leaflets stating that they would declare Bandung in central Java an 'open city'. This would give Bandung similar status as other open cities such as Paris and Rome and mean that it would not be attacked and that civilians could be moved there to safety. The Dutch took the Japanese at their word and packed the city with their women and children from all over Java. When the city was full, the Dutch were given twenty-four hours to surrender or Bandung would be bombed and razed to the ground.[1] They had no choice and on 8 March the surrender of Java was announced. One of the terms of the surrender required the Dutch to show the Japanese an undefended route to the positions in the mountains where MacCarthy and the remaining British, Dutch, Australian and American forces were busy preparing their last stand.

As a result, MacCarthy and his comrades were rounded up, disarmed, counted, recounted, shouted at, counted again and marched down from the mountains to the plains below.[2] In a surreal and sudden moment they had become prisoners of war. Their lives would be utterly changed by what was to come. They were marched down the mountain into captivity. Some of the prisoners joined local Dutch Indonesian troops and made a run for it; many were recaptured and shot but a few escaped into the jungle. Interestingly, of the twenty-seven Allied doctors captured when Java fell, nineteen were Irish.[3]

The heat and humidity grew more intense as they reached the plains where they were forced into the metal goods wagons of waiting trains. The trains then lurched eastwards in the tropical heat. The prisoners became more thirsty and frightened by the hour. Eventually they arrived at a railhead in the small city of Tasikmalaya where they were unloaded and marched to a large former Dutch military airfield. There, around 3,800 prisoners were herded in front of a row of low hangars, counted, recounted, and ordered inside. This would be their prison for the next two months.

The guards at the airfield were front-line troops, many of whom had been blooded and battle-hardened during the invasions of Malaya, Singapore and the Dutch East Indies. Others had learned their craft in the barbarity of the Sino-Japanese War, which began when Japan invaded China in 1937. The initial encounters between the prisoners and Imperial Japanese soldiers were surprisingly cordial and, following the immediate shock of capture, the prisoners suffered little animosity or abuse from the front-line troops.[4] The Japanese soldiers were curious. The prisoners were mainly RAF, Royal Australian Air Force and Royal Malayan Air Force personnel and many of the Japanese had never seen a Caucasian person before. They seemed almost apologetic towards the prisoners, and gave them cigarettes and items of food such as the tins of fruit they found.[5]

The prisoners still had plenty of Dutch guilders so were able to barter at the perimeter fences with local traders who were quick to oblige their captive market. The prisoners bought dried meat, fresh fruit, dried fish, soap, rice, vegetables and some poultry. They also bought alcohol, including cheap brands of whisky, gin and even bottled beer but no medicines or drugs were available, except for Tiger Balm, a herbal pain-relieving ointment popular at the time in South-East Asia. Probably the most important purchase they made at this time was pure yeast, which was rich in vitamin B. Without it they would have been unable to combat the various deficiency diseases they would soon encounter or the damage caused to the optic nerve by the lack of vitamins in their diet. This condition would become rife throughout the POW camp system and, if left untreated, could lead to blindness.[6] The chemists among the POWs, especially the Dutch, soon got to work and developed a number of separate yeast cultures from the original.

The overall effect of their initially lazy captivity, unmolested by the guards, well-fed from their trading at the fence, and washed by the heavy, warm tropical rains that fell each evening at almost exactly 6 p.m., lulled them into a state of naïve optimism about what lay ahead. Adding to this complacency was a conviction that the war would be over as soon as the Allies recovered from the initial surprise attacks, regrouped and began to fight back. Fifty years later, MacCarthy recalled that during the initial stages of captivity he was healthy and thought 'this will be an adventure'. He did not think it would be an unusual experience.[7] His opinion changed soon after, when the Japanese front-line troops were replaced by a cohort of designated camp guards, interpreters and administrators.

Discipline and brutality escalated immediately: 'everything was counting, shouting and marching'.[8] The new guards wanted to establish their authority: they kicked, shouted at and beat the prisoners if they did not react quickly enough to orders. They shot and beheaded a number of prisoners for attempting to escape.[9] On one occasion the prisoners were ordered to gather in a circle around an officer who was beheaded in front of them.[10]

On the second day after the arrival of their new guards, all of the POW flying personnel were ordered to line up on one side and write out a complete manual of how they had been trained.[11] Under the Geneva Convention the only information a POW was required to provide was their name, rank and number.[12] The senior British officer, RAF Wing Commander Edward Steedman refused to allow these forms to be completed and was taken to the guardroom and beaten.[13] The prisoners later heard the assembly bell and they ran to the square. Steedman was paraded before the prisoners and then shot by a firing squad.[14]

The order to complete the questionnaire was repeated. MacCarthy was terrified.[15] Eventually the aircrew decided to comply with the order, but consoled themselves by using their answers as a form of sabotage: if the Imperial Japanese Air Force pilots followed their directions they would be killed attempting the impossible.

The Japanese were outnumbered by almost two to one when they attacked Singapore and had not expected to win so easily. When Singapore and the Dutch East Indies were suddenly captured, the Japanese had no contingency plan to look after over 100,000 prisoners. The welfare of the POWs was the least of their priorities.

The prisoners from Australia, Britain, the Netherlands, Ireland, India and elsewhere were suddenly introduced to the concept of 'face', 'loss of face' and the restoration of 'face'. This was alien to them but hugely significant from an Asian perspective and quickly began to dominate every moment of their lives.

In the Imperial Japaese Army, prison camp guards were not selected for any particular aptitude or skill. They were the recruits who did not make the grade, on either physical or mental criteria, for combat or other more important roles. They were the runts of the litter – and they knew it.

Discipline in the Imperial Japanese Army was enforced through beatings: officers beat and humiliated men under their command daily. If, for any reason, a guard lost his temper and lashed out, it rippled down the hierarchy of command. If the commandant hit a sergeant, the sergeant hit a corporal, the corporal hit the nearest private, the private hit the nearest Korean guard and the Korean guard hit the nearest POW. This ritual of violence saved 'face' all the way down the line.

The Korean prison guards were regarded as racially inferior by the Japanese guards and were severely punished if they did not obey instantly. They were daily victims of ill treatment so passed their frustrations onto those of lower status in order to restore 'face'.[16] In this pressure cooker of violence, fear and insecurity, the POWs would inevitably suffer most.

MacCarthy described the Korean guards as being like prisoners in an open jail. In most, but not all, cases, they were conscripted and forced to serve the Japanese. Korea had been gradually annexed by Japan since the beginning of the twentieth century, and was forced to produce food and provide manpower for industries on mainland Japan and elsewhere, as well as soldiers and camp guards. As many as 60,000 Koreans are believed to have died in mainland Japan alone. Korean women (as well as women from other countries occupied by the Japanese) were abducted in their thousands and forced into sexual slavery as 'comfort women' to the Imperial Japanese Army. This was the reality of Japan's propaganda myth of the 'Greater East Asia Co-Prosperity Sphere', the slogan for a racist doctrine of subjugation and exploitation of those unfortunate enough to fall under Japan's control, either through invasion or the installation of puppet governments.

Although there were interpreters in the camps, their numbers were limited. One of the major difficulties of prison-camp life

Aidan MacCarthy's POW camp feeding bowl, made from a Dutch army water bottle. BARRY MURPHY

was that all commands were issued in Japanese. Most of the prisoners had arrived from Europe or Australia shortly before being captured and did not understand a word of Japanese or have an understanding of the culture. When inevitable misinterpretations occurred, it was regarded as a gross insult and loss of face by the Japanese guards. In order to restore face, the prisoner had to be punished violently. The penalty for any minor breach of the rules was an on-the-spot beating, usually with the guard screaming and shouting with rage.

If a prisoner was ordered to the guardroom, it usually meant the other guards would join in with punches to the face and blows to the head and back with bamboo sticks or canes. The victim had to keep to his feet because if he fell to the ground, more kicks would follow.[17] Throughout this daily ordeal, the prisoner could not defend himself or retaliate as it would mean further punishment or possibly death. It took incredible restraint for prisoners not to react violently when being beaten.

Psychologically, it was also hugely traumatising for prisoners to witness the ill treatment and execution of their friends and comrades. But brutality was not the only means by which a small number of Japanese guards were able to control large numbers of prisoners. As the POWs became progressively weaker over time through malnutrition and starvation, their ability to resist or defend themselves physically was further reduced.[18]

With the arrival of the new guards, all trading with the natives was forbidden under threat of torture and death for both buyer and seller. Without access to food from outside, conditions rapidly worsened. Signs of malnutrition became evident within weeks.[19] The POWs' food supply progressively deteriorated in quantity and nutritional value; meals consisted of dirty rice mixed with millet and sometimes half-rotten sweet potatoes and cabbage tops. Occasionally fish heads were mixed in. The rice was served as a pap, a watery rice pudding ladled out 'with a precision that would have shamed a computer'.[20] The aching hunger pains never ceased and the prisoners were living on their reserves as they made the terrifying transition from hunger to starvation. They became obsessed by food. They dreamed about it and discussed future meals and menus. This was unfamiliar territory to many of the prisoners who had lived in relative privilege before the war. They were now experiencing real hunger for the first time in their lives and there was no end in sight.

In the months following capture, as hopes of an early Allied counter-attack receded, the numbing prospect of the continuation of their starvation diet resulted in morale sinking ever lower. Tropical infections such as malaria and dysentery soon began to spread.

This was not the type of war for which MacCarthy had volunteered. The hot meals cooked by the MacCarthy family's housekeeper, Nora O'Shea, must have been a distant and gnawing memory. He had been raised in a household with an abundance of food, that sold and even exported food in vast quantities, and this made starvation all the more alien.

Every grain of rice became precious for the prisoners as they starved, in many cases to death. Survival instincts took over and getting their fair ration would dominate their existence for the remainder of their captivity. Prolonged starvation became evident in ways that none of them could have previously imagined. When prisoners lay on their backs, the bones of their spines could be seen through their stomachs.

Unlike the other prisoners, many of whom had been conscripted, MacCarthy had volunteered to go to war in search of adventure and had actually looked forward to seeing 'action'. He was now living in a nightmare from which the only escape seemed to be death. MacCarthy's war became a struggle against disease, infection, starvation and brutality. With no medical supplies and tasked with treating hundreds and often thousands of starving, diseased prisoners, his only weapons were his medical training and his strength of character.

The prisoners were organised into work parties and forced to do manual work for the Japanese war effort, first building an airstrip and often loading ammunition onto railway goods wagons. This ignored international rules on the treatment of POWs. The Japanese were consistent in their refusal to implement these rules throughout the war.

The Japanese needed the airfield for military expansion so, after being held for two months at the Tasik Malaya airfield in central Java, the POWs received news in May that a move to an unknown destination was imminent.[21] Immediately the POW chemists began to work on developing a means of distributing the precious yeast cultures to various groups of prisoners before they were transported. They came up with a clever solution whereby POWs were issued with a small amount of uncooked rice about the size of a golf ball. It was held together by a vegetable gelatine made by cooking a local root. The rice ball was then injected with an active yeast culture and wrapped in a large bay leaf. Each man was instructed to take his injected ball of rice to the next camp and hand it to a medical officer on arrival.[22]

A few days later they were ordered to parade at dawn. They were lined up, counted and, taking only what they could carry, were marched several miles in the tropical sun to a nearby rail terminal. The 3,500 prisoners were then forced onto three trains, locked into steel goods wagons, and a sixteen-hour nightmare journey in airless, filthy and overcrowded conditions began. When they arrived at their next destination – Surabaya in eastern Java – the first thing that hit them was the heat. Situated at sea level, Surabaya was far more humid than the previous camp in the more mountainous western Java. The prisoners were split into two groups and MacCarthy's was marched through the city, beaten with rifle butts and screamed at by the guards until they arrived at 'Lyceum Camp', a former girls' school which had been converted into a POW camp. They were crammed into the school building with Dutch troops already held there.

By this stage, several months into their captivity, the long-term effects of starvation were becoming evident with the increasing number of cases of deficiency diseases. Due to a lack of vitamins in their diet, cases of peripheral neuritis began to spring up. This causes damage to nerve endings, resulting in relentless pain in legs and feet.[23] One common disease was referred to as 'happy feet' or 'electric feet' because sufferers would experience burning 'electric shock' sensations. They would stamp their feet as a means of temporarily reducing the burning pain that the condition caused.[24] It was especially painful at night and prevented the sufferer from getting any rest, further adding to his exhaustion and disorientation.

Another common deficiency disease was wet beriberi, caused by a deficiency in thiamine or vitamin B1 and resulting in an accumulation of water in the tissues of the extremities. The prisoner's hearts were no longer physically strong enough to pump blood through their veins and remove waste from muscle tissue to be passed as urine.[25] Prisoners with beriberi found themselves breathless and they developed severe body swelling at the ankles, legs, scrotum and abdomen. Another common disease was dropsy, which also caused water to accumulate in tissues, especially feet and legs. These cases required numerous trips to the toilets, especially at night. If a POW suffering from dropsy failed to urinate, he would die.

> Those who made the lavatory trip were usually in a great hurry but first the permission of the guards on duty had to be obtained. POWs had to bow and say 'Banjo-ari-ma-sen' (Toilet please). On the return trip another bow to the guard was required and an 'Arigato' (Thank you). Some of the guards were bloody-minded and instead of allowing the man straight through they kept him waiting for no apparent reason. This delay was sometimes disastrous. The result caused great amusement for the guard and also earned the unfortunate man a few slaps on the face.[26]

In order for the prisoner's bodies to generate the energy needed to survive, the protein in their muscles began to break down. Known as autophagy, it is the process by which the body literally consumes itself in order to stay alive.

The vitamin deficiency also caused retrobulbar neuritis (papillitis), an inflammation of the ends of the optic nerves in the eye. This in turn resulted in a gradual loss of vision, which progressed, if untreated, to permanent blindness.[27]

Still, the Japanese relentlessly demanded that these sick and diseased prisoners worked long hours as beasts of burden. Passing men as fit for work caused a lot tension between the doctors and other prisoners, but the doctors had no choice. In the view of Japanese camp officials, sickness was equated with dishonour, shame and even with sabotage if it affected the completion of the day's work quota.[28] Food was issued on a per-capita basis for the number of men that worked, so the medical staff had no choice but to pass sick men as being fit for work, otherwise they would all die. Any man who was able to stand, however feebly, was considered fit for work by the Japanese.[29] Despite the fact that the prisoners were dying in their multitudes, and that people tend to work better if reasonably well fed, have access to medicine and are not grossly overworked, never challenged this doctrine.[30]

By the time the prisoners had arrived at Lyceum Camp in Surabaya, cases of bacterial dysentery had already begun to appear. This is a severe diarrhoeal disease caused by infection and the patient suffers from the passage of mucus and blood and severe abdominal cramps.[31] It spread quickly through physical contact because water and food became infected in the cramped, filthy conditions of the former school. It caused patients to lose even more weight and reduced even further their ability to absorb what little food they ate, exacerbating the effects of malnutrition and increasing the debilitation of their immune systems. In many cases it was a slow death of deterioration as the prisoner wasted away or contracted some other infection such as pneumonia and died. Very few Allied POWs avoided contracting dysentery at some stage during their captivity.

An isolation section for these cases was set up in the former school gymnasium at Lyceum Camp. Outside holes were dug in the ground for toilets and were laced with lime to try and limit the spread of bacterial infection. For weakened patients who had to stand or walk on the lime in their bare feet, the resulting burns and ulcers would trigger further problems in the future.

In order to reach the isolation section, MacCarthy had to walk through the entrance hall of the school where the guards sat on the porch in a half-circle of chairs with a pet monkey chained to a perch behind them. One day as he passed through the entrance hall on his way back from a visit to the isolation section, he found it empty. All the guards had gone for their midday meal, leaving only the monkey sitting on his perch. MacCarthy saluted the monkey, unaware that one of the guards was returning through the main door. The guard saw the salute and took the gesture as a grave insult. He was infuriated. He called the other guards and they attacked, as a screaming mob, beating MacCarthy senseless for ten long minutes. Only after he had collapsed into semi-consciousness did the exhausted guards eventually allow the other prisoners to drag their doctor away.

MacCarthy recovered but one of the many dangers of such a beating was the possibility of tropical ulcers forming on wounds. These became endemic throughout the POW camps. The origin of an ulcer was usually something fairly innocuous – a scratch from a thorn or splinter of bamboo, cuts due to poor or non-existent footwear, insect bites or a beating. In the tropical heat these became itchy, got infected and ulcerated, and, owing to reduced immunity as a result of poor nutrition, became chronic.[32] Dirt, sweat and inadequate dressings – often

87

just a piece of paper or a large leaf held together with a piece of string – contributed to a continuous series of ulcers that ate deeper into the flesh. Ulcers often extended down to the underlying bone, causing it to become infected – a condition known as osteomyelitis. The infected pus from these wounds fell on the surrounding area, or dried onto sheets, clothing or towels and created an endless cycle of infection.[33]

The strength of character that enabled MacCarthy to keep focused on healing, even though he was surrounded by death, saved countless lives and allowed many others to die with some dignity or solace. With no proper medical supplies, apathy would been understandable in the face of such circumstances but MacCarthy, like so many other POW doctors, had an almost super-human strength that sustained him and those under his care. Throughout the prison camps in the Japanese empire, POW medical personnel saved innumerable lives by putting systems in place to limit the spread of infection and disease as well as selflessly caring for the sick and dying with no resources and at all times exposing themselves to the risk of infection. This is one of the traits of humanity that shines brightly from the camps.

Food was a constant concern. Because the rice was unwashed, it was infested with maggots. These conditions provided an unlikely source of protein as the maggots floated to the surface when the rice was cooked. They were creamed off, collected and boiled separately to produce 'maggot soup', which supplemented the diets of the weakest prisoners.

As well as maggots, the dirty rice also contained earthworm eggs which, when eaten, often hatched in the POWs' stomachs and occasionally in their lungs. The hatched earthworm would travel up the passage from the stomach to the throat and then crawl into the POWs' noses or mouths. MacCarthy recalled seeing a man playing cards ask to be excused for a moment, pull a worm from his nose or mouth, and return to the table without anybody taking any notice.[34]

But the quality and quantity of food were not the only problems. The complete absence of flavour caused the prisoners to crave anything that would add some variety to their diet. Orange skins, chillies and salt, if found, were hoarded and used sparingly. Java is a volcanic island and as a result the soil is very fertile. Prisoners suffering from dysentery were often caught short before they could reach the makeshift toilets and consequently soiled the ground. Before long, the tracks to the latrines were blooming with chilli plants which sprouted from the seeds of those occasionally added to their food. The prisoners had no hesitation in eating their fruit despite their origin.[35] Such levels of desperation meant that creatures that would normally have been considered vermin were now delicacies: flying foxes, bats, snakes, lizards and rats were caught and cooked. The leathery meat would be divided into tiny morsels and chewed for hours.

One of the prized possessions that MacCarthy had carried from the first camp in Tasik Malaya was a 2 lb tin of sausages. When they reached the camp in Surabaya, the first thing he did was bury the precious tin in the corner of the school's sports field – both to hide it from the guards and to keep it at a relatively cool temperature. Desperately homesick, he had decided to save the sausages for their first Christmas morning in captivity. Early on 25 December 1942, accompanied by two medical colleagues, he went and dug up the tin, planning to give the men a treat to raise morale. When he opened it he found that it contained asparagus tips. He threw the tin away in disgust and cried. He never ate asparagus again.

In Java, the prisoners were tormented by insects – thousands of flies by day and by mosquitoes by night. Malaria, yellow fever and dengue fever are spread mainly by mosquitoes and before the war, the Dutch had combated mosquito breeding by implementing a system of water-level control in the rice fields. Mosquitoes need a static water level during their development and breeding so by raising and lowering the water level, their ability to breed was reduced. But with the war, the system had broken down so there was an increase in mosquito numbers and, as a consequence, a high incidence of malaria in the camps.[36] Those suffering from these diseases were still required to attend the numerous roll calls or Tenko, which meant their fellow POWs had to carry them on parade and prop them up during the counting.

The various nationalities suffered the same treatment but the British, Australian and Dutch prisoners became suspicious of the loyalty of some of the native Indonesian POWs to their fellow prisoners and former colonial masters. Indonesia had been a Dutch colony for centuries so there was resentment against the colonial world view of white Europeans. A number of the Allied POWs became convinced the Indonesian prisoners were not being treated as badly by the Japanese and were potentially being used as camp spies. Their suspicions ended abruptly when a Sumatran prisoner, whom the Dutch had previously regarded as untrustworthy, was caught near the perimeter fence, carrying on a shouted conversation with someone outside the camp. He was grabbed by the guards, beaten and tortured to make him reveal the name of the person he was speaking to on the outside, and the subject of the conversation. It soon became clear that the illegal conversation was about his sick wife.

The following day, the prisoner's head was shaved, and he was buried up to his neck in the centre of the courtyard. He was left there bareheaded, without food or drink, and at the mercy of the tropical sun, flies and mosquitoes. I watched him, unable to do anything. The Japanese refused to let me offer him any relief at all. At the same time they insisted that all the POWs walked past him dozens of times each day. Appalled, we watched their victim change in forty-eight hours from a young man to a geriatric. Insect bites set up immediate infection, his eyes began to close and his dried lips became set in a permanent snarl. It took two days and a night for him to die.[37]

From the beginning of their captivity the prisoners had been forced to adjust quickly to the social rituals of their captors. In Japan, hierarchy and its expression through etiquette is complex and varies greatly depending on the relative status of various individuals. Bowing is central to this and the longer and deeper the bow, the greater the respect shown. In an environment where camp guards were considered the lowest of the low in the Imperial Japanese Army hierarchy, many of them used the camp system to exact respect through violence. The paying of courtesies between the Japanese themselves and from POWs to Japanese or Korean guards was rigidly enforced. On meeting, guards bowed to officers with a loud sucking of breath indicating a form of respect. When a POW encountered a Japanese or Korean guard, he had to say '*Kiotski*' (attention) followed by '*Keiri*' (bow), then '*Neari*' (relax). Prisoners would shout '*Kiotski*' in order to alert POWs nearby of the presence of the guards. If a prisoner did not notice an approaching guard or failed to bow to the depth that satisfied the guard's whim, the result was an outburst of violence that could result in serious injury or death.

In October 1942 MacCarthy made this mistake whilst treating a dying airman at the dysentery ward in the gymnasium.

The patient was in agony with severe abdominal cramps and pains.[38] He had no control over his bowels or bladder and his emaciated body stiffened with each spasm. MacCarthy had no medicine to give him and knew his patient had only a matter of moments to live. He had his arm around him and all he could do was hold his hand, pray and whisper words of encouragement.[39] As the patient weakened, a guard entered the gymnasium. MacCarthy heard the call to attention but because the patient was about to die he did not give the bow and *Kiotski–Keiri–Neari* salute as was expected. The guard, having 'lost face', became apoplectic with rage and charged towards him, screaming in Japanese with his rifle raised. In a flustered mix of Japanese, Malay and English, MacCarthy tried to explain that the patient was about to die. Realising he was in the wrong, the guard hesitated. MacCarthy turned back to the patient and saw that he had just died. While MacCarthy's back was turned, the guard suddenly smashed his rifle butt onto his right elbow and fractured all the bones at the joint. MacCarthy writhed on the ground, gasping in agony as the guard casually walked away.

With his elbow smashed, he was transferred to a civilian hospital where a wing had been allocated for prisoners. The Japanese surgeon who examined him seemed reasonably competent. He ordered to have the elbow X-rayed and decided he needed to operate the following day.

Early the next morning MacCarthy was escorted from the ward and marched across the hospital grounds accompanied by two armed guards to the operating theatre. He was told to lie on the table as the two guards stood to attention nearby. An Indonesian orderly then strapped his legs and arms to the sides of the table. He was confused by this odd preliminary to the anaesthetic but then realised there was not going to be any anaesthetic.[40]

The 'surgeon', who turned out to be a third-year medical student eager to gain some practice before going to the front, made an incision on his elbow. MacCarthy realised he was making the cut in the wrong place and when the scalpel broke the skin he felt a searing blast of pain and instinctively struggled to break free of the straps until he passed out. When he eventually regained consciousness he looked up to see his butcher of a surgeon proudly holding in his forceps half the head of the radius bone of his forearm. The student then quickly lost interest and left. The Indonesian orderly took over and mercifully injected some local anaesthetic. The wound was sewn up, a dressing applied and MacCarthy was given a sling before being marched back to the ward. The operation seemed to have shaken even his guards as they silently lit up cigarettes and offered him one in sympathy.

Shortly afterwards, he woke up to find he had a streptococcal infection. Normally this would be a mild infection and not dangerous but in his debilitated state and without antibiotics, it was life-threatening. That night, a very brave Ambonese medical orderly risked his life by sneaking out over the roofs of the hospital and bringing him some antibiotics he bought on the black market.[41] Within about three days, the infection was gone but his elbow would never fully recover.

One of most precious things for all POWs, whether good or bad, was news from the outside world. This was a link with reality. It offered hope and boosted morale.[42] In order to access news, they had smuggled illegal radios into the camps, often piece by piece. The Japanese suspected the presence of radios and made every effort to find them – questioning, torturing and launching numerous surprise searches. Discovery of a radio meant death for the operators or, if they could not be identified, the people sleeping nearest to the point at which it was discovered would be executed. Ingenious hiding places were invented, including the artificial leg of an American civilian who had been in Java on business when he was captured. He had originally lost his limb as a sailor. A radio was fitted into his hollow wooden leg, with a cleverly hidden socket on each side (one for plugging in the power, the other for earphones). He took the radio on parade with him every day and was never discovered.

Meanwhile, on the other side of the world in Castletownbere, the MacCarthy family had received no news for almost a year. The RAF had recorded Aidan as 'Missing Believed POW' on 26 March 1942. For a year his family did not know whether he was dead or alive. D.F. had to keep the family businesses going and was able to occupy his mind through work. Julia, on the other hand, withdrew to the apartment above the shop, praying incessantly for her son's safe return.

The Imperial Japanese Army, although they kept meticulous records of their prisoners, generally did not pass details on to the Red Cross of whom they held in captivity. Throughout this first year and for the entire period of his captivity, Julia, normally so assertive in managing the family's affairs, became withdrawn. She would only emerge from the apartment to go to Mass every morning. Her friends and particularly her sister Kit would call around to support her. She never gave up hope.[43] She prayed constantly and refused to accept that her son was not alive. The entire population of the town was instructed by the local priest to pray for MacCarthy's safe return and he later credited this 'huge battery of prayer' as having an influence in saving his life.[44]

Out of the blue, a telegram came from the War Office in London with news that MacCarthy was a prisoner of war in Java but no further information was given. An entry in Julia's diary stands out: '*Got news of Aidan being a prisoner of war in Java, 3rd Feb 1943*'.

A page from Julia MacCarthy's diary, recording milestones in her family's lives, such as first holy communions, starting jobs and, sombrely, the news about Aidan being a prisoner of war.

It was a message that brought both joy and sadness for the family: their 29-year-old son and brother was alive but he was far from safe. He was imprisoned on the other side of the world by an enemy that had no regard for prisoners. There was nothing the family could do for him but hope and pray.

A month later, in early March, POW workers in the camp administration office at Lyceum Camp in Surabaya began to notice signs of what looked like plans to relocate the prisoners. A Japanese doctor subsequently arrived at the hospital compound to get a breakdown on the condition of every patient. This confirmed the rumours so the POW doctors quickly held a conference to decide which patients could be moved. They decided it was best that as many as possible should be moved because they were worried about what would happen to those left behind. They could not have known that the infamous 'Speedo' period from April to August 1943 was about to commence. This was during the construction of the Thai–Burma railway when thousands of prisoners were worked to death in order to hasten the completion of the railway intended by the Japanese to resupply their troops in Burma.

It was a lottery as to where POWs were sent and luck alone, not strength or guile or character, would decide whether a prisoner lived or died. MacCarthy was lucky to avoid being sent to work on the railway.

He recalled later that having endured such misery the prisoners had developed a deeper determination to survive. Their credo was to 'keep from getting dead, that was the only thing on your mind and you worked at it, twenty four hours a day'. By now, MacCarthy had been constantly exposed to death and suffering for over two years. He had survived the German onslaught in northern France, escaped at Dunkirk and treated wounded and dying airmen in England. He had seen their blood and body parts washed out aircraft after returning from bombing raids and believed that this had helped him to develop a level of immunity. Death was beginning to have little effect on him.[45]

Shortly after the impending move became known, the doctors, staff and patients were marched to the railway station in Surabaya. They joined POWs from two other camps and, as before, were all packed into closed goods wagons, with little space or ventilation. The doors were bolted from outside. The steel boxes with their cargo of misery soon heated up in the tropical sun and in the airless, baking semi-darkness, the nightmare journey began.

> Acute claustrophobia set in at once. Our bodies were pressed hard against each other and all that could be heard above the rumble of wheels on the track was the rasp of breathing and low, continuous cursing. As the temperature rose occasionally a man screamed aloud, unable to bear the congestion any longer. But he was sworn at and was soon reduced to whimpering silence. We could only guess at the countryside we were passing through. Some of us who were religiously inclined prayed aloud but I prayed inside. My prayer was very simple – 'Lord – let us all survive this night.' But not all of us did. Towards the end of the twenty-two hour journey several prisoners had died and in the stifling, inescapable heat their bodies began to quickly decompose.[46]

The train made the long journey of over 400 miles from east to west across Java and eventually arrived at the city of Bandung. At last the doors were unbolted and the prisoners spilled out, gasping for air and water. They were ordered to march to their next camp and although the journey was only 2 miles it seemed endless to the exhausted and dehydrated prisoners who were forced to carry many of their comrades on makeshift stretchers.

MacCarthy celebrated his thirtieth birthday in March 1943 and was about to receive an unexpected birthday present: as he marched to the camp he noticed with relief that Bandung was in the mountains so they would not have to endure the unbearable humidity of Surabaya. The camp turned out to be a former Dutch barracks with decent accommodation and plenty of space. It had a small, well-equipped and well-stocked hospital. He could hardly believe his good luck.[47] The resident POWs, mainly Dutch, looked reasonably well fed. They told the new arrivals it was a show camp set up for visiting representatives of the International Red Cross, to deceive the world that the Imperial Japanese Army treated prisoners in accordance with international rules of war.

Compared with the previous camps the conditions in Bandung were good, so the new arrivals made the most of their stay, building up their health and morale. Many years later, MacCarthy recalled that he and the other survivors owed their continued existence to the time they spent at Bandung. He was fully convinced that the brief respite saved his life by allowing him to regain some strength before facing a further two years of gruelling captivity.

The Bandung climate was as near to ideal as possible with day temperatures just above 32°C (90°F), dry and with a soft breeze that MacCarthy described as being like a pleasant summer's day at home. The nights were cool enough to need only a light blanket, and to think twice about taking a cold shower first thing in the morning.[48] The accommodation was in well-ventilated barrack buildings, with verandas, and there were also a number of bungalows. Life was bearable at last.

MacCarthy began work at the camp hospital as the resident British doctor. Now that they had more resources, he and his medical colleagues began experimenting with different diets to see if they could cure the beriberi, retrobulbar neuritis and various other deficiency diseases.[49] Other common diseases were those of the skin, bowels, eyes and ears, and in order to eradicate these they developed a strategy. The worst cases were selected first, particularly those with retrobulbar neuritis (papillitis), in an effort to save their sight.

> These cases were divided into three categories and fed (a) a full fat diet, (b) a full carbohydrate diet and (c) a mixed fat/protein diet. Within ten days there was a general improvement, especially with the (c) type diet, but the amelioration of eye conditions stopped short of full recovery. On this basis we decided to take a calculated risk: the patients were given an intravenous injection of a small amount of typhoid vaccine. This was normally given as a skin injection for protection against typhoid and paratyphoid. Given intravenously, it produced an artificial fever (102°F to 103°F) within thirty minutes. This lasted about an hour. Our theory was that the fever would increase the metabolic rate (i.e. it would accelerate the breakdown and absorption of fats and protein in the body). In the majority of cases it worked, and with continued treatment the vision returned to normal or near-normal. A small percentage, however, were too far gone and went totally blind.[50]

Several cases of leprosy occurred among the Dutch. This was the result of an infection they had picked up as children, from their Indonesian nannies. The voice would become husky, and as the disease progressed the face would assume the likeness of a lion owing to the enlargement of the facial bones. Proper isolation was impossible within the camp, and the doctors kept the disease a secret within medical circles in order not to alarm the rest of the POWs. Some precautions were taken, such as the patients using only their own utensils and clothing. This system prevented the lepers becoming outcasts as being a prisoner was lonely enough and MacCarthy insisted on maintaining social contact with the lepers. He kept them engaged by playing card games and one even became his regular cribbage partner.[51] The doctors could not predict the Japanese reaction to the presence of lepers in the camp, but were convinced that they would have killed them.

MacCarthy diagnosed a few isolated cases of tuberculosis and most of these patients did not survive long under the circumstances. Despite the relatively improved conditions at Bandung, a tragic yet avoidable episode occurred for about twenty diabetics, mostly Dutch, when the guards suddenly stopped the supply of insulin, claiming there was no more available. The doctors' complaints were ignored and they watched helplessly as, one by one, the diabetics lapsed into unconsciousness and died. One, a friend of MacCarthy's, was a qualified physiotherapist who had worked every day on his injured right elbow. During these sessions they had become close friends as they talked about their families, homes, hopes and their work before the war.[52]

On another occasion the POWs were forced to partake in medical trials as the doctors were ordered to inject a given number of POWs with a vaccine that had been manufactured for the Japanese in the Bandung Institute of Research. They did not know what the vaccine was for, but guessed it was some sort of anti-plague vaccine for front-line Japanese troops. They were told that some POW doctors would have to inject one another first so they pinched the skin and pushed the needle through the skin fold – in one side and out the other. They then sprayed the vaccine into the cupped palm of the hand that was doing the pinching. Luckily, the Japanese did not notice the deception.

With no end in sight and no hope of escape, the prisoners sought to leave their unbearable reality in more imaginative ways. They began to distil alcohol using improvised distillation equipment. The liquid 'dynamite' they produced was highly potent and caused terrible hangovers but the pain was worth it for the mental escape it provided. Inevitably, a guard noticed that a prisoner was drunk. He demanded to sample a whole bottle of what the prisoner was drinking. He liked it and a pact was agreed whereby the guards would turn a blind eye in return for a regular supply of the booze. Alcoholism is an unlikely disease to be associated with a POW camp, but owing to this arrangement it was rife in Bandung.[53]

The Japanese demand for working party quotas was not a problem at Bandung because although the work was hard and they were harassed all day long by the guards, those working on the outside found ample opportunities for pilfering food. They were working mainly at the railway yards so were able to tap rice bags, steal vegetables, and sometimes even remove beer and spirits from the cargos. They became experts at piercing a bag or barrel, extracting some of the contents and closing up the incisions. They smuggled food back into the camp between their legs, under hats or bandages, or in Dutch army water bottles.

The POWs' life at Bandung was in some ways similar to that in European prison camps. They played cards, read, organised debates, discussions and lectures on various subjects. They were allowed to stage plays and were entertained by musicians among them who had brought their instruments from other camps. For nine months, they were relatively well treated but that was about to change.[54]

6

Voyage to Hell

acCarthy spent his second Christmas in captivity at
Bandung, at the Red Cross show camp, but rumours of an
imminent move had, once again, begun to circulate from
prisoners working in the camp administration office. He and the
other officers began to prepare for the move by making lists of
the names and addresses of the living POWs as well as medical
records and concealing them in empty metal ammunition cases,
burying them under the stone slabs of the kitchen floors.[1] They
were anticipating future war-crimes tribunals that they were
confident would bring their captors to justice.

In early January 1944, again taking only the essentials
they could carry, the POWs were marched from the camp to
the railway terminal. They faced the now-familiar nightmare
process of prisoner transport in the Japanese Empire as they
were crammed into metal goods wagons in the stifling heat. This
time the train headed north-west towards Batavia (now Jakarta).
When it stopped the POWs were grateful that sympathetic
locals gave them some mangos and papayas. They eventually
arrived at Batavia and the complacency that had been induced
at Bandung was shattered the moment the doors of the wagons
were opened. At sea level once again, the heat and the humidity
were unbearable.

The brief respite they had had at Bandung was over: they were pushed, beaten and screamed at as they were marched to their new quarters – Cycle Camp, a former Dutch Army barracks with a terrifying reputation for cruelty. This was due to the camp commandant – Lieutenant Kenichi Sonei – a psychotic, drug-addicted maniac. Sonei was waiting for the prisoners at the gates, screaming orders and beating guards and prisoners alike. MacCarthy recalled Sonei's welcome to the POWs outside the main gates of the camp. In broken English he announced:

> This is a hard place – and you will be treated hard. Any breach of discipline will be punished by a beating. Any attempt at escape will be punished by death.[2]

They were marched through the gates and barbed-wire fences into the camp, lined up under the full glare of the tropical sun and counted again. Ordered to stand to attention without moving, they were denied water, use of toilets and rest. Anyone who moved was beaten. After two long hours Sonei, obviously enjoying the power he had over his captives screamed:

> You are all criminals and you deserve nothing. You are criminals because you are allied to the American bastards who are trying to destroy our glorious empire. In this camp we shall show you the error of your ways. In this camp you will learn how strong and invincible the Japanese people are.[3]

It was clear from Sonei's body language and outbursts that he was insane. All MacCarthy could do was pray for the strength to endure what lay ahead as his life was now in the hands of a maniac. After the war, it emerged that Sonei was in the grip of a degenerative mental illness brought on by advanced syphilis.

Shortly after their arrival at Cycle Camp, the prisoners discovered that Sonei was an opium addict and demanded that one of the POW doctors visit his quarters at six o'clock every second evening to give him an intravenous injection. When he was high he was even more unpredictable – he could be violent, sleepy or affable – there was no guessing which mood he would fall into.[4]

A Dutch POW, Frank Samethini, recalled that when a prisoner refused to allow his head to be shaved on arrival at the camp Sonei used a pair of scissors like a lever: wrapping tufts of hair around the blades, he forcibly pulled out all the prisoner's hair out by the roots until he collapsed unconscious, with a bloody pulp where his scalp had been. 'The most horrifying part of the ghastly performance is that Sonei's face had not for a moment lost its expression of loving care while manipulating the instrument.'[5]

The same prisoner recalled a day when two escapees: 'mere boys, are captured and brought before the closed ranks to die. Tied up to the barbed-wire fence, they are blindfolded and then butchered with bayonets. Their pitiful groans are blotted out by the hoarse shrieks from the thrusting, lunging robots who do their work according to some weird ritual: two thrusts in the throat, two in the belly and finally two in the heart.'[6]

On one occasion, Sonei had a painful ingrown toenail, which had gone septic and was very inflamed. He consulted a Dutch doctor who recommended removal of the nail. The doctor was ordered to return that evening. Petrified, he presented himself to perform the operation. In a bizarre display of bravado, Sonei refused a local anaesthetic and screamed '*Banzai*' throughout the operation. When it was over and the dressing had been applied, the trembling doctor was presented with some cakes and a bottle of whisky – then slapped on each side of the face before being allowed to leave.[7]

The Japanese guards were equally terrified of their commandant. Samethini recalled a guard being summoned to his office: 'Sonei closes the door with one hand, unbuckling his belt with the other. The sound of leather on skin and the moans are music to our ears.'[8] The satisfaction of the prisoners was tinged with fear because whenever a guard was beaten or humiliated by a superior officer, he would respond by lashing out at the nearest prisoner.

Sonei liked to consider himself a man of principles: 'One may torture or kill a prisoner of war for a little or big thing he is guilty of, but first there must be legal proof of his "crime".'[9]

As was the case in other camps, working parties were sent out to the docks of Batavia and, although the POWs hated the long, hard days of backbreaking work, it again offered the prospect of extra stolen food. It also meant they were away from Sonei for a few hours. Sonei's madness was compounded by periodic 'moon-sickness' which meant that he became increasingly violent and erratic during a full moon.[10] Sonei had developed a bizarre fixation with castor oil plants and every available piece of ground in the camp was sown with them. Each POW officer was allocated a certain number of plants to look after. The prisoners lived in fear that if anything happened to them or if they failed to grow Sonei would hold them personally responsible and they would be punished severely.[11]

The indifference of the Imperial Japanese Army to the suffering of the prisoners seemed limitless. One day the camp gates opened, and MacCarthy saw a sight he would never forget: a procession of 250 emaciated, filthy and completely demoralised 'scarecrows' stumbling into the camp. They were dressed in rags and led by the only member of the group who was not blind. Each man rested a hand on the shoulder of the man in front. They were all that was left of an original working party of 1,000 who had been shipped off to the tiny island of Haruku in the Ambon Sea. There they had been forced to dig and chip out coral to make an airfield runway using little more than hand tools.[12] Their blindness had been brought on by prolonged vitamin B deficiency and the glare of the tropical sun on white coral.[13] To protect themselves from the searing brightness they had improvised makeshift sunglasses from bamboo but these had little effect. On Haruku, they were completely dependent on food and water transported by ships. Storms, typhoons and shambolic organisation had often caused delays and many of the prisoners had starved to death. After twelve long months the survivors were transported back to Java in the overcrowded hold of a small coastal steamship. The journey of almost 1,500 miles in bad weather claimed a further 200 lives.

The other prisoners were not allowed any contact with them, but from their own scant resources they managed to pass some clothing, soap and food to them. The extra food was contributed mainly by those in the outside working parties, who had to increase their pilfering hugely and risked their lives to smuggle the food past the guardroom. Some of the new arrivals recovered, but many never regained their sight.[14]

A few months later, in April 1944, Sonei was moved to the civilian internment camp at Tjideng, which was mainly for Dutch women and children. There he became known as 'the Beast of Tjideng' and his treatment of the civilian internees there formed the basis of his post-war trial. A female Dutch internee recalled one of his bouts of 'moon-sickness':

> Heavy with sleep, we were led out to an ancient mango tree, in the eerie moonlight, was Sonei, dressed in only a

loincloth, doing a wild and strange barbaric ritual dance. We were grouped around him and made to watch. After he had danced himself into a frenzy, he ordered his soldiers to give us each a shovel to dig our own graves … After the appalling dance, Sonei would sink to the ground and was led away by his officers. Everyone was allowed to return to their beds.[15]

On another occasion, late one night, a group of women and children from another camp was brought to Tjideng:

The women and children were bewildered, tired and under-nourished. They were supposed to bow deeply before the guards at the entrance of the camp but in their condition and in the dark, they just could not function as the Japanese wanted them to. The demented camp commander noticed the sloppy way in which the bone-tired women and children greeted his soldiers. He worked himself into a frenzy again, frothing with manic anger. Suddenly he roared with rage and ordered his soldiers to strike the prisoners. In no time at all, screaming women and children were trying to parry blows from the soldiers. The children, whose blows were many but lighter than the savage beating of the women, screamed from exhaustion and fear and from seeing their mothers so brutally treated. When we saw them the next day, the women were badly bruised, some could hardly walk, and some could not move at all.[16]

Sonei was always looking for opportunities to dream up another method to frighten those under his control. The camp guards at Tjideng kept a number of large wild monkeys in cages outside the camp. As a form of amusement, Sonei ordered the monkeys to be starved before releasing them into the camp at night when the internees were distributing the evening meal. The hunger-crazed primates attacked and terrorised the civilian internees.[17] This was repeated again and again. On another occasion, a large truck filled with freshly baked bread was driven through the camp. The starving internees smelt the aroma and ran after the truck. It drove slowly through the camp and then it left. This was repeated a number of times until the internees stopped chasing the truck.[18]

Around the same time as Sonei was moved from Cycle Camp in April 1944, MacCarthy learned that he had been selected to be sent to another camp, rumoured to be on the Japanese mainland. By now there were almost 10,000 POWs in Cycle Camp, but the number was constantly being reduced as groups of prisoners were sent to Sumatra, Borneo and Japan.[19] Japan needed manpower for its heavy industries and mines as most Japanese men had been drafted into the army.[20] The POWs provided a convenient resource for the Japanese war economy so wherever manual labourers were needed, Allied prisoners of war were sent as slaves. They were usually transported in groups of around 1,000. In all, 36,000 prisoners were shipped to mainland Japan to work as slaves for companies such as Mitsubishi and Kawasaki, which profited from the war and went on to become household names.[21] In a twisted way, the fact that the POWs were 'useful' to the Japanese war effort may have been a factor in their survival. Had they been of no use whatsoever to the Japanese it seems likely that the death rate would have been far higher.

* * *

As on previous occasions, information about the imminent move came from the POW workers in the camp administration office.[22] A few days later the doctors were ordered to create a list of all so-called 'fit' men, who were then paraded naked before a Japanese doctor. The Japanese doctor took care to sit well away from the POWs as they were considered verminous. However, they needed to be examined because the Japanese did not want to send ill or diseased prisoners to their sacred homeland.[23]

The prisoners were apprehensive and wondered if the food situation would improve in Japan or if the survivors would return as blind, decrepit scarecrows.

They were now familiar with the departure rituals, which were always emotional occasions. Friends gathered for a final chat, wishing each other luck and promising to make contact after the war. They would exchange small gifts such as a spoon, a bit of soap, a badge or a book. They completed their farewells and on the morning of Friday 19 May 1944, MacCarthy's group was marched through the front gates into the unknown.[24]

He had mixed feelings, dreading the long and dangerous sea journey, but he was optimistic. Surely life in Japan would be a little better. Regardless, he was convinced he would not have survived much longer at Cycle Camp.

They were marched to Batavia's seaport at Tan Jon Priok. The 8-mile journey took the weakened, emaciated prisoners several long weary hours to complete. When they arrived at the docks, they were ordered into the holds of the Kiska Maru, a small cargo vessel.[25] As they clambered below they did not realise that they were descending into what would later be referred to as a hell ship – one of the many transports used by the Japanese to ferry POWs throughout their empire in appalling conditions.

MacCarthy would never set foot on Javanese soil again.

In all, 1,200 Dutch, Australian, American and British prisoners were crammed into the holds of the *Kiska Maru*, which had been fitted with wooden bunks like shelves, with a space in the centre and wooden ladders for access to the bunks. The layout reminded MacCarthy of illustrations he had seen as a child of eighteenth-century African slave ships. This is little wonder because that is exactly what they were. Hell ships had a uniform construction with tightly fitted bunks, wooden ladders leading to the deck and makeshift latrines slung over the side. Another defining feature was a complete disregard for human suffering. These vessels were one of the greatest hazards faced by Allied prisoners of the Japanese due to the frequency with which they were sunk by Allied submarines, whose captains were unaware of the human cargo on board their targets. The Japanese were supposed to put markings on ships to indicate the presence of prisoners on board but this rarely occurred.[26] The prisoners were secured below decks under battened hatches and when ships sank, any survivors were often machine-gunned in the water by the Japanese, possibly to eliminate witnesses to the crimes committed against them.[27]

On 19 May the *Kiska Maru* left the dock and sailed north towards Singapore via the Banka Strait.[28] Three days later at 4 p.m. on 22 May the ship arrived at Keppel Harbour in Singapore. As the prisoners emerged from the holds and onto the deck they saw a German U-boat tied up at the dock with two shell holes in the stern.[29] The German crew were assembled on deck, staring at the POWs in silence. More and more curious prisoners crowded to the ship's side to take a look at the U-boat. Then, without organisation or signal, spontaneous booing erupted from the prisoners with the jeering and shouting becoming louder and louder. The German crew, horrified by the sight and sound of the heaving crowd of filthy, emaciated skeletons above them, screaming and directing intense hatred at them, fled below decks. The prisoners stood back and cheered themselves – their small act of defiance was excellent therapy.[30]

Once unloaded, they were taken to River Valley Road Camp on the west side of Singapore island. The bare wooden huts provided the minimum of shelter and facilities, but, aware that they were destined for mainland Japan, they knew they would be there for only a short period.[31]

Their numbers were constantly declining due to illness, mental breakdowns and suicide.[32] Also, as the prisoners were about to be sent to Japan, the Japanese were especially careful about anyone who had an infectious disease. Any prisoner suffering from, or suspected of having an infection, was left behind. This reduced the draft to just over 1,000.

At 8 a.m. on 2 June they were marched back to the Singapore docks and put on board a large cargo ship, the *Bijou Maru*,[33] which was laden with aluminium ore.[34] They were ordered into the holds and had to lie, packed in like sardines, on the metal decks. Wooden stairs led up to the hatches, allowing prisoners to access the crate-like wooden toilets dangling over the sides of the ship. Every five minutes a group of men was allowed up on deck to use them, with a limit of five minutes for bowel movements. This was standard procedure on hell ships. The following day the convoy of twenty ships, three of which were carrying POWs, with an escort of four small destroyers, sailed out of Singapore Harbour.[35]

At exactly the same time on the other side of the world, all along the south coast of England, Allied forces were making the final preparations for the D-Day invasion of Normandy. Soldiers and equipment were being loaded onto ships in preparation for the imminent launch of Operation Overlord. The war was entering its final chapter. But for the prisoners leaving Singapore Harbour it was far from over. They were destined for slavery in the country that would be the last to surrender.

As the convoy set out, everyone was on edge, fearing attack from an Allied submarine at any moment. This was heightened when, three nights into the voyage, the lead destroyer was sunk by torpedo.[36] They were now being tracked by at least one submarine and it was assumed that others were gathering. The convoy warily made its way towards Manila in the Philippines, staying close to the coast of Borneo. It then made a break towards Manila. Whenever there was an air raid or submarine warning, all ships sounded their hooters. The hatches on the holds were slammed down and locked for the duration of the warning. If the ship was torpedoed, the Japanese were determined its cargo of slaves would not escape and would go down with it. Below deck the heat and general conditions in the holds were unbearable. The prisoners were packed so tightly into the hold that men suffocated to death.[37] Others died from sickness, thirst and starvation. In some cases cannibalism and even vampirism were reported as men, driven mad by thirst, killed their comrades to drink their blood.[38] The Japanese medics were often shocked by what they found when the holds were eventually opened. When a man died, his body was not removed until nightfall because of a convoy rule which stipulated that nothing that floated could be thrown overboard, except at night. So the body of a man that died early in the morning was 'ripe' by the time it was dark enough outside to throw the corpse overboard.[39] The trail of sewage that continuously emanated from the toilet crates did not seem to be covered by this edict.

In addition to this horror, many of the POWs suffering from dysentery could not hold onto their diarrhoea until their turn came to use the shipside latrines. This caused others to vomit, further adding to the squalor. The atmosphere was one continuous stench and MacCarthy wondered how long they would be able to survive.[40] Twice daily, food containers were lowered into the holds. The cooked rice and fish, usually with head, tail and guts intact, were washed down with tea that also tasted of fish. It was sickening, but it was their only sustenance.

The convoy arrived at Manila and anchored for a few days near the island fortress of Corregidor. Men returning from the latrines reported that local boats had tried to pass on some messages to them.[41] Hours of argument and debate ensued as they tried to interpret the meanings of these messages, as they were mainly delivered by sign language. Then the convoy set off from Manila and ten hours later was hit by a typhoon. Again the hatches were bolted down and in plunging, heaving darkness, the prisoners sweated, hoped and prayed.[42] Their lives were threatened by the Japanese, by American submarines and now nature itself seemed determined to destroy them. Eventually, after what seemed an eternity, the weather calmed, the hatches were opened and the wretched prisoners in the hold gazed up at placid blue skies, drinking in the cool fresh air.

When the first batch of prisoners who had been allowed on deck to use the latrines returned, they told the other prisoners that their ship was being towed by another. They later learned from one of the Korean guards that the propeller shaft had been broken during the storm and that they had been floating at the mercy of the elements for hours.[43]

Eventually they reached T'ainan in Formosa (now Taiwan) on 18 June. The cargo of aluminium ore was unloaded and they were transferred to yet another ship, the *Tamahoku Maru*.[44] This had previously been used to carry horses and mules to the Philippines and little effort had been made to clean up the ensuing mess. The holds were still filthy, stinking and infested with rats, which made conditions more terrifying, even by hell-ship standards. Despite this, it had been loaded with a cargo of sugar, which was soon discovered and systematically raided by the rats as well as the prisoners for the remainder of the voyage. The sugar improved the flavour of their food and tea but it was also nourishing the rats. There were also about 500 Japanese servicemen on board and, judging by their shoddy appearance, the POWs guessed they were survivors of a submarine attack.[45]

There were lifebelts on board, but most were not issued, despite protests from the prisoners. Instead, they were stacked against the ship's side forward of the guards.[46] The guards, mainly Koreans, kept watch in the hold from a special raised platform near the hatch but they went on deck for their food. Whenever the alarms sounded they climbed on deck and bolted the hatches shut from above.

The convoy was steaming up the Formosan Straits, between what is now Taiwan and mainland China. There were fourteen ships and two destroyers remaining.[47] On their first day out of port, two American bombers attacked and hit one of the oil tankers.[48] The entire ship exploded, scattering oil and debris over a wide area. The terrified prisoners locked into the holds braced themselves and considered themselves lucky when a bomb fell just 50 yards behind the ship. Every day there were a number of air and submarine alarms. The crews of the Allied bombers and submarines had no idea that one of the ships they were trying to sink carried almost a thousand weary POWs. While the Japanese routinely refused to place Red Cross markers on ships ferrying Allied prisoners, they did, however, put these markers on ships carrying munitions.

Whenever the alarm sounded, the hatches were slammed down and locked. The prisoners sat terrified in the steaming darkness, listening to the depth charges rattling like giant chains along the sides of the ship, expecting a torpedo to hit at any moment. In the sweltering filth of the hold, the naval officers among them could give a rough estimate as to how far away the depth charges were exploding. They assured their trembling comrades that as long as they heard these explosions, there was little chance of being hit.[49] They prayed that on this occasion the American submarines would miss their target.

The number of ships began to diminish as each night the submarines picked off the ships one by one.[50] On a number of occasions when the alarm was stood down, some of the crew requested the medical advice of the POW doctors. During these consultations a guard usually accompanied the crew as an interpreter. It became obvious that the Japanese merchant seamen had lost all interest in the war and were aware of the inevitable outcome. One of the crew informed a POW doctor that he had been torpedoed nine times. He was sure that the next would be his last. The doctors were paid with sake and food, which made a welcome addition to their ration.[51]

By the time the convoy reached the Ryuku Islands, several hundred miles south of Japan, only one oil tanker and six cargo ships, as well as a few escorts, remained of the original convoy. They passed the island of Okinawa, unaware that it would become the scene of one of the bloodiest battles of the Pacific less than a year later. It was to be used as the base for the final invasion of mainland Japan.

The convoy was due to reach its destination port of Kure Harbour in Hiroshima on Sunday 25 June. By that stage there were 880 POWs on board the *Tamahoku Maru*. The majority of the POW officers were lying in the holds on the metal under-deck with their feet towards the mast. On that final night of the voyage there was an air of almost universal celebration among prisoners, crew and guards. For the prisoners it was the end of a long and terrifying journey that began when they left the docks at Tan Jon Priok in Java over five weeks previously. For the guards and crew it meant they would soon be home with their families. The guards were all in high spirits, getting drunk on sake and singing. Some even shared their alcohol with the prisoners.[52] Lights illuminated the coastline: large-scale aerial bombing of the Japanese mainland would not commence for another few months and the country was not yet living under a blackout, even at this late stage of the war.[53] The crew felt so confident that, for the first time in weeks, the ships' lights were switched on. Locked below deck in the hold of the *Tamahoku Maru*, the prisoners began to sing the wartime songs made popular by Vera Lynn and for a finale before being ordered to bed down they sang an Andrews Sisters song that seemed appropriate to their destination: 'I'll Be With You in Apple Blossom Time'.[54] As the last chorus rang out above and below decks they ached with nostalgia but at least they felt safer than they had for many weeks.

7

An Unlikely Saviour

On the afternoon of 8 June 1944, an American submarine, the USS *Tang*, quietly slipped through the channel of Pearl Harbor on her third war patrol.[1] *Tang* sailed east on a 4,000-mile voyage to the East China Sea. The submarine captain was Lieutenant Commander Richard O'Kane and his mission was to hunt Japanese shipping in the waters between China and Japan. O'Kane would go on to become one of the most renowned American submarine captains of the Second World War. Two weeks later, on 24 June, *Tang* was going about its business of sinking ships off the coast of the southern Japanese island of Kyushu.[2] O'Kane knew that enemy shipping would have to pass through the area and he had received a radio report that a convoy was heading his way. Under the cover of darkness O'Kane ordered the crew to surface so that they could scan the horizon using binoculars in the hope of spotting the convoy. It also allowed O'Kane to increase *Tang*'s speed and close in on the convoy. They were just 25 miles south-west of Nagasaki when at 9.45 p.m. the radar operator announced over the speaker: 'radar contact, bearing one five zero, range twenty-five thousand yards'.[3]

The radar operator had detected a small convoy sailing north at full speed. Shortly after came a further report of 'a mess of ships, still twenty-five thousand yards'.[4] Then came the coded confirmation 'convoy'. The crew prepared to attack.[5]

The tension on the bridge mounted as six large transport ships in two columns became clear. On either side of the larger ships were six smaller escorts. *Tang* moved in slowly, its low profile on the surface making it difficult to be spotted from the higher decks of the ships. The submarine sneaked across the stern of the leading escort destroyer on the starboard side. Then it took the same course as the main convoy, travelling faster to overtake its prey and get in position to attack. By now *Tang* was within 1,500 yards of the main convoy and still had not been spotted. O'Kane decided to target two of the large freighters in the right-hand column. When the submarine was ahead of its target, O'Kane ordered the crew to 'make all tubes ready for firing' and swung *Tang* to port.

In the hold of the *Tamahoku Maru*, MacCarthy was trying to sleep. He had wrapped his mosquito netting around his feet to protect them from the rats that infested the area where the prisoners slept. He could not understand why for the previous four nights they had foraged around his feet when there was a whole cargo of sugar nearby for them to feast on. Suddenly he felt a rat close to his feet: it was stuck in the netting. He sat up, terrified, and tried to disentangle himself from the rat.

At exactly 11.50 p.m. O'Kane gave the order to fire. *Tang* sent a spread of three torpedoes towards the leading freighter. A similar spread was quickly launched at the second freighter. The crew held their breath for the run of one minute forty-eight seconds. 'Thirty seconds to go …'

On board the *Tamahoku Maru* MacCarthy did not know whether he or the rat was more frightened as they struggled to escape the netting. Then the torpedo struck.[6] The explosion lifted him violently off the metal deck as the torpedo hit directly underneath, just forward of the bridge on the starboard side.[7]

Away to starboard of the ship, O'Kane saw the flash, followed by an ominous rumble. He could see that the lead freighter had been hit twice: once in the stern and once in the middle. Its entire side seemed to have been ripped out. Then came more explosions as the second ship burst into flames. The escort ships began dropping depth charges to sink the submarine. O'Kane circled *Tang* around looking for the nearest deep water in which to dive.

The torpedo had blown off the front length of the keel that held the *Tamahoku Maru* together. The blast also blew the covers off the locked hatches but had destroyed the wooden stairways leading to the deck above. There was no escape for the prisoners below.[8] Then the lights went out and suddenly MacCarthy was plunged into pitch darkness. He called out to the officers on either side of him and was surprised when they did not respond. He was amazed that the explosion had not woken them. Then the awful thought occurred to him that they were either dead or unconscious. He later surmised that the explosion had caused a shockwave through the metal deck and that this had fractured their necks. He was lucky to have been sitting up – the rat's intervention had saved his life.

As water rushed into the hold, MacCarthy was initially overcome by a feeling of hopelessness and he was frozen with fear. The ship's engines had been turning at full speed at the moment of impact. With the keel blown off, the propellers were driving the ship faster and deeper into the incoming sea. Alone in the hold and surrounded by the lifeless bodies of his comrades, MacCarthy knew he had to find a way out or he would drown. No one would be coming to help him. From growing up in a busy harbour he knew his way around ships and from his recent trips to the deck to treat the crew, he knew there was a metal inspection ladder at the side of the hold which lead up to the deck. He scrambled towards it in the dark, found it and climbed upwards. Battling against the pressure of the water cascading down from above, he climbed upwards rung by rung. Suddenly a hand grasped his ankle. Spurred on by terror, he managed to pull them both to the top. Then, without looking to see who had followed him, he shook his leg free and hauled himself onto the tilting deck. All around 'ships seemed to be sinking everywhere' and the terrifying scene was lit by fires raging in the two oil tankers that had also been torpedoed.[9]

Without thinking, he jumped overboard and started putting as much distance as possible between himself and the rapidly sinking ship. The summers he spent in the cold waters of the Atlantic around west Cork came good as he 'swam the best fifty yards' of his life.[10] Then he paused, exhausted, and treaded water as he turned to survey the sinking ship. From his vantage point on the surface he could see the ship ploughing deeper towards the seabed. The stern tilted higher and higher. The propellers had stopped rotating but those who had jumped overboard immediately after the explosion had been dragged under. Their bloody remains were glued to the blades of the propellers. The ship's death struggle ceased abruptly. It shuddered and began to plunge downwards. MacCarthy took a deep breath and closed his eyes expecting to be sucked down after it but nothing happened. He realised that he was not going to die just yet.

As he kept himself afloat, he tried to come to terms with what he had just survived. Everything had happened so quickly. It was later estimated that the ship sank in a matter of minutes.[11] He guessed he had escaped from the hold about a minute before the ship sank.[12]

MacCarthy saw some wreckage floating by and swam to it, grateful to have something to cling on to. All around, above the crackle of flames from the burning tanker, he could hear the screams of surviving prisoners and crew. High above, he could see the stars shining down placidly, oblivious to the human carnage below. He later recalled looking up to the sky and calling out to God: 'you'll have to help me now – there is nowhere else I'm going from here.'[13]

He began discovering other survivors during the night and soon heard an Australian accent saying 'that you, Doc?' from a nearby piece of flotsam. He swam towards the voice and found two of the Australians with whom he had endured the previous years of captivity in Java. They were looking the worse for wear. One was badly injured, so he patched him up as best as he could. He then began the most unusual 'rounds' of his medical career, swimming from one piece of wreckage to another. In his open-water surgery, he bound broken collarbones, roughly splinted broken bones and stopped bleeding by putting clamps on severed arteries.[14] He managed all of this by using bits of rope, string and wood he picked up from the drifting wreckage.

Any guards found amid the floating debris during the night were killed as soon as they were discovered. Each POW took a turn beating the guard over the head with a piece of wood, so that one man could not be held responsible.[15] Whilst hanging onto a piece of wreckage, MacCarthy looked around and saw the Korean guard they had nicknamed 'Junior' floating nearby. Previously cruel and sadistic, Junior was now a very frightened man.

> He was grabbed by two of the Australians and hauled on to their piece of wreckage. They then started to address him using a combination of sign language and four letter words.

They asked him if he wanted to go to Heaven or Hell. As they posed this question they tested pieces of floating wood for strength. By now Junior was receiving the general message loud and clear. He pleaded in Korean, and even offered one of his tormentors his ring as a bribe for mercy.[16]

MacCarthy disapproved of what they were doing but shouted at the Australians to get it finished quickly before daylight in case they were spotted by some Japanese floating nearby. They counted 'one, two, three ...', swung the solid piece of wood and Junior's skull shattered with one blow. His body sank almost immediately. MacCarthy was unable to count how many former guards died in similar circumstances that night 'but there was a lot of them'.[17]

As they clung to the wreckage their bare feet often touched soft, yielding objects that turned out to be the bodies of women and children who had been on one of the passenger ships in the convoy.[18] They had been evacuated from the Philippines and Taiwan in preparation for the defence of those islands against the imminent counter-invasion by the Americans. MacCarthy was shocked when he dragged one of the bodies to the surface and found himself looking into 'the sightless eyes of a dead child, with its mouth fixed in an anguished scream'.[19]

When the sun finally rose it revealed the full extent of the carnage. The surrounding sea was a heaving, oily slick. The oil tanker was virtually burned out but still afloat in the distance. Post-war records later confirmed that two passenger-cargo ships and two freighters were sunk with a salvo of six torpedoes: the *Tamahoku Maru*, *Tainan Maru*, *Nasusan Maru* and *Kennichi Maru*. The attack was over within ten minutes and was later recorded as one of the most devastating submarine attacks of the war.[20]

Suddenly a periscope popped up out of the water: it was from an American submarine. The floating survivors started screaming and waving their arms frantically. They thought they were about to be rescued. Below the surface, the American submariners were either unaware that the POWs were desperately trying to get their attention or could not risk surfacing without putting themselves in danger. The periscope observed the night's work and the destruction that had been inflicted on Japanese shipping. Then it disappeared and the submarine dived. It was well timed as two Japanese naval planes appeared overhead at that moment and started dropping depth charges.

The prisoners were once again in the firing line. The exploding depth charges caused sudden, violent decompression on their stomachs. The underwater blasts crushed their chests and caused them to vomit. They had to react quickly and improvise in order to lessen the pain. Whenever the depth charges exploded underwater they grabbed the nearest piece of wreckage and levered themselves out of the water to avoid the worst effects of the decompression.

Eventually the sound of the planes faded into the distance and they were alone again. Time dragged on interminably as they clung to the debris and silently prayed to be rescued by anyone, Allies or Japanese. They had no water or food. It was decided that only the seriously injured could be allowed to lie on the rafts. If everyone climbed on they would sink. Fortunately for the terrified prisoners the sea was not terribly cold but after a while their skin began to look shrivelled and was turning a lifeless grey colour. MacCarthy thought of his family and prayed earnestly: 'Please God, don't let me die. Not now. Not after so much.'[21]

After floating aimlessly for twelve hours, the survivors – about forty in all – were picked up by a Japanese destroyer.[22]

The prisoners struggled out of the water and gathered on the deck. They were hungry, naked, thirsty and covered in oil and blood. Initially the Japanese sailors did not know who or what they were and gave them rice balls and some water. Then a naval officer with very poor English tried to question them but neither side had a clue what the other was saying. Eventually when it was clear that they were POWs the crew began systematically to beat the prisoners unconscious one by one and throw them overboard. When the lifeless POWs hit the water they were sucked into the surge of the propellers and pulped into a bloody trail behind the fast-moving destroyer. MacCarthy and two others saw what was happening and decided their only option was to dive overboard. With characteristic understatement he recalled fifty years later that 'a destroyer travelling at full speed is a difficult thing to get off'.[23]

Helping each other, the remaining survivors swam back to their bits of wreckage, now some distance away. They eventually reached it, exhausted and now even more frightened.

They had no choice but to swim either to the mainland about 20 miles away to the east or to a group of islands in the opposite direction, about the same distance away. They decided to paddle towards the islands, more in hope than expectation. As they paddled endlessly, the conversation turned to the possibility that even if they miraculously managed to reach the island, there was a chance that the Japanese islanders would decide to take revenge and kill them. They continued their struggle through the night and early the following morning five or six whaling ships appeared. The ships were returning from a six-month trip to the whaling grounds north of Japan.[24] The exhausted prisoners were relieved when the crew started plucking the survivors out of the water and sailed into Nagasaki Harbour.

At that time Nagasaki was a large and busy port city on the south coast of Kyushu island, the most southerly of Japan's four main home islands. In 1944 it was an industrial city with a population of around 270,000, many of whom worked in the steel mills, shipyards and armaments factories built by American and British corporations earlier in the twentieth century.[25]

When the whaling boats finally arrived at the docks, the military officials waiting for them on the pier insisted that the crew turn round and dump the POWs out at sea. But after their long and dangerous journey the whalers were determined to offload their catch and return to their families, so they refused.

An argument continued until eventually the port officials relented. They decided to allow the prisoners to disembark and be used for their original purpose, to work as forced labour for the Japanese war economy. MacCarthy recalled that in all, forty-two survivors out of the original 880 prisoners on board when the torpedo struck now stood naked on the dock.[26] Official accounts mention 212 survivors of the *Tamahoku Maru* but it is possible they did not all arrive in Nagasaki at the same time.[27]

The shrivelled and salt-encrusted bodies of the POWs were covered with cuts from the nails and sharp edges of the wreckage and their skin was wrinkled like new-born babies. They were then forced to sign a document stating that they had been sunk by the cowardly Americans and bravely rescued by the merciful Japanese. They signed, adding U/D after their signatures to denote 'under duress'. When MacCarthy looked at his signature he was shocked. He wondered if the handwriting was really his – was he still the same person? It seemed incredible to him to see his own signature for the first time in so long. He had been through so much degradation since he had last been asked to sign his name that he could barely even believe in his own existence.[28] He no longer felt like a person.

The prisoners were forced to march – or rather hobble – from the docks, through the streets of Nagasaki, carrying the badly injured on makeshift stretchers. Even though the crowds gathered to jeer and shout at them, the POWs were overcome by a sense of elation. Unable to fathom that they were still alive, now surely, after all they had been through, they could survive anything. A few of the Australians flicked their exposed penises towards the crowds or gave the V sign. Having experienced so much suffering they seemed to be losing their minds. Many of them would never recover, but at least now, for the first time in what felt like an eternity, they felt defiant.

They were led to the Urakami valley, the industrial centre of Nagasaki, which lies either side of the river that bears the same name. It stretches inland from the harbour and is bordered by steep hills. The upper slopes of the hills were, at the time, covered with terraces of lush green paddy fields.

Eventually, the POWs arrived at their destination – the Mitsubishi Steel & Arms Works. In the yard of the factory was a camp previously built for Japanese workers. When the workers were sent to fight for the Emperor it had been converted to a POW labour camp. Camp Fukuoka 14B would become MacCarthy's home for more than a year.

The prisoners were immediately packed into a large room with another group of prisoners. It measured about 40 feet square. They would remain stuck in this cramped prison-within-a-prison for weeks. There were no washing facilities, no privacy and the prisoners had no idea for how long they would be incarcerated there. It was late June. Summers in Japan are extremely hot and humid, so the cramped conditions became unbearable. The prisoners were given one meal a day and had enough water to drink, but the only toilet facilities were a few buckets in the corner. They congregated into different groups according to their various nationalities. These groups sat, talked and slept together all day. The days turned into weeks. Stress levels rose and the groups began to get on each other's nerves. Tempers frayed and fights broke out. The reason they were being kept in isolation was that the Japanese were paranoid that spies had been inserted into the group during their journey. As a result, the prisoners had to remain segregated from the rest of the camp until their names and numbers had been checked with the authorities in Java and Singapore.

The claustrophobic conditions became so unbearable that, in desperation, two of the Dutch Indonesian prisoners committed suicide by biting through their wrist veins. With no medical supplies, the rest of the prisoners could only watch as they bled to death. A number died from pneumonia and within a short period there were only sixty-five POWs left in the room. Eventually, after five excruciating weeks, their documentation arrived and they were 'released' into the main camp. Having not washed for so long, they were in a filthy state. Unsurprisingly, their first priority was to wash themselves and their clothes.

They soon discovered that most of the POWs already in the camp were Dutch and Indonesian. Ironically, there had been a historic connection between Nagasaki and the Netherlands for centuries. During 200 years of self-imposed isolation, from the seventeenth to the nineteenth century, the only European country Japan allowed trade with was the Netherlands. Today, a traditional local cake offered to visitors to the city is still known as 'Holland cake'. But during the Second World War there was no special welcome for Dutch prisoners.

MacCarthy found the main camp in reasonably good condition compared to those he had experienced in Java and Singapore. He was relieved to find a washhouse in the centre of the camp. It was fitted with a large cement bath that even had hot water where they could bathe at the end of work shifts.

They were initially assigned to the Mitsubishi Steel & Arms Works, adjacent to the camp. There they joined Indonesian POWs welding plates to the hull of an aircraft carrier.[29] In defiance of international rules for the treatment of prisoners of war, the Japanese forced officers as well as men to work.[30] Every working day in the camp began at 5 a.m. Bells clanged and the prisoners had to be on parade at 5.15 a.m. They were counted and recounted, as they shouted out their numbers in Japanese. At 5.45 a.m. they were given mixed rice pap, millet and hot water to drink. By 6 a.m. they were on parade again and then marched off to work. At twelve noon there was a half hour break for food (the same as breakfast but with pickled fish or pickled vegetables, or dried fish powder mixed with water from their water bottles). They went back to work until 5.30 p.m. when they were marched back to camp, paraded, searched and counted. Then the punishments were meted out. If there had been a complaint from one of their guards or a civilian foreman for misdemeanours – such as not working hard enough, talking at work, or being caught smoking – the prisoner's number was called out. Every POW knew the sound of his number in Japanese and had to step forward and wait either to be punched repeatedly in the face or beaten over the head and back with rifle butts or bamboo sticks. After this daily ritual they went for a communal bath and ate their food, which was the same as the other rations. At 9 p.m. the evening delousing ritual began and then they tried to sleep, knowing that the procedure would begin all over again in a few hours.[31]

This numbing routine was unending – day after day, month after month.

When they first arrived MacCarthy was surprised that the lights in the camp were left on all night. This was a common practice in Japan as late as 1944 and there was no form of blackout. However, this would soon change.

Before settling down to sleep after a long day of backbreaking work, each POW had to perform the same ritual, removing their clothes, and examining them seam by seam for lice.[32] They did the same with their tatami sleeping mats. Any lice that were discovered were crushed between their thumbnails. Fleas were accepted as an unavoidable inconvenience and the bites made them look like they were permanently suffering from measles.[33] When they eventually went to sleep, the prisoners were usually so exhausted that they did not notice the lights or remaining fleas or lice.

Work on the aircraft carrier involved riveting plates on to the ship's sides. The ship had high bamboo scaffolding on both sides. The prisoners worked in teams of five. One heated the rivet; it was then thrown into a metal bucket held by another, extracted by a third who wedged it into a hole in the plate that was held in place by a fourth. The fifth prisoner secured the rivet using a small jackhammer. They added a clever act of sabotage into their rhythmic pattern, immersing the red-hot rivet in cold water before it was inserted in the metal plate.[34] The intention was to weaken the rivet by the causing fragmentation of the metal as a result of the sudden change in temperature. Most of the rivets were sabotaged and the POWs gleefully imagined the plates bursting open on the sides of the carrier once it made it out to the open sea. They did not worry about getting caught because the guards never came near the scaffolding. Soon after starting work at the factory they organised a number of 'accidents' where guards were pushed from the high scaffolding onto the concrete dockyard below. They managed to kill about eight guards and from then on the prisoners worked on the scaffolding unobserved.[35]

The primitive toilet facilities at the camp were merely a pit about 10 feet in depth. The floor over the pit was a series of slits running the length of the building, over which they had to squat to relieve themselves. Once a week the floorboards were removed and any POW too weak to go out to work in the factory had to climb down into the cesspit and toil, knee deep in faeces, filling up buckets with raw sewage and surrounded by the nauseating stench, clouds of flies and thousands of maggots. The buckets of filth were hauled up and taken away in handcarts by local farmers to be used as manure in their paddy fields in the hills.[36] It was a job detested by the POWs who were already suffering from malnutrition, sickness and disease. Maggots got lodged in their hair, ears and clothing, where they competed with the lice and fleas for what sustenance they could get from the prisoners' bodies.

The exhausted prisoners were denied even the basic familiarity of a seven-day week. It was replaced by a ten-day cycle where every tenth day in the camp was known as *Yasume* day (rest day).[37] On these precious rest days they still had to work, as the struggle against disease and infection meant that the early part of the day was spent cleaning out and delousing their barrack rooms. When the weather was warm, clothing was washed, tatami sleeping mats and pressed paper blankets were cleaned and taken out into the sunshine and aired. This usually allowed about three days' respite from lice and fleabites.[38] With the cleaning and washing finished, most of the exhausted captives slept. Others played cards, which had been secretly handmade from pressed cardboard or pieces of tin, and marked with the name of the card rather than the suits. It was clear that their tedious, numbing routine could not last forever but perhaps they would have found those endlessly repetitive days easier to endure had they known the horror that was to come.

8

A Slave in Nagasaki

In autumn 1944, the Japanese moved all of the senior
Allied POW officers to their puppet state in Manchuria,
or Manchukuo, as the Japanese named it, where they had
an army of almost a million. They planned to use the Allied
officers as bargaining chips in the event of an American invasion
of Japan. This left doctors, dentists and clergymen as the senior
ranking Allied officers in the camps. MacCarthy suddenly found
himself the senior ranking officer in Camp 14B. Now he was in
charge of the prisoners and responsible for their actions as well
as their medical care. This put him in a dangerous and nerve-
wracking situation.[1]

When the daily work shift at the Mitsubishi factory ended,
the prisoners were marched back to the camp to begin the
usual routine of being lined up and counted. Then the beatings
commenced. From the time he became the senior ranking
POW officer, MacCarthy received the same punishment as
each offender because they were his responsibility.[2] These daily
beatings would take their toll many years later.

For their dangerous, backbreaking slave labour, the POWs
received a nominal payment from the Mitsubishi Corporation.
The daily rate was thirty cents for officers, twenty cents for
senior NCOs and ten cents for regular army, naval and air force
personnel. Those who were too sick to work received no pay

and their food rations were reduced, so their food had to be supplemented from the rations of those who were able to work.[3]

The work lists were added up daily and at the end of the week the total of their pay was doled out. As they queued to receive their pay, the Japanese prepared to distribute the cigarette ration of ten cigarettes a week. By cruel coincidence, the cost of the cigarettes almost always equalled the exact amount of their total pay. This weekly charade meant that the prisoners were effectively working for a salary of ten cigarettes per week. The only winner in this situation was the non-smoker who was 'able to exchange his cigarettes for extra food from the heavy smokers, whose craving for tobacco took precedence over everything'.[4]

MacCarthy was astonished to see half-starved nicotine-addicted men:

> selling part of their already meagre food ration in exchange for cigarettes. I could do nothing to stop this form of trading, although I pleaded and argued with the suppliers as well as the eager recipients. The staring, defiant eyes of a man who had sold all his rations for cigarettes haunt my memory. He had turned his back to avoid watching the other eat, puffing away at his all too expensive cigarette.

Cigarettes were the main currency of the camps. The men gambled and played cards to try to win more cigarettes. Over time this currency increased in value as each cigarette was cut into three equal parts.

During the war the Red Cross distributed parcels to prisoners in POW camps throughout the world. These contained tinned food, condensed milk, chocolate, tea, soap and such. In Japanese POW camps they were usually not passed on to the intended recipients and if they were, they were rarely intact. The first indication of the arrival of a shipment of Red Cross parcels at Camp 14B was when the guards handed out tubes of American 'Barbisol' shaving cream – one tube to every five men. The shaving cream was distributed but the food in the parcel was not.

Soon the reason for the generosity became clear. With the ever-deteriorating sanitary conditions, the Japanese were afraid that the filthy lice-ridden prisoners could spread diseases among the local population. The POWs were ordered to use the shaving cream, with sharpened knives and bits of steel to shave their heads and faces. Being forced against their will to shave their heads added further humiliation and degradation to their captivity.[5]

On studying the ingredients of the shaving foam, MacCarthy noticed that it could be used for more than just shaving. One of its ingredients

> was a substance called salycilic acid (a main constituent of aspirin) and this was known to be good for certain skin diseases. To our absurdly limited medical stores Barbisol was heaven-sent. We used the cream to dress the numerous cases of open and weeping tropical ulcers, which were then covered with cloth or paper, tied together with string.[6]

In October 1944, as their first winter in Japan began, the prisoners were assigned to work at another factory. This was the Mitsubishi Ordnance Works, situated about a mile further up the valley. The Type 91 aerial torpedoes that were dropped on Pearl Harbor had been manufactured at this facility.[7] MacCarthy was set to work casting and polishing bronze propellers for naval ships. The work was not as physically demanding as in the shipyard and despite being monotonous and dusty, it had the advantage of being warm. As outside temperatures began to fall, the heat from the furnaces and large charcoal braziers provided a welcome relief from the cold. Also, the civilian workers ate at the factory and would occasionally slip some food or a cup of tea to the starving prisoners.[8]

The Ordnance Works also provided opportunities to improve their almost non-existent medical supplies. As was the case throughout his captivity, MacCarthy's responsibilities required him to coordinate the theft and manufacture of medical supplies when opportunities arose. The only stocks issued by the Japanese were some poor-quality bandages, a primitive form of red dye disinfectant and, for some reason unknown to him, vast amounts of safety pins.[9]

Despite the limitations of his circumstances, MacCarthy was still able to perform life-saving operations. He was especially proud of his work on two cases of lung abscesses (emphysema), when, 'because of the rapid deterioration of the prisoners concerned, it was decided to take a gamble and operate. First I cut into the lung over the site of the abscess with a razor blade, taking care not to puncture the lung. Then I planted a drainage needle, which was inserted through a hollow tube (tracula).'

The drainage needle and tracula had both been handmade in the factory out of sight of the guards. These had been sterilised by immersion in a chemical used in the factory – potassium permanganate – which the prisoners managed to steal. A home-made syringe, also secretly made in the factory, was used to suck the pus out of the wound. The protruding tracula tube was left to bubble through water in a bottle and, every three days MacCarthy would remove the equipment, sterilise it and reinsert the tube. 'Three weeks later my efforts were rewarded, as both abscesses dried up. The incision was allowed to heal and both patients survived their captivity.'

As the senior Allied medical professional in the camp, he had no choice but to improvise when an emergency arose. He had not studied dentistry but, when a rotten tooth had to be removed, he was the only person the prisoners could turn to. Such operations, he later noted, 'required courage, from both doctor and patient, and drastic action'. Four men would hold the prisoner down. MacCarthy would use an ordinary pair of pliers, also stolen from the factory, and pull the tooth out without the benefit of an anaesthetic.[10]

As the weather began to grow colder, the prisoners were issued with captured British Army greatcoats. This brought an unexpected bonus as they discovered that the decorative buttons were popular as souvenirs among the local civilian workers at the factory. They exchanged these in return for rice and cigarettes.[11] One prisoner even managed to persuade a local worker that the buttons on his coat were, in fact, made of gold and he graciously traded these precious items for even larger amounts than the usual exchange rate.

Overall, these minuscule additions could not improve the general situation and as winter 1944 progressed, the POWs were surviving on the very last of their reserves. None of them had any illusions about their chances of living through a second winter in Japan. Far different from their previous experiences in Java, Japanese winters are cold and long. This was the first time MacCarthy had experienced such cold since France and England several years earlier in the war. The POWs were grateful that one of the few comforts at Camp 14B was a pot-bellied stove, which provided plenty of warmth. It was in constant use, the metal glowing red hot as sawdust was continuously fed into it. The stove became the prisoners' focal point throughout the winter.[12]

All the while it was becoming clearer that the Allies were getting the upper hand and this gave them hope. There were more and more American bombers in the skies and the frequency of the air raids was increasing. The Mariana islands of Guam, Tinian and Saipan had been captured by the Americans in July and August 1944, and the airbases on the islands were operating by November 1944. This meant that the Japanese home islands were now within range of American B-29 'Superfortress' bombers. The US Air Force's Strategic Bombing campaign against Japan was about to be brought to bear on a population for whom the war had been a distant reality. Japan's air and naval power had been depleted after years of ceaseless war, leaving it defenceless against the sustained air attack it was about to face.

Meanwhile, the death rate of the prisoners increased as winter temperatures dropped. Death seemed to be the only escape from the misery of their captivity. When a prisoner died, the men were ordered to strip him quickly and, while still warm, the emaciated body was curled up and stuffed into an empty wooden barrel before rigor mortis set in.[13] A lid was then hammered onto the barrel and prisoners would be selected to take it by handcart to the crematorium. The ashes were placed in an urn, which was marked with the dead man's rank, name and number and then carried back to the camp. Every two weeks the urns were collected from the four POW camps in the area and brought to the crypt of the nearby Urakami Catholic cathedral. As they cremated more and more of their friends, the prisoners found each day a battle for survival. They wondered if their corpse would be the next to be shoved roughly into a wooden barrel and burnt without a hint of dignity.

In December there was an increase in deficiency diseases such as beriberi and dropsy.[14] MacCarthy was himself now suffering from beriberi and a diary entry hidden in a hand-bound note-book gives a rare glimpse of the true extent of his suffering.

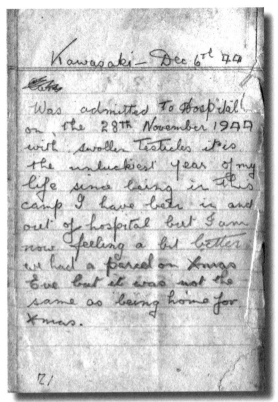

Kawasaki – Dec 6th 44

Was admitted to hospital on the 28th November 1944 with swollen testicles it is the unluckiest year of my life since being in this camp I have been in and out of hospital but I am now feeling a bit better we had a parcel on Xmas Eve but it was not the same as being home for Xmas.

121

An entry from Aidan MacCarthy's prisoner-of-war camp diary.

(Interestingly, the notebook mainly includes the lyrics of songs but has diary entries hidden among them. MacCarthy's daughters discovered it in 2015.)

> Was admitted to hospital on the 28th November 1944 with swollen testicles, it is the unluckiest year of my life since being in this camp I have been in and out of hospital but I am now feeling a bit better.

One of the most distressing conditions he treated was also a side effect of poor blood circulation caused by sustained

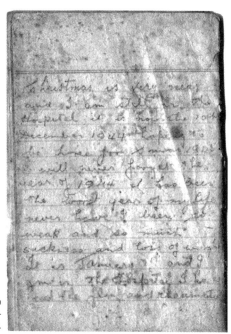

A page from Aidan MacCarthy's prisoner-of-war camp diary.

malnutrition. This was dry gangrene of the toes due to cellular thickening of the extremities, blocking the blood supply. The physical appearance of the condition was revolting as the affected area was basically dead. Under the circumstances there was no cure for the condition and cases were typically fatal.

> But we still went ahead and removed the dead toes with a quick snip of our pliers. Though this did nothing to prolong the patient's life, it certainly helped psychologically.

As 1944 drew to a close, his will was being tested beyond anything he had experienced before.

> Christmas is very near and I am still in the hospital. It is now the 10th of December, hoping to be home for Xmas 1945. I will never forget the year of 1944 it has been the

worst year of my life. Never have I been so weak and so much sickness and loss of weight'.[15]

As their third Christmas in captivity approached, the prisoners appealed to the guards to allow them to visit the local Urakami Catholic cathedral. At first, the commandant refused. The concept was alien to the camp administration, so the prisoners tried a different approach. They told the camp officials that it was their local Shinto shrine, a place where the prisoners wanted to honour their dead. When they mentioned the ashes stored in the crypt, they were finally allowed to go.

Nagasaki was unique in Japan in that it had the country's only Catholic cathedral. It had been the centre of Japanese Catholicism for centuries. The origins of the community went back as far as the sixteenth century when Jesuit missionaries, following Portuguese traders and led by Francis Xavier, arrived to spread Christianity. They were later persecuted by the local shogunate and the imperial government when Christianity appeared to be gaining too much influence. As part of this persecution, twenty-six Christian martyrs were executed at the end of the sixteenth century. They had been crucified on Nishizaka Hill – overlooking Camp 14B from a distance of about 500 yards. In 1945 there was a Catholic congregation of around 22,000 in the city.[16] Unusually for Japan, the sound of the cathedral bells ringing out across the Urakami valley was a familiar part of the city's daily routine. Many people believed that, for much of the war, Nagasaki was spared intensive Allied bombing because of its Christian heritage. But the real reason would emerge later.

The fact that the Christian community in the city was founded by the same Jesuit order that had educated him in Clongowes Wood must have given MacCarthy some solace as he led his men out through the gates of the camp towards the cathedral. They were under a heavily armed guard and accompanied by many non-Catholic prisoners who simply wanted a glimpse of what the rest of Nagasaki was like. The walk took their weary bodies thirty minutes through the stark, depressing city streets. The journey gave them a bleak impression of life in wartime Japan. Huge swathes of shack-like houses had been demolished to create fire lanes intended to reduce the effectiveness of American incendiary bombs. There were far more fire lanes than they had expected.

> Many additional waterpoints and power lines were being erected. High voltage cables were slung on flimsy poles and were spread haphazardly all over the place. They constituted a major hazard and when typhoons struck they snapped in the high winds. Their lethal electrically-charged cables whipped and crackled as they flailed about, causing appalling damage and severe burns to anyone in their path.[17]

When they arrived at the cathedral they found the main body of the church completely empty of seats. Although still a functioning cathedral, it was also being used to store munitions.

> The choir loft and the back of the nave were packed with cases of shells. In the nave a group of women were filling and sorting the shells into rows on long tables. The high altar was intact, and decorated with candles, a white cloth and flowers. A red oil lamp was burning to the side of the altar. We knelt down and said a rosary in English and Dutch. During the course of this our guards stamped around the bare floor of the Cathedral, smoking, laughing

and spitting. Our praying seemed to cause them great amusement. Some Catholic priests arrived in the church while we were praying. Two of them were Italian, but when we asked them for rosary beads, they apologetically said that they were forbidden to speak to us.[18]

Despite this, one of the Japanese priests kept apologising to the prisoners and when one of the guards spotted him he became enraged. The priest was viciously beaten before the altar.

MacCarthy always credited his strong faith with giving him the strength to persevere throughout his captivity. He had served as an altar boy in his youth and had spent so much time in churches that to see a cathedral desecrated in such a way affected him deeply. Unable to intervene on behalf of the priest, he knelt there praying and tried to retreat into his inner sanctuary. He tried to visualise the family pub and grocery in Castletownbere and picture his parents, siblings and the faces of friends and locals, remembering their voices, stories and mannerisms. Throughout his years of captivity, he had developed this technique to keep himself focused on survival and escape the horror of his surroundings. To delve deeper into memories, he would begin a mental stocktake of the products on the shelves – the shelves that had been made by the Italian craftsmen over thirty years previously. Starting on the top shelf, he would move from left to right, remembering the labels, the quantities and where each item was placed. When he had worked his way across from left to right, he moved on to the shelf below and repeated the process. He would continue on down the six shelves, reliving a task he had done so often for his father whilst growing up. This was the place where he was raised and the Japanese could never take that from him. His memories gave him the strength to believe that one day he would make it home.

But as he knelt praying in the Urakami Cathedral he tried to conjure up this image and he could only see shadows and:

> faintly stirring images of the past. But I could make out no detail. Not a single item stood out and the familiar village personalities were indiscernible. Worse still, when I tried harder to visualise them, they turned towards me becoming all too familiar. Suddenly the shop was full of Japanese officers, posturing mockingly at me. I rose from my knees, shaking. Now there was not even mental escape from the brutal environment about me.[19]

He thought he was beginning to lose his mind. The camp guards had finally taken over his sanctuary and he could no longer escape.

9

Final Reserves

As the New Year began, around the world the war was going well for the Allies. The Americans had secured most of the Philippines and were retaking one Pacific island after another. In Europe, the German air force had effectively been wiped out and the Soviet offensive against the Germans had begun again in the east.

For MacCarthy, Christmas 1944 passed with a greater sense of dread and homesickness than he had ever known. In his diary he noted: 'We had a parcel on Xmas Eve but it was not the same as being home for Xmas.'[1]

The New Year brought no reason for the POWs to be optimistic. It was the same as their previous years of captivity and the daily struggle to survive continued.

They did not have a radio in Nagasaki as they had had in Java, but they knew the Allies were winning the war. The increased frequency and scale of the air raids, the wholesale demolition of houses to create fire lanes, the irritability of the guards and a continuous atmosphere of tension all made it clear that the war was nearing its final stages. They could work it out from the small maps in newspapers discarded by civilian workers. From what they knew of their enemy, they were certain that the Japanese government was feeding the public a more positive version of how the war was going.

However, not everyone in Japan believed what their government was telling them. The POWs had become suspicious about activity in a separate area of the factory. This section was strictly out of bounds but an English RAF sergeant, who looked Japanese, was mistakenly ordered into the area to move some heavy machinery. He managed to escape notice for a while and to his surprise found that the machines were not, in fact, dealing with war work:

> Instead the workers were casting knives, forks and spoons, washing boilers, window frames, metal lockers, ladders and other household items. Seeing the surprised look on his face, a Korean guard laughed and intimated by signs and bits of Japanese that the factory bosses had already accepted the inevitable defeat of the Japanese Empire.[2]

Having profited hugely from supplying the Japanese war machine, the great Baron Mitsui was preparing to cash in on the post-war shortage market. It is worth noting that the Mitsubishi Corporation profited more from POW slave labour than any other Japanese company during the war.[3]

The level of desperation of the Japanese government was growing with every ship American submarines and bombers sank. The country was running out of raw materials and food. But even though Japan's eventual defeat was becoming more obvious, the attitude towards prisoners did not improve; if anything, it deteriorated. The more the Japanese were starved into submission the less sympathy they had for the prisoners, so their rations were continually being reduced.[4] A rumour had begun to circulate that rice was being transported from Korea by submarine.[5] This gave the POWs mixed feelings because, if true, it confirmed that the Americans now controlled the Sea of

Japan. However, this would be of little consequence to them if they starved to death before being rescued.

A diary entry on 18 January 1945 conveys MacCarthy's exasperation with his captors:

> Conference with camp Commandant. They came to a decision to issue the Red Cross Parcels as an emergency ration. There was three and a half parcel (deliveries) arrived in the camp and we have only had one that was at Xmas and they arrive at the decision above.

The POWs had no idea precisely how desperate Japan had become or the new tactics to which they were resorting until one afternoon when a few prisoners returned from work outside the camp. They reported that they had seen young Japanese cadets in full dress uniform. Instead of caps, they wore white headscarves with a rising sun emblem. They carried large swords at their sides and were strutting about the streets being treated like royalty. The POWs guessed that they must have been royal princes but there were too many of them for this to have been possible. When one of these cadets arrived at Camp 14B he was feted with VIP treatment by the entire camp staff, including the commandant. Later the interpreter told the prisoners that they were *kamikazi* pilots, who would be going on suicide bombing missions. For a week prior to their one and only flying mission, they were treated like gods. In MacCarthy's opinion, they deserved it.[6]

Later in the spring, the prisoners were transferred to work in coalmines located about 2 miles outside the city, beyond a line of steep hills. After the incidents on the bamboo scaffolds of the Mitsubishi Steel & Arms Works, the guards did not risk supervising the prisoners in the tunnels in case an 'accident'

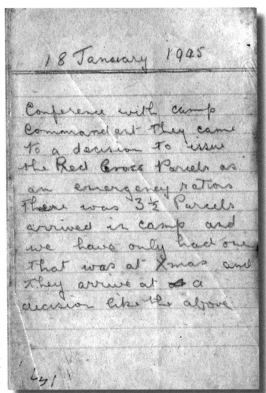

18 January 1945

Conference with camp
Commandant. They came
to a decision to issue
the Red Cross Parcels as
an emergency rations
There was 3½ Parcels
arrived in camp and
we have only had one
that was at Xmas and
they arrive at a
decision like the above.

An entry from
Aidan MacCarthy's
prisoner-of-war
camp diary.

was arranged for them.[7] The prisoners took advantage of this
to let the weaker men rest whilst the fitter men produced the
required number of trucks of coal. The type of coal in the
mines was of very low-grade quality and the quota for the shift
was specified by the civilian foreman. The POWs were forced to
stay in the mines all day, with no sight of sky or sun, until the
quota was complete. After finishing the day's work they faced
the exhausting climb up the steep steps from the coal tunnels to
the surface before trudging back over the hills to the camp.

Forced to work in such hazardous conditions, the POWs
had to be extremely careful: the hastily constructed mines were
prone to collapse and the guards had no interest in the well-

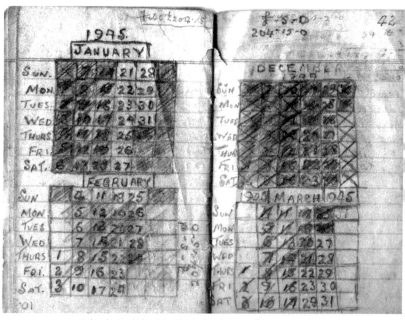

Calendar in Aidan MacCarthy's prisoner-of-war camp diary.

being of their labour force. On one occasion a shaft collapsed, trapping a group of Chinese prisoners. The POWs were ordered to continue working and the guards prevented them from making any attempt to rescue the trapped Chinese.[8]

There was, however, one benefit of working in the coalmines: the tunnels attracted snakes which the POWs caught. The snakes were cooked for hours and hours in order to make them edible.[9] Even though the sinewy meat retained its pungent taste, smell and toughness, for the prisoners the taste of meat of any form was a delicacy to be savoured.[10]

When Germany surrendered on 8 May, the news was known in the camp almost immediately. The Japanese did nothing to disguise the animosity they now felt for their former ally. The hatred they bore towards them even temporarily overshadowed their bitterness towards the Americans.[11]

For the increasingly irate Japanese, America was personified by the commander of the American forces in the Pacific, General Douglas MacArthur. Unfortunately for MacCarthy, his surname sounded, to Japanese ears, like MacArthur and towards the end of his captivity, he recalled, 'I think I was hit or slapped every time I spoke my name.'

Throughout their years of captivity the prisoners had no contact with the outside world apart from a few mail deliveries. They had received no letters during their two and a half years in Java because the Japanese were not forthcoming with details of which prisoners they had, where they were or whether they were still alive. Then, out of the blue, they received their first mail delivery in Nagasaki. The letters initially caused great excitement in the camp, but then they realised the letters had been sent a year or two previously. Around 60 per cent of the intended recipients were already dead and 10 per cent were unknown to them, probably located in other camps.[12] For the remaining 30 per cent, the arrival of the letters was an emotional experience they could not bear. After years of captivity their morale was at its lowest ebb. Their dignity and self-worth had been eroded through the unending suffering and humiliation. Reading news from home reminded them how much they had changed from the people their families once knew. Their loved ones surely would not recognise the skeletal, diseased and demoralised wretches into which they had been transformed.

The letters had the opposite effect to the one for which they had been written and caused a sudden and dramatic drop in morale. The prisoners became lethargic and no longer cared if they were beaten.

> Many of them hardly spoke at all from the time they awoke until the time they crawled wearily into bed. They had

lost the will to live. Ironically those who got no mail felt depressed for completely opposite reasons.[13]

The reaction to the arrival of the mail worried the officers and a meeting was organised for the heads of the various nationalities. They made a unanimous decision not to distribute future mail deliveries. They would burn them unopened instead. They did this when two further deliveries arrived. Although they were worried that if the rest of the men discovered what they had done, their motives would not have been appreciated, MacCarthy was convinced it was the right thing to do, based on the reaction to the first delivery.

Maybe because the outcome of the war was becoming clear, the Japanese made a token gesture of proper treatment of the POWs and allowed them to send postcards home. This happened on a number of occasions.[14] One such was in May 1945:

> We addressed the cards to our families. There were twelve POWs in our camp with Southern Irish addresses and, after the first batch of outgoing mail had been sorted, we were summoned to the office of the Commandant. We were harangued at length. Through an interpreter we learned that we were 'very bad people indeed'. We Irish had, it seemed, joined forces with the British to wage war against the Japanese people, who were only defending themselves against the brutal attacks of the American and Commonwealth warmongers. Because of our bad actions we must be punished. So all thirteen of us received an old-fashioned beating from the Commandant himself.[15]

Fortunately for MacCarthy, his postcard was selected to be read out in English on Tokyo Radio by the female propaganda

GERRARD 9234

TELEPHONE:
Extn...............

Any communications on the
subject of this letter should
be addressed to :—
THE
UNDER SECRETARY
OF STATE
and the following number
quoted :— P.367297/42/P.4 P/W B.5.

Your Ref...............

AIR MINISTRY

(Casualty Branch)

73-77 OXFORD STREET

W.1

1 3 June 1945.

Sir,

I am directed to inform you that the following letter
written by your son Squadron Leader Joseph Aidan MacCarthy
23425, was read over the Japanese controlled Tokio radio on
2nd June, 1945 and picked up in Canada.

"Dearest Mom and Dad and all the family Hello.
I am broadcasting this message from Japan where I am
now a prisoner of war. I hope you are all in the best
of health and praying for my early return. I expect
Barrie is ordained and Sta married by now. I regret
having missed both these happy occasions. I hope
to be home in time for Brian's ordination and Sheila's
wedding. Eileen, Michael and Jim are a great comfort
to you at home. You are all constantly in my thoughts
and prayers and I dwell often on our reunion which
will be soon with God's help. Please don't worry
about me. My health is excellent and my chin is
well up. I am anxiously looking forward to some news
from you. Goodbye and God bless you all. All my love."

I am, Sir,
Your obedient Servant,

E. F. Crasle

for Director of Personal Services.

D.F.MacCarthy, Esq.,
The Square,
Berehaven,
Co.Cork, Eire.

The note sent by the Air Ministry in London following the broadcast of
MacCarthy's postcard on Tokyo Radio in June 1945.

broadcaster 'Tokio Rose'. The broadcast took place on 2 June
and was picked up by listeners in Vancouver, Canada. A copy
of the broadcast was posted to the Air Ministry in London and
a message was then sent, addressed to Denis F. MacCarthy, The
Square, Berehaven, County Cork. The letter informed D.F.

that the following had been broadcast over Japanese controlled Tokyo radio:

> Dearest Mom and Dad and all the family, hello. I am broadcasting this message from Japan from where I am now a prisoner of war. I hope you are all in the best of health and praying for my early return. I expect Barrie is ordained and Ita married by now. I regret having missed both those happy occasions. I hope to be home in time for Brian's ordination and Sheila's wedding. Eileen, Michael and Jim are a great comfort to you at home. You are all constantly in my thoughts and prayers and I dwell often on our reunion which will be soon with God's help. Please don't worry about me. My health is excellent and my chin is well up. I am anxiously looking forward to some good news from you. Good bye and God bless you all. All my love.

The previous year the Air Ministry had informed the MacCarthys that Aidan's name was included among the survivors that had been rescued from a ship torpedoed en route to Japan. They had heard nothing since then. The details MacCarthy mentioned in the broadcast confirmed that he was still alive. The news brought the family a rare moment of joy and hope that their prayers would be answered: that their son and brother would make it home alive. But their joy was muted because MacCarthy mentioned that he expected 'Barrie has been ordained'. His younger brother had indeed been ordained. That had happened in January 1943 but he was killed on 3 March 1945 by the last German bomb to fall on London. Barry was just thirty years old when a V2 rocket landed on the presbytery of the Catholic church at Dockhead, Bermondsey shortly after 11 p.m,[16] killing him and two other priests from County Cork. Barry's death and the years of worry during Aidan's captivity were already taking a huge toll on Julia's health as she remained bed-bound in Castletownbere.

The reality of MacCarthy's situation was far different from the optimism conveyed in the postcard. After more than three long years of starvation, brutality and disease, the odds of him escaping alive were looking increasingly unlikely. The prisoners had learned that the island of Iwo Jima had been captured at the end of March. They also knew that a savage battle was being fought on Okinawa. It lasted for almost three months until the island finally fell to the Americans on 22 June.

The POWs rightly guessed that the Americans planned to use Okinawa as the launch platform for the final act of the war, the invasion of Japan.[17] They were able to piece together this picture of events using the little inset maps from discarded newspapers and from loose comments made by the Korean guards. After Okinawa was captured the Japanese knew it was only a matter of time before Nagasaki would come under attack. The prisoners were terrified at the prospect of being killed by American bombs, so they were relieved when the camp commandant allowed them to dig makeshift air-raid shelters.[18] This meant they had to continue working after a long day in the mines but nobody objected: they had struggled for too long to be killed by their own side. Soon the shelters were completed. They were basic constructions, trenches measuring 20 feet long by three feet wide and five feet deep, and covered by a thin layer of concrete with square entrance holes every six feet.

As the summer months wore on the continuous air raid sirens made a full night's sleep impossible:

We had to get up and go to the shelters every time they sounded. Eventually we slept in the shelters all the time, not minding that they were badly ventilated and severely cramped. After all we had been through we were now determined to survive.[19]

The weary prisoners watched joyfully as vast numbers of B-29s flew northwards on their way to firebomb Japan's major cities. The Japanese called the bombers *B-nee-ju-kus,* the Japanese translation of B-29. The scale of the raids caused the camp guards to become increasingly aggressive and unpredictable. On one night alone, 9 March, around 300 B-29s bombed Tokyo, killing over 140,000 of the city's inhabitants.[20] The city became such a cauldron of fire that the water in the canals began to boil.[21] There no longer seemed to be any effective Japanese resistance – either by anti-aircraft fire or by fighter aircraft – so the American planes could attack with impunity. As if mocking their enemy, they flew at low altitude and usually in close formation.[22]

Hundreds of thousands of Japanese civilians were killed as the Strategic Bombing campaign stepped up a gear between July and August 1945. With numbing regularity, every two to three days, raids by vast formations of up to 600 bombers visited a holocaust of destruction on heavily populated cities. The densely packed wooden buildings ignited like matches when struck by a new type of weapon invented by the Allies, a form of jellied gasoline known as napalm. It would become a weapon synonymous with indiscriminate destruction and killing of civilians. Napalm incendiaries were designed to start vast numbers of smaller fires which were then whipped up into hurricane-force firestorms as high-explosive bombs were dropped by later waves of bombers. The goal, according to the US Strategic Bombing Survey, was 'either to bring overwhelming pressure on [Japan] to surrender, or to reduce her capability of resisting invasion … [by destroying] the basic economic and social fabric of the country'.[23] The architect of the campaign, General Curtis LeMay, and Robert McNamara, who served with the Office of Statistical Control and later became US Defense Secretary, agreed that had America lost the war they would both have been prosecuted as war criminals. They recognised that what they were doing was immoral but deemed it necessary to bring the war to a swift conclusion.

Just a year previously, when MacCarthy had arrived in Nagasaki and before the large-scale bombing of mainland Japan had begun, the country seemed immune to such destruction. At that time, the Japanese had not yet implemented a blackout of its cities to reduce their night-time visibility to bombers. Nagasaki, right up until July 1944, had escaped the intense massed bomber attacks. This was because the Americans wanted to use the city and its harbour as a landing base for the invasion of Japan.[24]

The Americans needed Nagasaki and its infrastructure intact, but every now and again, a plane returning from a raid elsewhere would drop a 'hang-up' bomb on the city.[25] These were bombs that failed to release during the initial bombing run elsewhere and had to be dropped before returning to base because they were already primed to detonate on impact.

For the last few months of the war MacCarthy remembered that he always seemed to be digging. First in the coalmines, then the air-raid shelters and then one day they were sent out to dig a large pit. It was about six feet deep and about twenty feet square. As they were digging they noticed civilian carpenters erecting a long wooden platform about fifteen feet from the edge of the pit. Suddenly they realised that the platform was for machine guns that would be used to execute them. They were digging a mass grave.[26] MacCarthy was overcome by numbness, unable to believe what was happening. 'To dig one's own grave is an extraordinary sensation,' he later recalled. He imagined his own shot-up corpse lying in the watery mud. Having survived for so many years, it would all come to nothing. The POWs' suspicions were later confirmed to them by one of the Korean guards.[27]

The Japanese were preparing for the implementation of the 'Kill All Policy'. This was a general policy developed towards the end of the war and was to be carried out in the event of an American invasion. A copy of the order was written down and later discovered during investigations of war crimes in Formosa (now Taiwan). The order was transmitted by radio from the Japanese War Ministry to POW camps in Formosa on 1 August 1944 and instructed camp officials to prepare for the final disposal of their POWs. The methods to be used were at the discretion of the local camp officials:

> Whether they are destroyed individually or in groups, or however it is done, with mass bombing, poisonous smoke, poisons, drowning, decapitation, or what, dispose of them as the situation dictates.
>
> In any case it is the aim not to allow the escape of a single one, to annihilate them all, and not to leave any traces.[28]

As the war drew to a close, mass graves were dug at camps throughout the Japanese Empire: in Java, Taiwan, Thailand, Burma, the Philippines, mainland Japan and elsewhere.[29] The Vice War Minister sent an order by secret telegram to camp commandants on 17 March 1945:

> Prisoners of war must be prevented by all means available from falling into enemy hands. They should be either located away from the front or collected at suitable points and time

with an eye to enemy air raids, shore bombardments etc. They should be kept alive to the last wherever their labour is needed.[30]

One of the motivations was to prevent the 123,000 prisoners of the Japanese from becoming a hostile force. Another was to get rid of witnesses to the crimes that had been committed against the prisoners. There are examples where this order was carried out. The Japanese garrison on the island of Palawan, south of the Philippines saw an American convoy approaching in December 1944. Believing Palawan was about to be invaded (the convoy was, in fact, on its way to invade the Philippines), Japanese officials invoked the 'Kill All Policy'. They herded the POWs into bomb shelters, which were then doused in petrol and set on fire. They then threw in hand grenades. 'As men engulfed in flames broke out of their fiery deathtraps, the Japanese guards machine gunned, bayoneted and clubbed them to death'.[31]

In the summer of 1945 the final date for implementation of this policy became known. Prisoners in camps on mainland Japan were informed by their civilian interpreters and prison guards that an execution date for all prisoners had been decided: 22 August 1945.[32]

The Japanese had made their decision: there would be no escape – unless something dramatic happened.

As the prisoners dug their mass graves, the Japanese were also digging. They were preparing for the American invasion expected to begin in November 1945. There would be no surrender and the defence plan was called 'Operation *Ketsu-Go*', which translates as 'Operation Decisive'. A volunteer fighting force was mobilised and civilians were drilled in the use of sharpened bamboo spears and Molotov cocktails to fight alongside soldiers in defence of their Emperor and sacred homeland. A slogan coined during the summer of 1945 roughly translates as 'the sooner the Americans invade, the sooner 100 million will die proudly'. The military government was prepared to sacrifice the population in an act of national *hara-kiri* rather than endure the shame of surrender. With chronic shortages in manpower, weapons and resources, the Japanese did not expect the operation to defeat the invasion. However, fanatical resistance would make it so costly in terms of casualties that the United States would be forced to negotiate terms favourable to Japan rather than insist on unconditional surrender. This would ensure that the military government and the Emperor would remain in place.

The Allied invasion would have involved a force of 5 million men. The Japanese plan was to confront the attacking force before it landed with kamikaze planes as well as suicide boats and submarines. When the invasion force landed and had the Emperor ordered his subjects to resist, they would have responded to the command from their god and fought dutifully with the same dogged determination that had been witnessed on Saipan, Okinawa and Iwo Jima.This would have resulted in huge numbers of casualties for soldiers on both sides as well as the civilian population for whom there was no evacuation plan. When the Americans invaded Saipan in the summer of 1944, Emperor Hirohito ordered his subjects to commit suicide rather than submit to the enemy and they obeyed in their thousands. The government lauded the example set by civilians throwing themselves from cliffs as a model of defiance against the invaders. A third of the civilian population of Okinawa, 100,000 people, died during the capture of the island.[33] Extrapolating a similar death toll for the invasion of the main islands suggests that the number of Japanese civilian casualties could have been in the millions. It also seems likely that, had an invasion been necessary, the *Ketsu-Go* operation would have delivered the intended outcome for the Japanese.

MacCarthy was left to ponder an image of himself lying in the mud at the bottom of a mass grave, unaware that on the other side of the world in New Mexico, the first atomic explosion had taken place on the morning of 16 July. As a mushroom cloud rose over the Alamogordo Desert, it heralded the arrival of the atomic age. The following day the leaders of the United States, Great Britain and the Soviet Union met at Potsdam near Berlin. The war in Europe was over but the continent was in ruins. Truman, Churchill and Stalin met to determine its new borders (Churchill was replaced by his successor Clement Atlee shortly afterwards). Japan's Imperial Empire was crumbling and the Allies had to decide on a strategy to bring the war in Asia to a swift conclusion. Before the Soviet delegation set out for Germany, the Japanese Foreign Minister sent a message to Moscow indicating that the Emperor wanted to bring hostilities to an end, with certain preconditions. American intelligence intercepted the message. However, certain elements within the US administration were in no mind to discuss terms.[34] Anything other than unconditional surrender would not be considered. During the initial meetings at Potsdam, Truman was handed a note confirming that the atomic bomb test at Alamogordo had been a success. Truman was ecstatic and commented that the US had invested in the 'greatest scientific gamble in history' and won.[35] Two billion dollars and years of research had been spent on developing the technology that would place America at the apex of the post-war world. Churchill and Stalin agreed with Truman's intention to use the bomb.

The morality of using such a weapon to destroy entire cities indiscriminately had been blunted by years of war and a public appetite for revenge. Sixty-three scientists who had worked on the bomb, including Oppenheimer and Einstein, petitioned Truman not to use the weapon against the cities of Japan. But it was too late. Flushed with the success of being the first country to have developed the atomic bomb, the US president and many others in his administration were anxious to test its effectiveness, to demonstrate the supremacy of the United States. US General Eisenhower and many of the naval commanders in the Pacific, including admirals Nimitz and Leahy, were vehemently opposed to its use. They considered it a barbaric weapon and its use would place the US on an ethical standard more appropriate to the Dark Ages. They knew that the Japanese were on their knees and had made overtures for peace via Moscow. Churchill later recalled that at Potsdam there was unanimous, unquestioned agreement that the atomic bomb should be deployed. He claimed there was never any suggestion that they should do otherwise.

On 26 July the Proclamation Defining Terms for Japanese Surrender – the Potsdam Declaration – was announced. This followed the meeting of Truman, Churchill and Chiang Kai-shek of the Nationalist Government of China. The declaration called for the unconditional surrender of Japanese forces. It was an ultimatum: if the Japanese government did not surrender unconditionally, the country would face 'prompt and utter destruction'. Truman, knowing the destructive power he now held, warned in a broadcast picked up by Japanese news agencies that Japan could 'expect a rain of ruin from the air, the like of which has never been seen on this earth'. The official Japanese response to the declaration was referred to as *mokusatsu,* which was translated as 'to kill with silence'. Apparently they were waiting for a response from Moscow but the Japanese Prime Minister Suzuki went so far as to assure the Japanese press that his government intended to ignore the Allies' demands and fight on. This response hardened the Allied leaders' determination to deliver the final blow to end the war.

* * *

On 1 August 1944 Nagasaki experienced its first mass bombing when a flight of about fifty B-29s attacked the city. It was heavily bombed, especially the industrial area, and the Mitsubishi Steel & Arms Works was badly damaged, but the POW camp escaped being directly hit.

A large number of smaller naval dive-bombers also attacked the harbour and shipyards in low-level attacks. The prisoners knew that the dive-bombers must have been launched from nearby aircraft carriers, so it was clear the Americans were closing in. The dive-bombers sank the aircraft carrier that the prisoners had so diligently sabotaged when they were first put to work at the Mitsubishi Steel & Arms Works. It had been moored in Nagasaki Harbour while a flight deck and armaments were being installed.[36] The POWs' dreams of it folding like a deck of cards on the open seas were never realised.

The following day all coal mining was suspended and the prisoners were ordered to help clear up the bomb damage. They spent the following week at this work. At least they were out in the fresh air and MacCarthy, for one, was relieved. It was better than digging his own grave.

A few days later, unknown to the prisoners, Truman made good on his threat: the first nuclear attack in an act of war took place on the morning of 6 August. The uranium-based atomic bomb, 'Little Boy', was detonated above Hiroshima and initially killed approximately 80,000 people. Many thousands more would die in its aftermath.

'Fat Man', the atomic bomb that was dropped on Nagasaki. WIKICOMMONS

Two days later, on the night of 8 August, the Soviet Union declared war on Japan. About an hour later, shortly after midnight in the early hours of Thursday 9 August, Soviet forces attacked the Japanese in Manchuria and Korea with an army of over a million men. The greatest fear the Japanese had was that they would be invaded by the Soviet Union. They knew that if the Americans invaded they would reconstruct the country and eventually repatriate their troops. The Russians, on the other hand, would never leave, and Japan would become a colony of the Soviet Union.[37]

As Soviet forces poured across the borders of Manchuria, taking the Japanese by surprise, the crew of an American B-29, *Bockscar*, gathered in darkness on Tinian island in the Pacific Ocean. They were preparing for what they knew was an important mission. An enormous plutonium-based atomic bomb, over 12 feet in length, was loaded into the bomb bay of

Map of Japan showing Nagasaki, Keisen and Kokura.

Bockscar. The bomb was named 'Fat Man' in honour of Winston Churchill and had the destructive capacity of 20,000 tonnes of TNT high explosive. It was almost twice as powerful as the bomb dropped on Hiroshima. The captain of the mission, Major Charles Sweeney, aged twenty-five, had flown on *Enola Gay* when it dropped the first atomic bomb on Hiroshima. The *Enola Gay* had also taken off from Tinian island so the crew were well aware of the destructive power of what they carried. They also knew it would not be a straightforward mission as the weather forecasters warned Major Sweeney of tropical lightning storms all the way from Tinian to Japan, a distance of 1,500 miles.[38]

Before *Bockscar* took off, Father George Zabelka, the military chaplain on the island, prayed over the crew: 'Almighty God … let your grace come down upon the men who will fly in this night. Give us all the courage and strength for the hours that lie before us, and reward us according to the hardships they will bring. But above all … give your world peace.'

Shortly before take-off, Sweeney was told that one of the fuel-transfer pumps was not working, so it would not be possible to use the fuel in the reserve tanks. He was ordered to proceed with the mission as it was too dangerous to transfer the bomb to another plane because it was already live.[39] At 3.49 a.m. the plane took off 'against a background of threatening black skies torn open at intervals by great lightning flashes'.[40] *Bockscar* flew north-west through the violent electric storm towards Japan and its primary target, the city of Kokura on the northern tip of Kyushu island. Kokura was a large industrial city housing one of the few remaining large arsenals in Japan. The weapons and munitions stored there would be vital for Japanese efforts to repel the imminent American invasion. The city had also been the secondary target for the atomic bomb attack on Hiroshima just three days previously.

The first signs of dawn came shortly after 5 a.m. With sunrise, the weather calmed and they approached Japan from the south to rendezvous with a second B-29. This was an observation plane assigned to deploy the instruments that would record the explosion.

For the prisoners in Nagasaki the day started bright, calm and windless, with just a few clouds away in the distance.[41] All along the Urakami River the chimneys of the munitions factories belched white smoke as usual.[42] An air-raid alert was sounded at 7.50 a.m. as two B-29s – *Bockscar* and the observation plane, *The Great Artiste* – passed high overhead. They were flying north at high altitude. Throughout the city people hurried to air-raid shelters but it was a false alarm and an all-clear signal was given at 8.30 a.m.[43]

By the time *Bockscar* reached Kokura the city was obscured by smoke from the nearby city of Yahata, which had been firebombed the previous day by 200 American bombers. Yahata and Kokura were just a few miles apart (so close that they are now considered wards of the larger city of Kitakyushu). Three times Major Sweeney flew over the city with the bomb bays of the B-29 open, desperate to release 'Fat Man' and be rid of the most destructive weapon ever made. But each time his bombardier Captain Kermit Beahan, aged twenty-seven, could not find a break in the smoke and haze to allow him to identify the target. After the third run over the city, the fuel shortage was becoming critical. Sweeney was short one fuel tank and had already made the decision to return to Okinawa instead of Tinian because it was closer.[44] At this rate it was unlikely he would have enough fuel to make it even to Okinawa. With anti-aircraft fire bursting around them and fighter aircraft approaching, Sweeney decided to make for the secondary target: Nagasaki.

Kokura's luck would be Nagasaki's downfall.[45] Sweeney had enough fuel for only one run over the city. The third and final option would be to drop the bomb at sea before landing on Okinawa.

At 10.45 a.m., it was a typical hot August morning. A line of worshippers made their way in a procession towards Urakami Cathedral, their white umbrellas shining as they walked solemnly in prayer.[46] A few hundred yards away MacCarthy and the other prisoners were given a ten-minute break from their work clearing the rubble from the previous air raid. Some of the men had gone back to their camp nearby to get a drink of water and a cigarette. They looked up, squinting at the bright sky. High above the city they saw eight vapour trails showing two separate four-engine bombers in the distance. This time they were heading south.[47] The prisoners recognised the silver shapes as the same bombers that had flown over earlier that morning.

They were flying at about 25,000 feet when suddenly one of the planes changed course and flew towards the city.[48] This meant only one thing: it was about to attack.

The air-raid sirens began to wail as the prisoners scrambled for the bomb shelters.[49] Despite MacCarthy's urging, several POWs insisted on staying outside the shelter to watch the city being bombed.

On board *Bockscar*, Sweeney told the crew to put on their welder's goggles. Captain Beahan was trying to locate Urakami Cathedral, which was the target for the bomb. The cathedral, which the POWs had been permitted to visit the previous Christmas, was the midpoint between the Mitsubishi Steel & Arms Works and the Mitsubishi Ordnance Works. Now the objective of the mission was to destroy these arms factories. In the makeshift bomb shelter of Camp 14B, without realising it, MacCarthy and the rest of the prisoners were within the target that the atomic bomb was intended to destroy. They prayed that they would be spared a direct hit.

10

'The End of the World'

bove ground outside the shelter, seven Dutch and one British RAF prisoner, Ronald Shaw, prepared to watch their enemy suffer. They had refused to listen to their doctor and commanding officer. From within the bomb shelter, MacCarthy could hear one of them describe what he saw. One of the planes had just dropped three parachutes.[1] These were from the observation plane and attached to the parachutes were cameras and other instruments which would record the blast. On board *Bockscar* at 11.01 a.m. Beahan released 'Fat Man' onto the city below. Its descent took forty-three seconds and when the bomb was about 1,500 feet above the city it detonated.[2] Inside the bloated dark metal body of 'Fat Man' sixty-four detonators in a geometric design similar in appearance to a giant football suddenly drove pieces of plutonium together in the core, creating an instantaneous critical mass. This split the atom and triggered a nuclear chain reaction.[3] There was a massive, searing blue flash, similar to that of a giant camera. It was quickly followed by a sustained bright, magnesium-type flare which immediately blinded the prisoners sitting above ground outside the bomb shelter. A few seconds later:

[there] came a frighteningly loud but rather flat explosion which was followed by a blast of hot air. Some of this

could be felt even by us as it came through the shelter openings, which were very rarely closed owing to the poor ventilation.[4]

The most violent explosion that had ever been unleashed by humankind began its destruction of the city.[5] In one second a bright ball of fire rose above the Urakami district and reached a diameter of about 1,000 feet. The heat at the core of the fireball instantly reached around 300,000 degrees Celsius.[6] It momentarily had the same brightness and temperature as that of the sun.[7] In grotesque irony, a man-made sun rose above Japan that morning.

When this awful force was released above the valley, it sent air molecules outwards in all directions in a massive shockwave that pulverised everything in its path. This, in turn, created a vacuum in the epicentre, which filled with intense heat. The extreme heat was caused by the sudden, massive exchange of energy.[8] The shockwave reverberated off the hillsides – which explains why MacCarthy described hearing two flat-sounding explosions,[9] the direct sound from the bomb and the echo as it reflected off the mountain.

Miles above the city the shockwave hit the B-29s, causing them to tremble from nose to tail.[10] Many of those on the ground who were not burned but who were within a certain radius of the blast had their internal organs ruptured by the massive shockwave.[11] Broken bodies were thrown at thousands of miles per hour through the flaming, rubble-filled air.[12]

The intense heat consumed everything below the fireball except concrete and steel. The great outward movement of air pressure then reversed, drawing in hurricane-force winds travelling at a speed of over 4,000 miles per hour.[13] As the searing fireball rose upwards, cooler air was drawn in from below. The

Mushroom cloud over Nagasaki. WIKICOMMONS

thermal air currents drew the soot, ash and dust of the charred city upwards like the updraft of a chimney, into a column of fire and debris several miles wide. It towered over the city to a height of around 10 miles. Its lower portion was 'brown, its center was amber, its top white'.[14]

The enormous column continued to swell as it rose upwards. Inside it a red fire seemed to be blazing and electric lights flashed incessantly like lightning. The colour of the flashing light seemed to change from red to yellow to purple. The column rose higher and higher and the cloud took on the shape of a mushroom. From the observation plane it looked like a giant 'living totem pole, carved with many grotesque masks grimacing at the earth'.[15] Also on the observation plane was RAF pilot Leonard Cheshire, one of the official British observers of the mission. He was unaware that fellow RAF servicemen were on the ground below and what he witnessed had a life-changing effect on him. He described the bomb as 'obscene in its greedy clawing at the earth, swelling as if with its regurgitation of all the life that it had consumed'.[16]

Fragments of the bomb itself had fallen as balls of fire varying in size from that of a fingertip to that of an infant's head. These flew through the air with a whistling sound, emitting a bluish white light and inflicting horrific wounds on those struck by them.[17]

The mass of debris drawn up into the air caused the sky to turn dark. The temperature dropped as the light of the sun was blocked out. The initial tsunami of destruction was then followed a few minutes later by disturbing silence. In Camp 14B, suddenly 'the world was all black', like a train that had entered a tunnel.[18] An Australian POW stuck his head out of one of the openings of the bomb shelter. He uttered one word – 'Jesus' – as he slumped back into the makeshift shelter in disbelief.[19] This sent MacCarthy and the rest of the prisoners scrambling for the exits to see for themselves. The sight before them stopped them in their tracks: 'there was no camp, it was gone,'[20]

> As we slowly surveyed the scene around us, we became aware that the camp had to all intents and purposes disappeared. Mostly of wooden construction, the wood had carbonized and turned to ashes. Bodies lay everywhere, some horribly mutilated by falling walls, girders and flying glass. There were outbreaks of fire in all directions, with loud explosions recurring as the flapping, live electric cables fused and flared. The gas mains had also exploded, and those people still on their feet ran round in circles, hands pressed to their blinded eyes or holding the flesh that hung in tatters from their faces or arms.[21]

There were fires everywhere and the air was filled with smoke and screaming. The camp guards who were usually sitting in a circle around the stove on wooden chairs were now lying dead with the stove sticking up in the middle.[22] The brick guardhouse was gone. The chairs had gone and the wooden camp buildings they had lived in for the previous year had vanished. Every piece of wood had been burnt instantaneously. The soot and ash that was all that remained of the camp was being sucked up into the mushroom cloud now towering over the city.

In the eerie twilight, where factories had previously screened their view, they could now see right up the length of the valley. The city was completely destroyed.

> A forest of discoloured corrugated sheets [clung] to twisted girders. Burst waterpipes shot fountains of water high in the air. The steel girders stood like stark sentinels, leaning

Two aerial photographs showing Nagasaki before and after the atomic bomb explosion. The scale of the devastation is clear. GETTY

over a series of concrete 'tennis courts' that had once been the floors of factories. But most frightening of all was the lack of sunlight – in contrast to the bright August sunshine that we had left a few minutes earlier, there was now a kind of twilight.[23]

The prisoners who had been above ground and to whom they had spoken moments previously were now burnt almost to ashes. Others who survived but had looked directly at the atomic flash were blinded. They would all die later as a result of radiation sickness.[24] The prisoners came to the conclusion that the world was coming to an end:

[We] had finally arrived at Judgement Day. An angry God was devastating the Japanese for their sins – and mistakenly including us in the destruction.[25]

The terrified prisoners understood conventional bombing, but this was different. They had heard of just three parachutes being dropped and there had been only two bombers. The sun had lost its light and was now a reddish brown disc in a dark sky.[26] They could not have known what an atomic bomb was or even have begun to comprehend the devastation that humankind was now capable of. For some, what they were witnessing seemed to be closer to what they had learned about the End Days, prophesised in the Book of Revelation: 'He opened the sixth seal, and behold, there was a great earthquake; and the sun became black as sackcloth … the sky itself will disappear like a scroll being rolled up and all the mountains and islands will be shaken from their places.'

Standing there speechless and not knowing what would happen next, panic soon took hold. MacCarthy's instincts told him to get far away as quickly as possible. He turned and ran, followed by the other prisoners. First they raced towards the harbour as water seemed to offer the most immediate prospect of safety. But as they ran towards it, they met crowds of terrified civilians running towards them. The prisoners were 'physically sickened by the endless stream of burnt, bleeding, flesh-torn, stumbling people, many unable to rise from where they had fallen'.[27]

Thousands of people scrambled, pushed, shoved and crawled across the shattered landscape in a crazed attempt to escape. Occasionally someone went berserk, driven mad by the horror of what they had witnessed. The city was strewn with thousands of corpses, many naked as the heat had burnt their clothes. Some were cooked alive, others charred beyond recognition. In the area beneath the epicentre all that remained of many victims was a just collection of dry bones. The whole atmosphere was permeated with blind terror and the nightmarish twilight was illuminated by the many fires that raged, engulfing what remained of Nagasaki in a sea of fire.[28] The crackling of the flames mixed with the screams of the dying and injured in what was later referred to as the Unforgettable Fire. Against the backdrop of eerie silence, this sounded all the more horrific. The silence was caused by the fog of soot, dust and ash that had been thrown up by the blast. There was no wind; all insects, birds and other traces of nature had been destroyed.

Temperatures on the ground directly below the fireball had hit between 3,000 and 4,000 degrees Celsius.[29] Concrete melted and roof tiles had turned to glass.[30] Anyone within a thousand yards of the blast was killed instantly or in the minutes after. MacCarthy and the rest of the POWs survived because they were a few feet underground and around 1 mile from the epicentre of the explosion.

An image of Nagasaki the day after the atomic bomb. The ruins are still burning. The gate to the Torii shrine somehow remained standing. YAMAHATA

A civilian crawls through the wreckage of Nagasaki. YAMAHATA

LOCATION OF POW CAMP 14B

The devastated city of Nagasaki with Mitsubishi Steel & Arms Works in the background and the location of Camp 14B marked. Getty

The ruin of Urakami Cathedral after the atomic bomb. Getty

Molten metals and glass had been sent flying through the air and landed on many of the city's inhabitants. This burned into their flesh, then cooled, so that some of the people MacCarthy encountered were 'half glass'.[31] At first they tried to help the wounded but there were just too many so they decided to join the people trying to flee to the mountains.[32] In the hellish remains of the city thousands of people were desperately looking for an intact bridge across the Urakami River to get to the nearby hills.

As they tried to get across the river some of the prisoners got stuck in the mud at the riverbank. It was filthy with ash and soot but they eventually pulled themselves out. In many places the river was covered with a blanket of dead bodies. Anywhere in the city where there was water – fountains, streams and ponds – were later found covered with corpses as dying victims had instinctively made their way towards water in the hope of finding relief from the fire.

Now and again the POWs stopped to help people but it was useless: there were dying and wounded people everywhere. One of the prisoners tried to pull a woman out of the mud and all of the skin came off her face. Another tried to help a child whose arm came away complete.[33] Everywhere people writhed in agony, the powerful radioactive rays having burnt the hypodermic system of any area of skin exposed to the flash. This meant that the cooked skin peeled away, exposing the raw flesh beneath.[34] Those unfortunate enough to have been exposed to the heat rays of the detonation and then the blast of air which followed had their skin torn off.

The situation was beyond anything they could cope with so, in order to escape to the hills, MacCarthy jumped into the filthy water and swam. The rest of the group followed and they got stuck again in the black glue-like mud on the opposite bank. Eventually, they got clear of the river and ran as fast as they could towards the mountains. They could see that around the valley the top of the mountains still looked green, but everything below was scorched bare.[35]

Despite the fact that 'Fat Man' was far more destructive than 'Little Boy', its lethal impact was curtailed by the mountains on either side of the Urakami valley.[36] 'Little Boy', the atomic bomb dropped on Hiroshima, was a smaller, uranium-based bomb. It killed between 70,000 and 140,000 people while 'Fat Man' killed between 40,000 and 80,000 within a few months of detonation. 'Fat Man' was primed with just over 13 lb of plutonium while 'Little Boy' carried ten times that amount of uranium. However, due to its design, the energy released above Nagasaki by 'Fat Man' was far greater (equivalent to 22 kilotons of TNT as against the 15 kilotons over Hiroshima). The mountains surrounding Nagasaki had shielded the more populated residential areas in the adjacent valleys from the worst effects of the blast.

Had the skies been clearer over Kokura and had 'Fat Man' been dropped on its primary target the casualty rate would have been far higher. It is likely that few of the city's 130,000 inhabitants would have survived and the name of Kokura would have been the one enshrined in memory as a symbol of atomic devastation.

As MacCarthy and the rest of the prisoners crawled up the slopes of the mountains, they grew worried at how the traumatised locals would receive them. Would they blame them for the destruction and take revenge?[37] But the people they met were even more frightened than they were. When MacCarthy told them he was an *isha*, or doctor, they were welcomed into caves and tunnels, which had been dug in the hillsides in preparation for the expected siege of Nagasaki.[38] He set to work immediately, splinting and tying up broken bones, but soon

Civilian victims of the Nagasaki atomic bomb. YAMAHATA

realised that his efforts were useless. Most of the people being brought in were dead and most of the people treating them were themselves already dying.[39] The worst injuries were burns – fire burns and flash burns – and he had no medical supplies with which to treat them. The locals were using some native fern-like leaves to ease the pain and these seemed to provide some relief, but overall the situation was completely hopeless.

About forty minutes after the explosion another biblical omen arrived: black rain began to fall. Initially it was welcomed because it would help to quell the fires.[40] Then the people became even more frightened when they noticed its colour. Each oily, sticky droplet was about the size of a fingertip. In MacCarthy's mind the black rain was further confirmation that they were witnessing the end of the world. Fifty years later he described the way he felt as more than fear. It was absolute terror.[41]

The black colouration was caused by the soot, dust and ash drawn upwards into the mushroom cloud. It met with colder moist air at high altitudes and formed water droplets. Unknown to the prisoners and Japanese, mixed in with the black rain were large amounts of radioactive material. This spread particles of plutonium far beyond the epicentre of the explosion.[42]

Later in the day, as word spread about the makeshift surgeries in the caves, more and more injured people began to arrive, many on improvised stretchers. MacCarthy treated people that had been injured by falling debris. Others were badly lacerated by flying glass and he did his best to help them. Probably the most horrific cases were where molten glass had burned into flesh and fused with the underlying bones and tissues.

Many of the wounded had their skin torn from their face and arms. The exposed flesh was contaminated by fragments of concrete, wood and glass, which would later cause infection. Amidst this scene of horror, the survivors, both Japanese civilians and the prisoners, were united by the unknown terror of what they were witnessing. But worse was to come.

Radioactivity, which over time would prove by far the deadliest effect of the bomb, was of two kinds: initial and residual.[43] The initial gamma radiation, a form of electromagnetic radiation, was similar to an extremely powerful X-ray. This caused what was initially termed 'Disease X' but was later identified as 'radiation sickness' or 'atomic sickness'. It was by far the more destructive. Gamma rays are high-energy ionising rays that pierce human bodies. They affect human tissue at an atomic level and can alter or mutate the DNA structure of cells. This can cause a cell to die through irreversible damage or to develop cancer at a later stage.

MacCarthy began to notice that those who initially showed no outward signs of illness suddenly began to vomit and feel nauseous. They suffered headaches, dizziness and became weak. For many of these victims, the sanctuary of the hills was now their final resting place as they lay by the shade of a wall, rock or tree unable to move. This condition was found in those who were physically exposed to the initial flash as the bomb detonated. Although it had lasted less than a second, the exposure caused a fatal dose of gamma radiation.[44] The rays easily passed through the wooden walls of Japanese houses and people who had managed to escape the devastation of the city and made their way to the mountains were soon overcome by radiation sickness.[45] No doctor in medical history had previously encountered the disease on such a scale.[46]

The visible symptoms of radiation sickness were bleeding under the skin, pus-filled blisters around the mouth, diarrhoea passed as blood, vomiting of blood, nose bleeding as well as inflammation of the mouth and throat. Exposure to such levels of radiation reduced the capacity of bone marrow to produce blood cells. This caused unfinished white blood cells to be sent into the bloodstream. If patients bled, their reduced blood platelets prevented coagulation and they died as a result of fatal haemorrhage. In many cases this was from something as simple as small cut, a graze or a needle prick. One by one the prisoners who had stayed outside the bomb shelter and survived the initial blast succumbed to the effects of radiation sickness.[47]

The residual radiation would last longer than the initial blast of gamma radiation. The residual radiation originated from the radioactive isotopes, the particles of plutonium released by the detonation of the bomb. These were ingested by inhalation or through contaminated food and water supplies, leaching into blood and vital organs.[48] The POWs who were in the bomb shelter were not physically exposed to the gamma radiation and also escaped the worst effects of the residual radiation because they were at the edge of the main damage zone. They had been lucky because they were in a valley, on the seaward side of the explosion. The wind from the harbour had pushed the atomic fallout up the valley away from them instead of blowing it in their direction.[49]

Over time, radiation sickness also damaged internal organs, caused leukaemia, stopped menstruation in women, caused sterility, loss of hair and deficiency in sperm production as well as birth defects.[50] The ionising radiation transformed neutral atoms into charged atoms, altering the structure of the original molecule. This led to the deformed plants, flowers and other living organisms that added to the terrifying legacy of the bomb.[51]

When the sun rose on the morning of 10 August the sky had cleared. The cloud of debris had blown away and revealed that what had happened was not some awful dream. The Urakami valley, which had looked so blissful in the sunshine of the previous morning, was now a smoking grey ruin of rubble, ash and human remains.

It was not long before MacCarthy and the rest of the prisoners were rounded up by the Kampetai, or military police. They were marched down to the city and put to work cremating corpses and body parts.

In and around the main blast zone cremations were not required – the bomb had taken care of this – but elsewhere the city was littered with the bodies of at least 40,000 people.[52] Human beings who had been going about their daily lives the previous morning had been vaporised in an instant. Grief-stricken survivors searched where their houses had been, looking for members of their family, often gathering up and burying bones in the hope that what they found were indeed parts of their loved ones. Others identified mangled bodies by the clothing, the person having been mutilated or burned beyond recognition.[53]

> Parties of women and children carried in loads of wood, which were then laid in long piles. After a half-hearted attempt had been made at identification, the bodies were laid on the wooden piles, sprayed with oil and set alight. The smell of burning flesh was overpowering; it permeated our bodies and our clothing, and it took several weeks to get rid of that smell from our noses. It remains one of my most horrific memories of those charnel days.
>
> In another area, further away, the tall administrative building, which had been the head office of the Mitsubishi empire, had been toppled in the blast. Nearly five hundred girls had been working in these offices, and when the building had been hit, they had been catapulted out. They were spread in a human carpet up to a distance of nearly a thousand feet, giving the impression of a nightmare doll factory. The majority lay as if asleep, unmarked and

unburnt, still in their trouser suits, and seeming as though they were waiting to be replaced on a massive shelf.[54]

The prisoners gathered up the bodies and cremated them in rows of fifty. This work continued for several days. The POWs slept at night in a small schoolhouse on the outskirts of the city.[55] They, like the Japanese survivors, were now *hibakusha*, a term still used in Japan, which translates as 'bomb-affected-people'.

In Tokyo, it was a solemn moment in the Imperial Palace as Emperor Hirohito considered his options. His decision would determine if the entire population of the country also became *hibakusha*. The members of the Supreme Council, or 'Big Six', who effectively controlled the government, were divided on whether to end the war or not. Three were hoping they could avoid the shame of unconditional surrender and wanted to come to terms. The other three were determined to fight on until the end. Only the Emperor's intervention could break the deadlock.

But the atomic bomb attacks on Hiroshima and Nagasaki brought home to most Japanese with utmost clarity the reality that the war was lost and that the country had to choose between survival and utter destruction. If one American plane could deploy a weapon that inflicted more damage than hundreds of conventional bombers, then Japan indeed faced utter annihilation before a single GI set foot on a Japanese beach. The Americans claimed they had more atomic bombs primed to detonate over other Japanese cities. The Japanese had to take them at their word but in reality it would have taken several weeks or months to prepare another bomb. In any case, the Americans had hundreds of B-29s with which they could continue to pulverise Japanese cities by day and night. This new reality put the tragic jingoism of the *Ketsu-Go* operation into stark perspective – Japanese

Korean martyr man house

Korean asylum

Yoshikuma village

cleaning ground

United States Air Force aerial map showing Camp 26, Keisen, Japan (top of photo).
KEISEN POW CAMP RESEARCH GROUP

civilians were sharpening bamboo spears to repel an enemy that could drop nuclear bombs at will.

In Nagasaki, the former inmates of Camp 14B needed to be moved somewhere, their prison for the previous year having been obliterated. The Japanese decided to disperse them among various camps in Kyushu province. MacCarthy was separated from many of the prisoners with whom he had spent the previous years of captivity. He and a group of others were put on a train and travelled overnight to Camp 26 at Keisen in the north of Kyushu island. This camp was attached to a mine owned by the Aso Mining Corporation. They were still prisoners and were forced to work. However, in the aftermath of the destruction of Nagasaki, their new guards were almost friendly. This lasted until a few of their previous guards arrived, but even they were now very much subdued. MacCarthy was surprised and quietly relieved to see that all saluting and bowing had ceased.

They continued working for a few days until the morning of 15 August, when they were prevented from going to work. All of a sudden the guards became very nice to them. For MacCarthy the only significance of the date was that it was the Feast of the Assumption, when in the Catholic tradition the Virgin Mary is believed to have ascended into heaven. Coincidentally, the Urakami Cathedral in Nagasaki had been dedicated to her.

But he knew something was happening when the prisoners were given some extra food.[56] Suddenly all the guards disappeared:

> But about 11.45 a.m. they reappeared, dressed in their best uniforms and proceeded to line up outside the Commandant's office. A radio set was brought out and placed on a table in front of the assembled men. Then the Commandant emerged, also in full dress uniform. They all came to attention and, sharp at noon, there was a blast

of martial music, followed by the voice of the Emperor of Japan. Immediately they bowed low towards the radio.[57]

At twelve noon, Japanese standard time, the broadcast began. It was the first time the Japanese people had ever heard the voice of the Emperor, their god.[58] Hirohito's speech was notably understated as he began by outlining, in Japanese, that 'the war situation has developed not necessarily to Japan's advantage'. At Camp 26 the guards remained bowed until they were told to relax and the voice continued.[59] Hirohito explained his decision to end the war, adding that 'the enemy has begun to employ a new and most cruel bomb, the power of which to do damage is incalculable … Should we continue to fight, it would … result in the ultimate collapse and obliteration of the Japanese nation.'

The Emperor never mentioned the word surrender. He simply made a vague reference to accepting the terms of the joint declaration of the powers (the United States, Great Britain, China and the Soviet Union).

MacCarthy turned to the interpreter and asked him what was happening. The interpreter now addressed him as 'Major'; he had previously been referred to as 'ichiban' or Number 1. As soon as he said it, MacCarthy knew he was crawling. MacCarthy said 'It's over, isn't it?' and the interpreter said 'yes'. A sacred Imperial decree had ended the war.[60] The Second World War, a conflict which had been fought on every continent and touched every human life on the planet, had come to a sudden end.

11

Liberation

When the Emperor's address finished, the guards ran for the gates and the commandant, 2nd Lieutenant Isao Kusuno, quickly disappeared into his office. MacCarthy turned to the other senior Allied officers. They ran to the commandant's office, tore open the door and saw Kusuno disappearing through the window. MacCarthy told the interpreter that he had two hours to get him back.[1]

MacCarthy rang the assembly bell and gathered all the POWs onto the parade ground. In a voice faltering with emotion, he announced the news.

> I phrased it as simply and directly as I could, but inevitably I found proper articulation almost impossible. We were all in a state of shock. We cried, hugged each other, shook hands, dropped on our knees and thanked God. A few of us began to sing hymns.[2]

MacCarthy had spent a total of 1,257 days in captivity – three years, five months and eight days. Now he was free. He had survived and the war was finally over. But it would take more than three months before he would finally arrive home.

The interpreter brought 2nd Lieutenant Kusuno back within an hour. He was a very frightened man and had good reason to be. The tables had turned and when he was brought to the camp a number of the POWs, especially the Australian prisoners, were determined to hang him. Although Kusuno received a beating, MacCarthy locked him in a cell for his safety.[3] He decided that it was outside his power to condemn any man to death and felt the right thing to do would be to leave the decision to the Americans.

At some point during this period, the former commandant of the camp presented MacCarthy with his military sword. Aidan later told his family that the officer had given him the sword in gratitude for saving his life from the POWs as they attempted to kill him. The fact that a Japanese officer gifted MacCarthy his sword was remarkable because, in Japan, a sword was far more than just a weapon: it was an officer's spiritual support and a symbol of his homeland.[4] It was unheard of for a Japanese officer to present his sword to his enemy. The officer also gave him an inscribed portrait photo to mark the event.

MacCarthy's focus turned to the practicalities of maintaining order and ensuring that the hundreds of men under his command made it home safely. Their main priority was food and they were relieved to find a supply of rice and fish powder at the camp stores. They also came across the remnants of several hundred Red Cross parcels. These had been intended for the prisoners but had all been opened and looted by the camp staff. Had Red Cross parcels been distributed as intended throughout the war, there is no doubt that many more prisoners would have survived.[5]

MacCarthy told the men that they were not to leave the camp unless they were armed and in groups of six because they did not know what the reaction of the local population would be.[6] At this stage they were still in danger. The initial reaction

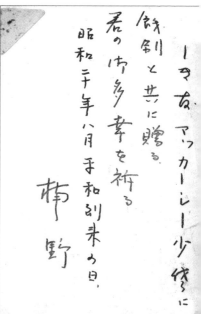

一寸右、マッカーレー少佐に

餞別と共に贈る。

君の御多幸を祈る

昭和二十年八月平和到来の日、

楠野

ABOVE The photo of 2nd Lieutenant Isao Kusuno, Commandant of Camp 26, given to Aidan MacCarthy in August 1945, and (*right*) the inscription on the back which reads: 'To my dear friend Dr MacCarthy, this is with my parting gift to you on this day the arrival of the peace, August 1945. Kusuno.'

The Japanese military sword presented by 2nd Lieutenant Isao Kusuno to Aidan MacCarthy in August 1945 at Camp 26, Keisen, Japan.
BARRY MURPHY

for many Japanese was one of dejection that their country had lost the war. Having been told that their years of suffering would lead to victory, it was now clear they had been lied to. The survivors had to bear the shame of surrender.

Up to the very end, the Japanese had been told by their leaders that they could win the war or at least come to an honourable settlement. But the Emperor, a god, had ordered them to agree to unconditional surrender. This was a sacred order so it had to be obeyed. In some areas the local military police refused to accept that the broadcast by the Emperor was genuine and a rumour was circulated that it was a trick of the Americans.[7] As Japanese soldiers demobilised, many were told by their officers to obey the Americans for the time being, and, just as Germany had risen from the ashes of the First World War, Japan would soon be ready to rise again.[8]

Allied commanders were taken by surprise when the surrender happened so suddenly and it took several weeks for them to liberate most of the camps. The formal surrender was not signed until 2 September. In the meantime, the former prisoners were on their own and at the mercy of the defeated Japanese.

On the evening of 15 August American B-29s dropped leaflets all over Japan instructing the POWs to paint PW on the roofs of their camps.[9] The following morning MacCarthy woke as a free man to the sound of B-29 American bombers again flying low overhead. He had enjoyed his first trouble-free sleep for three and a half years. Instead of bombs, the planes flying from Tinian island now dropped food, clothing and medicines on the camps by parachute. They also dropped pamphlets warning the Japanese that they would be shot if they were caught with even an empty tin of rations. If they found any of the parachutes they were to bring them to the nearest camp.[10]

This warning proved so effective that it became impossible to persuade the local women and children to accept even a chocolate bar or sweets. If they did accept, these goodies were swallowed on the spot and never carried away.[11]

MacCarthy kept as a souvenir a note, handwritten in pencil which was included with one of the supply drops, from the crew of 'Lucky 13', a B-29 with the United States Air Force 444th Bombardment Group:

Hi ya fellas,
Here's some good old army chow, don't know when we'll be back again. Hope you enjoy all the drops and hope there's plenty for all. How's our aim anyway? We hope its better than usual. Our crew 'The Lucky 13' wish you all a very speedy trip home which we know you're all waiting eagerly for, but believe me everything possible is being done to get you boys back home as swiftly as possible. The sooner MacArthur steps on Japanese soil the quicker you'll leave.

Well I hope you find this letter is all I can say, that'll depend on our aim.

Well I'll close now so the crew of the Lucky 13 say so long and may God be with you and Bless you all.

Lucky 13

The food in the airdrop was the first time the POWs had experienced abundance in years, but it was dietetically unplanned and included too much by way of animal fats and protein. It contained tins of Spam and dried milk, coffee, chocolate, fruit juice, sugar and bacon. After being starved for so

The note from the crew of Lucky 13, a B-29 used for a supply drop.

long their digestive systems were overwhelmed. Tragically, two young American servicemen died after gorging on chocolate. They had survived captivity but their emaciated bodies were overwhelmed by the foods they had craved for so many years.

The clothing included US army shirts, trousers, socks, shoes and underwear. After wearing lice-infested rags for years, their new outfits seemed like the height of elegance. Amongst the scented soap, razors, razor blades, toothbrushes and toothpaste there was one item they considered most thoughtful: deodorant.

レンゴウグンノホリョヘ

ALLIED PRISONERS

The JAPANESE Government has surrendered. You will be evacuated by ALLIED NATIONS forces as soon as possible.

Until that time your present supplies will be augmented by air-drop of U.S. food, clothing and medicines. The first drop of these items will arrive within one (1) or two (2) hours.

Clothing will be dropped in standard packs for units of 50 or 500 men. Bundle markings, contents and allowances per man are as follows:

BUNDLE MARKINGS

BUNDLE MARKINGS

50 MAN PACK	500 MAN PACK	CONTENTS	ALLOWANCES PER MAN	50 MAN PACK	500 MAN PACK	CONTENTS	ALLOWANCES PER MAN
A	3	Drawers	2	B	10	Laces, shoe	1
A	1-2	Undershirt	2	A	11	Kit, sewing	1
B	22	Socks (pr)	2	C	31	Soap, toilet	1
A	4-6	Shirt	1	C	4-6	Razor	1
A	7-9	Trousers	1	C	4-6	Blades, razor	10
C	23-30	Jacket, field	1	C	10	Brush, tooth	1
A	10	Belt, web, waist	1	B	31	Paste, tooth	1
A	11	Capt. H.B.T.	1	C	10	Comb	1
B	12-21	Shoes (pr)	1	B	32	Shaving cream	1
A	1-2	Handkerchiefs	3	C	12-21	Powder(insecticide)	1
C	32-34	Towel	1				

There will be instructions with the food and medicine for their use and distribution.

C A U T I O N

DO NOT OVEREAT OR OVERMEDICATE

FOLLOW DIRECTIONS

INSTRUCTIONS FOR FEEDING 100 MEN

To feed 100 men for the first three (3) days, the following blocks (individual bundles dropped) will be assembled:

3 Blocks No. 1
(Each Contains)

2 Cases, Soup, Can
1 Cases Fruit Juice
1 Case Accessory Pack

1 Block No. 5
(Each Contains)

1 Case Soup, Dehd
1 Case Veg Puree
1 Case Bouillon
1 Case Hosp Supplies
1 Case Vitamin Tablets

1 Block No. 3
(Each Contains)

1 Case Candy
1 Case Gum
1 Case Cigarettes
1 Case Matches

3 Blocks No. 2
(Each Contains)

3 Cases "C" Rations
1 Case Hosp Supplies
2 Cases Fruit

1 Block No. 7
(Each Contains)

1 Case Nescafe
1 Sack Sugar
1 Case Milk
1 Case Cocoa

1 Block No. 10
(Each Contains)

3 Cases Fruit
2 Cases Juice

The contents note of a United States Airforce supply drop.

Text on reverse of photo (handwritten):

*... octors in front
13 R.A.F. and Dutch
doc at right.)
4 Warrant officers behind
Royal Navy – British Army –
Royal Navy – Australian
Camp 26 Fukuoka
Kyushu Island
: Japan
September 1945*

ABOVE: A photo of the POW officers at Keisen, August 1945, with Aidan MacCarthy seated, second from right, and (*right*) the reverse of the photo.

POWs at Camp 26, Keisen, Japan, August 1945.

It provided relief from the stinking filth of camp life because, despite the availability of showers, there was a particular 'camp smell' that was impossible to escape.

With the arrival of the airdrops, the prisoners suddenly felt themselves to be in the lap of luxury. They were no longer living under threat of violence from the guards and did not have to bow to anyone or work as slaves. They made improvised sunshades from the airdrop parachutes and lay around semi-naked, well supplied with food and saki. MacCarthy described it as 'a period of utter and complete tranquillity'. He found it impossible to believe that the atomic bomb attack was real and not just a nightmare.

> Home seemed even less real. It was like being in a void. We lived for the day, neither able to look back into the past – nor look forward into the future. Later I realised that we must have been in a state of shock. Our survival was against all possible odds, and our miraculous escape was something we still found amazing every waking moment of our lives. But this state of dazed trance could not continue and gradually we became aware of the existence of another world outside our void. [12]

Shortly after the surrender, American *Nisei* troops were parachuted into Japan. These were second-generation Japanese American soldiers tasked with preparing for the arrival of the main occupation force. [13] For the first time in its history, Japan was about to be occupied by a foreign power and the familiar appearance of the *Nisei* paratroopers was intended to soften the blow. Ironically, in most cases, their families had been interned in America for the duration of the war. They delivered radios to the POW camps and twice daily, at 9 a.m.

Message from the Commander of the Fukuoka Prisoners of War Camps.

Aug. 22nd 1945.

I am pleased to inform you that we were instructed by the Military Authorities that hostilities ceased on Aug. 18th.

During your long stay in Japan as prisoners of War you must, I fear, have endured many hardships. Having survived these difficult times, however your dream of repatriation is soon to be realised. Your hearts must be full of joy at the thought of greeting your loved ones, parents, wives, children and friends.

I offer to you my sincere congratulation, and at the same time express my regret for those who have passed away as a result of disease or some other unfortunate mischance, without ever having the joy of greeting this happy day.

Obeying instructions, the Camp Staffs and I, have done all in our power to help and protect you, but owing to the difficult interal War conditions, we regret we were not able to do half as much as we wished. Nevertheless I trust that you will understand the predicament in which we found ourselves.

Several days ago at one camp the prisoners presented the Camp Staff and factory foremen with part of their valuable relief foodstuffs and personal belongings, while at others camps prisoners have asked for permission to help civilian War sufferers with their personal belongings. This is an example of your generous and understanding spirit and gentlemanliness. For all this we, the Camp Staffs and I, express our deepest gratitude.

Until you are transferred to Allied hands at the port which will be designated later you must wait at your respective Camps.

Therefore I sincerely hope that you will wait quietly taking care of your health and still obeying the rules of your camp as before, thus maintaining the honour and dignity of your great Nations.

Message from Commander of Fukuoka POW camps following the Japanese surrender, 22 August 1945.

and 6 p.m., MacCarthy received instructions broadcast from
Okinawa. Each camp was addressed by a known codeword and
was issued with instructions. These were then communicated
to local police chiefs who had taken over civilian administration
from the military. The former prisoners instructed the local
police where to stockpile and itemise guns, ammunition, tanks,
military vehicles, clothing, equipment, petrol, oil and food.[14]
The following day they would check that the orders had been
carried out and then radio this information back to Okinawa.

As the ground was prepared for the arrival of the occupation
forces, reality began to dawn on the former camp officials. They
would be held accountable for their abuse of the prisoners
under their care. On 22 August the overall commander of the
Fukuoka POW camps (all camps in Kyushu province came
under this command) issued a statement. He congratulated the
former prisoners for having survived 'these difficult times' and
expressed his 'regret for those who have passed away as a result
of disease or some other unfortunate mischance'.

He made a very deliberate effort to distance himself from
the brutality inflicted by the administration for which he was
responsible. Instead he asserted that 'obeying instructions,
the Camp Staffs and I have done all in our power to help and
protect you, but owing to the difficult internal War conditions
we regret we were unable to do half as much as we wished'.

There is no mention of the slavery, starvation, torture,
looting of Red Cross parcels or the numerous other abuses for
which he was responsible. Neither does he mention the 'Kill All
Policy' and the mass graves that his administration instructed to
be dug in preparation for the 'disposal' of the prisoners once the
appointed date of execution arrived.

The precarious state of limbo in which the POWs found
themselves went on for weeks. It was not until 2 September

<u>No. 26 CAMP ORDERS   No. 1.</u>

issued 3rd SEPTEMBER 1945

by

<u>SQUADRON-LEADER J. A. MacCARTHY. R.A.F.   COMMANDING.</u>

At 0745 hours yesterday, 2nd September you ceased to be Prisoners of War. This Camp is now a British Military Establishment under my command. From the very beginning I want it to be understood that the rules and regulations as laid down by me together with military discipline will be maintained.   I am now responsible to our governments for each one of you and I intend to see to it that you return home safe and sound and without a cloud of any sort on your military records. I know I will have the co-operation of practically everyone of you in this matter and that only a few may not co-operate. To those few I want them to understand clearly that they may expose themselves to the full punishments of Military Law which can be inflicted in this camp by me. Furthermore, a point of international law states that known now that hostilities have ceased anyboffence committed outside of this camp against the inhabitants of this country is a civil offence and subsequent punishment must be carried out or served in <u>this</u> country. Thieving outside this camp is equivalent to looting and looting is punishable by death. In cases of any serious breaches of discipline in this camp I will have no hesitation in handing the offenders over to the occupying troops for disposal.

   Routine Orders will be published daily and issued to each hut ; ignorance of orders will not be accepted as an excuse.

(J.A. MacCARTHY)
Squadron-Leader. Commanding.

Squadron Leader J.A. MacCarthy's first orders to POW Camp 26, 3 September 1945.

that representatives of the Empire of Japan signed the formal Instrument of Surrender in Tokyo Bay on board the USS *Missouri*. On that day, MacCarthy officially ceased to be a prisoner of war. The following day he formally took over command of Camp 26. His first orders to the former prisoners made it clear that he intended for each one of them to get home safely. But he also revealed a sterner side of his character as he outlined how he would deal with those who did not follow his orders. His suspicions about the discipline of some of the men under his command were obvious: he warned the few who 'may not co-operate' that they would be subject to the full punishments of Military Law. He warned them that thieving outside the camp was equivalent to looting, and punishable by death. He also made it clear that, because the war was over, any offence committed outside the camp was a civil offence and punishment would be carried out in Japan. This was remarkably clear-headed and fair-minded coming from a man who had just spent almost four years at the mercy of an administration that paid no heed to international rules of war.

Shortly after the surrender MacCarthy received a note from a group of prisoners, mainly Australians, in one of the nearby camps. Together they had survived captivity in Java, the hell-ship journey to Japan, the sinking of the *Tamahoku Maru* and the atomic bomb. After the destruction of Nagasaki they had been sent to different camps. The high regard they had for their doctor is clear from their note:

> Dear Doc,
> Just a line to let you know that we are all OK.
> Glad that you made it OK. It was a long pull but it's worth it now.

Dear Doc,

Just a line to let you know that we are all OK

Glad that you made it OK. It was a long pull but its worth it now.

Some of us might see you if we don't start shifting. There are 700 men in this camp and have only had 2 drops. Not much but maybe it will improve

Just health and lots of luck if we don't see you again. Don't forget to write to us

(Over)

Best ever —

Jack E. Turner
Jack Van Allen
B. L. Lowe
H. L. Logan
J. B. Brankenberg
E. Kamens
Tony Marcinkus
Shorty Porchia
Leo Callahan
Joe Holder
"Pete" Piercy
George D'Ambrose
J. T. Patterson
Kenneth Pride
Charlie Young

Letter from POWs in a nearby camp to Aidan MacCarthy, August 1945. Many of their names also appear on the roster for POW Camp 14B (see p. 204).

Some of us might see you if we don't start shifting. There are 100 men in this camp and have had only 2 drops. Not much but maybe it will improve.

Just hello and lots of luck if we don't see you again. Don't forget to write to us.

Many of their names appear on documents from June 1944 when they arrived at Camp 14B, and a roster from Fukuoku 14B also records that they were survivors of the *Tamahoku Maru*.

Among the medicines in the supply drops was a new drug that MacCarthy had never seen before: penicillin. Soon he had an opportunity to test its effectiveness when a local police chief in Fukuoka prefecture approached him. Superintendent Kobayashi and his wife asked through an interpreter if he would examine their sick daughter. She was critically ill with double pneumonia so MacCarthy gave her a dose of penicillin and stayed with her through the night. At about 8 a.m. the following day he was delighted to see that the fever had broken and she had started to improve. The parents were overjoyed. MacCarthy was impressed with the effectiveness of the new drug.[15] Over the following days his visits to monitor the child's recovery became uncomfortable. Her parents would meet him at the front door of their home and, despite his protests, they kept bending down and kissing his feet as he removed his shoes before entering the house. Before MacCarthy left Japan they gave him family photographs, which he kept for the rest of his life.

As the former prisoners roamed the local countryside they discovered several other POW camps nearby, which, similar to their own, were in appalling condition. MacCarthy learned that there were two large Chinese forced labour camps about 2 and 3 miles away.[16] Three very agitated Chinese had arrived

The photographs of the Kobayashi family presented to Aidan MacCarthy by the grateful parents of a young girl whom he cured with penicillin.

番号	氏　名	国籍	前歴	年月日	年月日	備考
6327	LOWE, PLUMER, P ロウ, プルマー, ピ	米	比	19・3・24	死亡・送還・(移動) 20・6・30	福岡第8分所へ
6328	ALLEM, VAN, JACK アレン, バン, ヂャツ	米	比	19・3・24	死亡・送還・(移動) 20・6・30	福岡第8分所へ
6329	BRANDENBURG, T.B (Jmr) ブランデンブルグ, ゼ,ビ	〃	爪　哇 19.6.24 長崎 港外で遭難	19・6・25	死亡・送還・(移動) 20・6・30	福岡第8分所へ
6330	CALLAHAN, Leo 　　Augustus カラハン, レオ, オーグステス	〃	〃 〃	19・6・25	死亡・送還・(移動) 20・6・30	〃
6331	D'AMBROSE, Ernest 　　William ダンブロス, エルネスト, ウリアム	〃	〃 ・ 〃	19・6・25	死亡・送還・(移動) 20・6・30	非軍人
6332	HOLDER, Joe, Neal ホルダル, ジョ, ニ―ル	〃	〃 〃	19・6・25	死亡・送還・(移動) 20・6・30	〃
6333	KAMINS, Eric カミンス, エリク	〃	〃 〃	19・6・25	死亡・送還・(移動) 20・6・30	〃 非軍人
6334	LOGAN, Wifred 　　Edward ロガン, ウイルフレド, エドワルド	〃	〃 〃	19・6・25	死亡・送還・(移動) 20・6・30	〃
6336	PATTERSON, J, T パツテルソン, ゼイ, テイ	〃	〃 〃	19・6・25	死亡・送還・(移動) 20・6・30	〃
6337	PEREZ, Fredereck, T ペレズ, フレデリツク, テイ	〃	〃 〃	19・6・25	死亡・送還・(移動) 20・6・30	〃
6338	PORCHIA, John 　　Michael ポルチア, ジョン, ミカエル	〃	〃 〃	19・6・25	死亡・送還・(移動) 20・6・20	非軍人
6339	PRIDE, Jerry, Kenneth プライデ, ゼリー, ケンネス	〃	〃 〃	19・6・25	死亡・送還・(移動) 20・6・30	〃 非軍人
6340	TURNER, Jack, Eudy ダルナル, ジャツク, ユデ―	〃	〃 〃	19・6・25	死亡・送還・移動 20・6・30	〃 非軍人
6341	YOUNG, Charles, Joseph ヤング, チャルレス, ジョゼフ	〃	〃 〃	19・6・25	死亡・送還・(移動) 20・6・30	〃 非軍人
6342	MacCARTHY, Joseph 　　Aidan マツカシイ, ジョゼフ, エイダン	英	〃 〃	19・6・25	死亡・送還・(移動) 20・6・21	福岡第27分所 軍医少佐
6343	THOMPSON, Noel, James 　　William トンプソン, ノ―ル ゼ―ムス ウイリアム	英	〃 〃	19・6・25	死亡・送還・(移動) 20・6・21	福岡第27分所 軍医大尉す

A roster from Fukuoka 14B. Aidan MacCarthy's name is second from the end.
POW RESEARCH NETWORK JAPAN

at Camp 26 and asked him to come to their camp quickly. One spoke some English and he described what they had suffered as forced labourers in open-cast coalmines. When the surrender was announced, the Chinese had taken the law into their own hands and murdered their guards. MacCarthy sent a group of six armed men to verify the story. They returned a few hours later and asked him to return to the Chinese camp with them. There, he found the camp so overcrowded and filthy it reminded him of the hell ships, but worse was to come. In the centre of the camp, MacCarthy found the bodies of around twenty-two guards kneeling with their heads lying on the ground in front of them.[17] The victims were unrecognisable. The heads had been beaten to a pulp and were crawling with insects.

The leader of the Chinese camp nervously explained that each one of the 750 prisoners had stuck a blow so that no individual could be held responsible.[18] The Chinese were now worried that the bodies would be found and provoke retaliation by the local population. MacCarthy told them to bury the corpses and called the entire camp on parade. They gathered in the drizzling rain and, speaking through an interpreter, MacCarthy told them he believed what they had done was wrong but that he understood why it had happened. He then told them they must stay confined to the camp for their own safety.

In the other Chinese camp the prisoners had also taken revenge and murdered their Chinese overseer. They submitted a statement to MacCarthy on 11 September claiming that the overseer was regarded as a traitor to his country and a Japanese spy. The statement makes clear his mistreatment of the men under his command and the fears of the Chinese labourers once MacCarthy and the others left.

In many ways the Chinese had behaved similarly to the POWs when they killed their guards in the sea following the

STATEMENT from the CHINESE CAMP.

_hy_ we killed the Chinese Officer in command of our Camp.
(A) The Officer's previous record. In the past he was classed as a Japanese Spy and a traitor to his country.
(B) He treated the sick men very badly. Men who were injured in the Coal Mine were restricted to one loaf of bread per day. this combined with the cold caused men to die. There were 18 men who died. In the Mine when men were not physically able to work and sat down to rest the Japanese reported them to this officer. He then punished them by beating. In cases where a man stole another man's food in the Mine he would be punished by being deprived of food at night . He would then leave the camp and would not be seen again. This happened in four cases.
(C) This Officer hoped to be a wealthy man when he returned to China. Previously in China he was a poor man so he came to Japan to control all the Chinese who worked in the Mine. He would give them half of their cigarette ration,soap and other goods, keeping back the balance so that when he went to China he could trade them for Chinese money and personally profit thereby.
(D) When this Officer said that 200 coal skips were to be filled and the task was not completed owing to a fall in the coal shaft the gang concerned were punished by the stoppage of food and all men were beaten.
(E) The reason why no drastic action was taken against this Officer before the Japanese capitulation was that the men in this Camp had no protection against the Japanese.
(F) (A)   Now, the Chinese of this Camp ask k for protection from the Japanese soldiers and police when the British soldiers leave Japan.
(B) While the British soldiers are in this Camp (as Guard) the food is very good and sufficient. But after they leave for their homes we are afraid that they will be reduced very much.
(C) Yesterday (10/9/45) the Japanese policemen had a secret conference and said that only 25 killed the Officer. But this is a false statement. All of the Chinese participated in killing this man.
(D) Now we have the British Guard in the Camp every day and they help us and advise us. Consequently the Japanese cannot catch the 25 men and punish them by Japanese Law. But we are afraid what they will do when the British Guard is withdrawn when they leave Japan.

Statement from Chinese labour camp whose overseer was murdered by the former prisoners.

sinking of the _Tamahoku Maru_ or pushed them off the scaffolding at the Mitsubishi factory. Perhaps it was the brutality of these executions that horrified MacCarthy. He left a small group of armed guards to protect them and promised as much food as could be found locally and that they would receive all their supplies when they were due to be shipped out.

There had been a delay in getting the American troops and supplies on land because there were no charts of the mines in Nagasaki Harbour. The Americans speeded up the clearing process by offering $100 to naval personnel to race across the harbour in empty landing craft wearing just swimming shorts and a life jacket. If they hit a mine and survived they were to dive overboard. A few men were lost but the harbour was quickly cleared, and occupation forces began to arrive in greater numbers.[19] Their arrival meant that the former POWs no longer had any duties to fulfil and became redundant.[20] Two days later, on 13 September, medical teams began arriving at the former prison camp in Keisen. The very sick were evacuated immediately by air. Because MacCarthy was in relatively good health he was among the men assigned to leave by ship via Nagasaki. He packed his bags, said his farewells and boarded the train for Nagasaki.

When the former prisoners arrived at Nagasaki docks, they were in a far better condition than when they had stood there in June 1944. They were ushered through a wooden building, which had been set up as a decontamination centre. MacCarthy's nine kitbags of souvenirs were removed for inspection but he was anxious not to lose his precious sword, feeding bowl, documents and the rest of his hoard. The men were told to strip and were showered, deloused, sprayed, tested and given new clothes. Then Geiger counters were passed over their bodies and inserted into cavities to test for radiation contamination. MacCarthy was still terrified of radiation sickness and was haunted by the fear that the same symptoms he had witnessed in Nagasaki would suddenly appear in him. He waited anxiously for the results. The Geiger reading was clear. He had miraculously survived the atomic bomb unscathed. Reunited with his kitbags he climbed up the gangplank of the

US navy landing ship to begin the first leg of the long journey home.

They sailed south-west and three days later disembarked on Okinawa island. The carnage of the battle that had been fought there was clear. The capital of the island, Naha, had been completely reduced to rubble and it lay in a desolate wasteland. As they approached the shore, the sea around them was full of half-sunken ships and landing craft. The burnt-out hulk of an aircraft carrier lay slumped on the shore.

The former POWs were accommodated at a tented camp. They settled into their new surroundings and enjoyed the facilities. A mess hall was open all day and they could help themselves to the food. One morning, MacCarthy was approached by an American who asked him if he could help identify the nationality of a former Japanese prisoner. They were trying to make arrangements to repatriate him but could not work out where he was from. In a mixture of Japanese, broken English and a strange language they had never heard before, the man tried to explain where he was from. Eventually they figured out that he was an Inuit who had been caught fishing by the Japanese. He had been interned for two years but his main concern seemed to be what he would tell his wife when he got home.[21]

MacCarthy was invited by an American naval officer to the Navy Club for a drink. Whilst he was there chatting to a group of officers he was introduced to an American submarine commander who had spent the last months of the war as a prisoner of the Japanese. They got talking and the officer turned out to be Richard O'Kane, the captain of *Tang*, the submarine that had sunk the *Tamahoku Maru*. MacCarthy regretted telling him how many Allied POWs had died as a result of his attack the previous year. O'Kane's immediate reaction was to get very drunk.[22] He had been captured in October 1944 when *Tang*

Japanese war currency signed by American servicemen in Okinawa, dated 22 September 1945.

was sunk by its own defective torpedo that had boomeranged during an attack in the Formosa (Taiwan) Strait. Most of the crew died but O'Kane was among a few survivors who were taken prisoner.

The former POWs enjoyed the relative luxury of Okinawa before being flown to Manila in the bomb bays of a B-29. Sitting on temporary wooden seats fitted in rows, the thought that one of the crew could accidentally pull a lever at any second and drop them into the Pacific was never far from MacCarthy's mind. After four long hours they arrived at Manila.[23]

Their patience began to wear thin as they waited in Manila before beginning the next leg of the journey. To avoid boredom they wandered around and again were shocked by the scale of the destruction. The intensity of the fighting that had obliterated much of the city was clear. They were invited to see one of the American 'Liberty Ships' in the docks. These were made of concrete and had been hurriedly built to transport supplies to the American forces for the invasion of Japan.[24] When MacCarthy was invited on board he was told that the first officer on the ship was also Irish and from Castletownbere. Anxious for news of his family, MacCarthy searched the ship and eventually found him. It was then that he learned that his younger brother Barry was dead. He had been killed six months previously by the last German bomb to fall on London.[25]

News of his younger brother's death weighed heavily on him and he was now even more anxious to see his family. Eventually they boarded an American troopship and were brought across the Pacific to San Francisco via Hawaii. When the ship entered Pearl Harbor, MacCarthy saw the destruction caused by the Japanese attack almost four years previously. One of the half-submerged wrecks was that of the USS *Utah*. The last time he had seen the huge battleship was in Castletownbere Harbour almost thirty years earlier during the Great War.

When the troopship arrived in San Francisco they were transferred to a hospital train, which brought them up the west coast of America. At the Canadian border they were met by Canadian trains and began the long transcontinental journey east.

At each provincial boundary we had a complete change of drivers, crew, cooks and stewards. Each province tried to outdo the others in courtesy, attention and the food provided. The trains often stopped in small towns *en route*, where the mayor, and a welcome party always met us.[26]

Eventually they arrived in New York where they boarded the *Queen Mary*. It had been requisitioned as a troopship and as they crossed the Atlantic they noticed that the crew were very wary of them. They seemed to make every possible effort to avoid contact with the former POWs. It turned out that the crew had been warned that former prisoners of the Japanese were mentally unstable as a result of their experiences and were to be handled with care. MacCarthy later discovered that the same impression was circulated by British authorities. He was annoyed because most of his relatives seemed to regard him 'with a kind of compassionate apprehension'.[27]

Around 18 November, as the *Queen Mary* approached the docks in Southampton, euphoria enveloped everyone on board. Although the war in Europe had ended six months previously they still received a huge welcome with boats and ships of all sizes. Hooters were blaring, sirens and church bells rang out from the shore. This was an emotional homecoming for the men who had spent so many lonely days on the far side of the world and had missed their families desperately. They lined the rails and hung out of portholes as welcome speeches were read out.

From there they were brought to RAF Cosford to be catalogued, medically examined, provided with ration cards, travel warrants and civilian clothing. Liberation questionnaires had to be completed, detailing where and when they had been captured, and where they had been imprisoned.

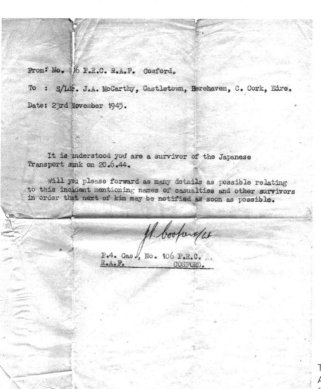

EX-P~~RISONER~~ OF WAR

LEAVE FOLLOWING ~~RELEASE~~ ~~FROM~~ ~~CAPTIVITY~~ OVERSEAS. No...... 19.NOV1945

No.106 P.R.C.

R.A.F. COSFORD

LISTS IN BLOCK CAPITALS

NO... R.3425 .... RANK... S/LDR ....

NAME. MAC CARTHY. A.A... BRANCH OR TRADE.................

ADDRESS ON LEAVE..
.... Castletown. Berehaven. Co. Cork. Eire .....
....

RAILWAY STATION TO WHICH WARRANT SHOULD BE ISSUED).............

Return to Unit 30/12/45

Leave permission slip from RAF Cosford, November 1945.

From: No. 106 P.R.C. R.A.F. Cosford.

To : S/Ldr. J.A. McCarthy, Castletown, Berehaven, C. Cork, Eire.

Date: 23rd November 1945.

It is understood you are a survivor of the Japanese Transport sunk on 20.6.44.

Will you please forward as many details as possible relating to this incident mentioning names of casualties and other survivors in order that next of kin may be notified as soon as possible.

P.4. Cas /, No. 106 P.R.C. R.A.F. COSFORD.

The RAF request to Aidan MacCarthy for information on the sinking of *Tamahoku Maru*.

Within forty-eight hours of their arrival in England they were cleared to go home. MacCarthy received instructions to return to his unit on 30 December but he had absolutely no intention of obeying the order. He was not going to miss his first New Year at home with his family for seven years.

Although he was desperate to get home, he delayed his departure for Ireland by a day so he could speak to some of the wives of those who had drowned when the *Tamahoku Maru* was torpedoed. They were clinging to the hope that their husbands were still alive and it was up to MacCarthy to explain that this was not possible. Their husbands were among the hundreds of unlucky POWs who had drowned almost eighteen months previously.[28] Finally he boarded the ferry that would bring him home. On 24 November the ferry approached Dún Laoghaire harbour in County Dublin. He walked down the gangplank and set foot on Irish soil for the first time in many years. His father, brothers and sisters had travelled from Castletownbere to welcome him. Everyone was there except his mother. As he walked towards his family, they did not recognise him until he smiled. He had been fourteen and a half stone when his family last saw him and despite having gorged on food during his two-month journey, he was only seven stone when he arrived home.

The fact that his mother was not there to greet him worried him as it was very unlike her, but the years of worry had taken their toll and she was gravely unwell.

They gathered up his collection of kitbags containing the hoard of souvenirs he had brought home from the war. In his hand he had the samurai sword gifted to him by Isao Kusuno. In his bag was the precious food bowl he had improvised, cut from a Dutch water bottle and with his name engraved on the side.

The family made their way into the city and checked in to the Clarence Hotel on the quays where Aidan received a

The telegram sent by Julia MacCarthy to her son on his return to Ireland.

message from his mother, wishing him 'a thousand welcomes'. Coincidentally, the day of his arrival was the anniversary of his baby sister Aine's death in 1918.

The journey from Dublin to Castletownbere was short compared to the odyssey he had experienced. But now MacCarthy was anxious to get home to see his beloved mother. Stepping across the threshold of MacCarthy's Bar was not the joyous occasion he had hoped for. He went straight upstairs to see his bedridden mother, not realising how ill she was until he saw her. Unable to bear the years of heartache when her son was a prisoner, Julia had aged considerably. When Barry was killed she had lost the will to live. She held on for Aidan to arrive home but died a month later, on Christmas Eve 1945. She was sixty-six years old and yet another casualty of the war. The happy Christmas that Aidan had longed for during so many years as a prisoner turned to more sadness and grief.

12

Post-War Life

After just a few weeks at home MacCarthy had to face reality again in early 1946. He would turn thirty-three a few months later and he had to move on. The first decision to be made was whether to remain in the RAF, but realistically he did not have too many other options. Before he joined the RAF, having experienced life as a GP in poverty-stricken Welsh valleys and the shilling surgeries of London, the workload and pay had turned him off general practice. There was no work available for him in Ireland because he did not have any family connections in the medical profession, so the RAF was the obvious choice. The service suited his personality and it offered excitement and opportunities for travel that he could not find elsewhere. Despite what he had been through, the air force was the world he knew and felt safe in. In a strange way it offered him security. He was also grateful that all the pay he had accrued during his time as a prisoner and the amount deducted whilst he was 'missing presumed dead' had been reinstated.

MacCarthy had given the RAF exemplary service during the war in Britain and overseas; he had been decorated highly for bravery, was revered for his work in the POW camps and had a huge standing within the organisation. He knew he would do well in his career if he stuck with it. He also liked the fact that because the air force was relatively new, it did not have the same level of formality as the centuries-old Royal Navy with its stuffy traditions and rigid discipline.

The long years of captivity and the short, euphoric weeks and months following his release were over. After some initial reluctance MacCarthy joined the other former POWs drifting back to RAF Cosford for rehabilitation and resettlement.

> But I faced life with a very different attitude. For a considerable period I had lived from one day to the next, rejoicing in the fact that I was surviving in the short term. Now I was able to plan in the long term. Even now I thank God for the miracle of being alive.[1]

There were medical staff on site with teams of educational and technical officers who were busy preparing the former prisoners' minds and bodies for the outside world. The psychiatrists soon realised that their experiences with POWs who had been incarcerated in German camps had not come near to preparing them for the prisoners of the Japanese.[2] The death rate for Allied prisoners in Europe was 4 per cent but 27 per cent of prisoners held by the Japanese died.

The British military failed to grasp the reality of what life had been like for prisoners of the Japanese. Every former POW was required to complete a Liberation Questionnaire in which they were asked for details about the number of 'Escapes or Attempted Escapes' during their captivity.[3] MacCarthy drew a pencil line through this question. However, the question itself reveals how little the authorities knew about their circumstances. The questionnaire went on to request an outline of each escape attempt, the prisoner's experiences during periods of freedom and the manner of his recapture. The questions read more like a report on a school outing.

There had been a few successful escapes but for the majority of prisoners of the Imperial Japanese Army there was simply nowhere to escape to. The only option would have been to trek through hundreds of miles of jungle, with no food. Many attempted but succumbed to starvation and disease. If they were caught, the torture and execution they faced was intended to discourage others from following their example. Any prisoners who succeeded in getting out of a camp were invariably turned over to the Japanese by terrified natives who faced savage reprisals if caught helping them. Also, there were rewards for turning over any Allied escapees to the Japanese forces.

The official attitude towards the returned POWs was dismissive; they were encouraged not to speak about what they had experienced and just get on with it. But this was impossible for men who knew the depths of humanity's capacity to inflict suffering on others. They carried unspeakable memories of torture and humiliation and the vulnerability that came with knowing how easily they could be disempowered and dehumanised.[4] Their dignity had been replaced with a deep sense of shame and worthlessness from which many would never recover. Thousands of former POWs spent the rest of their lives in isolation and loneliness because no one they knew could understand what they had endured.

What made the situation worse was that people knew that many of them were psychologically damaged; the stigma of having been a Far East POW followed them after the war.

A 1954 study found that in the two years following the end of the war, former Japanese POWs died at a rate four times higher than expected for men of their age.[5] A 1987 study found that 80 per cent of former Pacific POWs had a psychiatric impairment. They were 30 per cent more likely to commit suicide.[6]

In the years immediately after the war MacCarthy was badly affected and, like most former POWs, suffered flashbacks and nightmares. They relived their experiences sometimes on a daily basis, waking up screaming, sobbing or lashing out.[7] MacCarthy recalled many years later that these were particularly bad if he had a few drinks or got very tired.[8]

Each former POW had to chart his own course back to normality, with varying degrees of success. MacCarthy used to bring a number of Irish former POWs to Castletownbere each year to help them recuperate. They had been less fortunate than him: one would pace the town square for the duration of the visit whilst another could not sit in a room unless all of the windows and doors were left open.[9] They were broken men and whether MacCarthy escaped this fate through luck, faith, mental strength or some other factor is unknown, but he was grateful that he escaped long-term psychological effects.[10]

He applied the fortitude that had sustained him in the camps in his struggle to regain a normal life. Maybe his ability to forgive also helped him to leave his experiences behind, so that his war ended in 1945. Despite everything he had gone through he felt little bitterness towards the Japanese.

> The totally different culture and religion of the nation made them so alien that I could hardly regard their actions as immoral. Everything my own world stood for had been turned on its head during my imprisonment.[11]

MacCarthy made a point in his memoir that many of the former inmates of Cycle Camp in Batavia were pleased to find out later that their former drug-addicted camp commandant Lieutenant Sonei had been captured. He had not followed the Bushido example of committing *hara-kiri* and, in September 1946, the trial of the 'Beast of Tjideng' began. Without his daily shot of heroin he had become a gibbering wreck.[12] The formerly brutal prison camp commander sat with downcast eyes and apologised for all the horrors and intense pain, both physical and emotional, that he had inflicted on his prisoners.[13] His pleas for clemency were ignored and on 7 December 1946, he stood before a Dutch firing squad and was executed.[14] It is believed that his body parts were shipped to the Netherlands for medical studies.[15]

Over time MacCarthy put on weight and once again regained the stocky build that had earned him the nickname 'Tubby'. He was not tall but was very broad and barrel-chested. Shortly after he returned to England a friend of his, a priest from Castletownbere, introduced him to Kathleen Wall. She was three years younger than him and from Ballinamore Bridge, County Galway. Kathleen was training to be a nurse but did not really like it. At the time she was dating an Englishman who was very keen to marry her. MacCarthy and Kathleen quickly became friends. They bumped into each other occasionally and over time Aidan fell in love with her.

Eventually it came to the point where Kathleen had to decide between her English suitor and Aidan. She preferred Aidan but it was well known at the time that many of the former Japanese POWs had been damaged psychologically, and at the time there were plenty of young men to choose from. But Aidan was persistent and eventually she fell in love with him. This changed the rest of his life. As their relationship grew more serious she became worried about marrying him as more stories circulated about how strange former prisoners were. However, she stuck with him because he did not seem as badly affected by his experiences as the others. Kathleen observed that all of the former prisoners were very quiet when you met them initially and they seemed to be struggling to get back to normality, to regain their humanity.

The day before his thirty-fifth birthday in March 1948, MacCarthy received a letter informing him that he was to be awarded an OBE for his medical work in the POW camps. This was a huge occasion and his family, including uncles and cousins, travelled to London for the ceremony. A few months later, on 19 June 1948, Aidan and Kathleen were married at Westminster Cathedral. It was another huge family occasion with D.F. and the rest of the family travelling from Castletownbere. The newly-weds went to Cornwall on honeymoon for three weeks. On their return they started RAF life together. They were first posted to a medical training school in Gloucestershire. It did not seem a very glamorous introduction to the air force for Kathleen. Their accommodation was very basic as they lived in war-era Nissen huts covered with corrugated iron sheeting.

In the years that followed the war he avoided any discussion of what had happened to him. In Kathleen's words his night-mares were 'ferocious' and it was better not to ask him about his captivity because it would bring the memories flooding back.[16] It took some former prisoners many years before they could tell anyone what they had experienced. The reality for many was that they lived out the rest of their lives without ever uttering a word about it.

MacCarthy was very fortunate in that his busy working life allowed him to focus his energy on something positive and gave him an outlet. He did not have any interest in the POW associations because, like many others, he did not want to dwell on his memories. Instead, he preferred to leave them in the past and move on.

The MacCarthys spent their first year of marriage in Gloucestershire, after which Aidan was posted first to Sandringham, and then Lincolnshire, before their first overseas posting to Hong Kong in 1952. This coincided with the Korean

A formal photograph taken at RAF Little Rissington in August 1948. Aidan MacCarthy is fourth from left, front row.

Wedding photograph of Aidan MacCarthy and Kathleen Wall on the steps of Westminster Cathedral, 19 June 1948.

War.[17] Kathleen took the longer route by ship while Aidan travelled by plane and he was there to greet her when she arrived in Hong Kong. They stayed in a hotel before moving into a service flat in Kai Tak where he was the medical officer at the RAF base. They quickly settled into the expat lifestyle and enjoyed it to the full. A number of the local police were Irish and years later Kathleen recalled their social outings, such as the time they were on a boat in the South China Sea having drinks as the sun went down. It was a far more attractive lifestyle than working in general practice in the Welsh valleys or in Ireland.

After some time in Hong Kong they were due to go on holidays. They weighed up their options and incredibly MacCarthy decided that he wanted to return to Japan. This took a huge amount of courage. Travelling on a troopship, retracing the same route he had travelled just eight years previously on the *Tamahoku Maru*, he made his way back to the country where he had suffered so much. Maybe it was the beginning of a process of confronting the demons within. The fact that he was able to return to the people and the culture that only a few years previously had inflicted such suffering on him and his comrades is hard to fathom. He could have met one of his former camp guards. While they were there Aidan and Kathleen became friendly with a local doctor who acted as their guide and showed them around and one of the highlights of the trip was a visit to Kyoto.

They returned to Hong Kong and although happy there, their family life did not feel complete. They had been married for a number of years, they both loved children and wanted their own. They were devastated when they were told that, due to MacCarthy's exposure to the radiation of the atomic bomb, the chances of them having children were unlikely.

Aidan (right) and Kathleen MacCarthy (second from left) in Hong Kong, early 1950s.

Their lives changed a few years later when Kathleen told Aidan in Hong Kong that she was pregnant. He was ecstatic and was determined his child would eventually play rugby for Ireland. With that in mind, he wanted the birth to take place in Ireland so they left Hong Kong and made their way home. Their first child, Nicola, was born at the Glenvera nursing home in Cork city.

When the proud parents left the hospital they stayed with Aidan's sister Ita and her husband before travelling west to celebrate Christmas around the large table at the family home in Castletownbere. It was their first Christmas without D.F. who had died the previous March. After Christmas they returned to England where MacCarthy took up his next appointment at the RAF medical rehabilitation centre at Headley Court in Surrey. As it was a facility for wounded RAF personnel including former prisoners of war, his personal experience was invaluable.

During this posting the family lived at Epsom Downs and MacCarthy found that his commanding officer shared his love of horse racing. They would both disappear whenever there was a racing festival in the south of England. One of the reasons he liked the RAF was because there were others like him in the organisation and he could get away with things that he could not elsewhere. One of his superior officers, an Irishman whom he addressed by his first name, pointed out that he should address him by his officer title, 'Commodore'. As MacCarthy walked out the door he turned and replied, 'of course I will, Commodore, *agus póg mo thóin*' ('kiss my arse' in Irish).[18]

Kathleen was a brilliant hostess, always cheerful, and she loved people. She suited Aidan perfectly and fitted comfortably into the RAF lifestyle. Everyone was welcome in their house, regardless of rank, and particularly anyone of Irish extraction. MacCarthy believed that many visiting air marshals and vice-air marshals would remember Kathleen as the commanding officer of the medical facility and not himself.

On a practical level, MacCarthy often said that if an officer's wife did not like the lifestyle then there was no way her husband's career could progress. As an officer in the RAF, social contacts were essential for career advancement. Kathleen helped him to pursue his ambitions: her sociable and relaxed personality meant she was able to converse with everyone and their married life seemed to be an endless round of socialising and celebration. This was fortunate because, after all he had been through, MacCarthy felt blessed to be alive and was determined to enjoy life to the full.

A few years later, Kathleen gave birth to their second daughter, Adrienne. The following year MacCarthy completed his four-year tour at Headley Court. Their next move was to France where the family moved into a house outside the village of Chartrettes. MacCarthy was stationed at the Allied Air Forces Central Europe military base at Fontainebleau, 25 miles from Paris. This was at the height of the Cold War and Fontainebleau was to be the control centre for NATO air forces in the event of war with the Soviet Union. Against this more serious backdrop, the family enjoyed four blissful years. The children settled in to a local *petite école* and the parents, as usual, enjoyed the local hospitality, food and wine. They lived in a beautiful house where each bedroom had a balcony. They had a large garden at the bottom of which the Seine flowed towards Paris.[19]

MacCarthy's sister Ita came to visit them on one occasion and they brought her to see the famous Fontainebleau Palace where MacCarthy spotted a group of English-speaking tourists who seemed lost so he offered them a guided tour, for free. He then led them from room to room, making up the details as he went along. Ita and Kathleen followed, very impressed as the tourists were fully taken in by his ad-libbed knowledge of the palace. MacCarthy made a particular mention of a giant table on which Napoleon had signed the Treaty of Fontainebleau and told the tourists that he had commissioned an exact replica, which was in pride of place at his home in Castletownbere. When he was a medical student he had been a member of the Cork Little Theatre Society and this experience came in handy on occasion.

After four years in France they returned to England and settled in Lincolnfield briefly before MacCarthy was posted to Rheindahlen, Germany, in July 1965. He had been promoted and was in charge of the RAF hospital at Wegberg. According to Kathleen he was an appalling cook and could not make a cup of tea but he was a very effective administrator. He had developed a reputation for being able to get things done and run large organisations.[20]

Kathleen MacCarthy with baby Adrienne.

(*L–r*): Nicola and Adrienne MacCarthy in France.

(*L–r*): Adrienne and Nicola MacCarthy.

Aidan and Nicola pose outside her school in Chartrettes.

Aidan (*left*) and Kathleen (*second from right*) at a party in France in the 1950s.

This pattern became normal for the family. Every few years they moved to a new house for the duration of MacCarthy's tour, then packed up and moved to his next posting. Nicola and Adrienne would settle in at a local school while their parents made new friends and enjoyed the air force social life. Throughout her childhood Nicola attended a total of twelve different schools. To her this seemed normal and they assumed it was how everyone lived.[21] They lived in a succession of twenty-one houses, each of which Kathleen quickly managed to turn into a home. Significantly, there was one constant feature in each house – MacCarthy's Japanese sword always hung on the wall as a reminder of what he had survived.

Another constant in their life was west Cork. Every summer the family returned to Castletownbere on holidays for a fortnight in August.[22] They would drive across England in their green Ford Consul and then sail to Ireland by ferry. It was a pilgrimage that MacCarthy loved because he could catch up with his brothers, sisters, relatives and friends. The August bank holiday weekend would be in full swing and culminated with the regatta that had been such a feature of his childhood. He was always very proud to show his daughters around the place where he grew up and tell them stories from his childhood. These visits home were always centred around MacCarthy's Bar. Word would go out that 'the Doc's home'. People would go to the bar and join the queue to see 'Dr Aidan' as he set up an informal clinic, dispensing old cures, which always seemed to work.[23] His approach was possibly inspired by his mother and the remedies she compiled in her notebook. It was the simplicity of the homemade cures that appealed to him. Everyone from the town drunk to old fishermen and farmers would arrive with various illnesses, itches, rashes, back pains and other conditions. MacCarthy might tell them to apply a particular salve and bathe in the seawater twice a day. He did all of this for free and was delighted to be able to help people.

Another part of his holiday routine was to play cribbage with a former POW from Liverpool. This had been one of the games POWs had played to pass the time. Former POW George Roberts had survived the horrors of the Thai-Burma Railway and had been very badly affected. When he returned home from the war, he would sit cross-legged in the local pub in Liverpool where he worked. Staff would give him a bowl of rice and the locals were told not to disturb him. He ended up marrying a woman from the Beara Peninsula. They retired to the area and the shared understanding he had with MacCarthy meant a lot to him.

At night, MacCarthy loved the singsongs in the bar and joined in whenever he could. For the children, these holidays were heaven because their relatives owned a pub and this meant an endless supply of delicacies unknown where they lived; Tayto crisps, red lemonade and Lucozade in glass bottles.[24]

They spent much of the holidays on the nearby beaches in Allihies and Garinish. This allowed MacCarthy to indulge his love of swimming, which was good for the elbow that had been smashed by a Japanese camp guard in Java. The family holidays would usually end with a visit to the annual horse-racing festival that takes place at Allihies, west of Castletownbere, on 15 August. MacCarthy would begin the day by going to Mass to celebrate the Feast of the Assumption. It was also the anniversary of the day he heard Emperor Hirohito announce the surrender of Japan. He would sometimes mention that it was the day the war ended – the day he was liberated.

As his daughters were growing up they knew that he had been in the war but he never spoke about it. They knew their father as a caring, quiet and gentle man who could be the

Kathleen and Aidan (*second and third from left*) at Headley Court in the 1950s.

Aidan, Kathleen and Adrienne at Headley Court in the 1950s.

Two images of Aidan MacCarthy: in the 1950s (*left*) and 1960s (*right*).

Aidan and Kathleen MacCarthy (*front row, far right*) on a visit to Lourdes in 1956.

life and soul of the party when he wanted to be. From time to time Kathleen would tell them quietly that he had had a bad nightmare the night before. His daughters knew he had experienced something terrible and that he kept these memories bottled up inside. Any time they asked him about it he would just say, 'I'll tell you when you're older.'

In 1969, MacCarthy was fifty-six. He had been stationed in Germany for four years and it was time to return to England. It was summer, so Kathleen and Aidan decided to take the children to Bavaria on holiday. As they drove through the pristine countryside they passed near Dachau. MacCarthy decided he wanted to visit the former Nazi concentration camp. Kathleen tried to persuade him not to go but he insisted. They walked around the former camp looking at the huts with rows of bunks, photos and records of the victims. They were not there long when they noticed that Aidan had disappeared. When they eventually found him he was crouched over, vomiting. He was very upset and mentioned a particular 'camp smell'. Kathleen and the girls could smell nothing out of the ordinary. It may have been the scent of freshly cut wood, the wire fences, wooden bunks and the nauseating feeling that came with the knowledge of what had taken place there. All of this brought the memories of his own captivity flooding back.

They left Dachau and continued on to a town called Ruhpolding, staying in a pretty Bavarian B&B with flowers in the windows and a swimming pool. The following morning they had decided to go to Salzburg for the day. They had driven a long way the previous day, the engine needed water and the windscreen was covered with flies. After breakfast MacCarthy said, 'I'm going to go and tidy the car, Kath.' A short while later, twelve-year-old Adrienne was in the back seat of the car as her father was putting something in the boot. He suddenly started swaying. Adrienne began to laugh because she thought he was joking. He then called to Kathleen: 'Kath, I'm dying ...' and collapsed. He was having a fit. People quickly gathered and he was taken to the local hospital by ambulance.

The owner of the B&B offered to look after the girls and Kathleen gave them money to go to the shops to get some sweets. She told them that the lady would look after them, they could stay by the pool and their daddy would be fine. She got in the ambulance and went to the hospital with her husband. The doctors detained him for a week but could not figure out what was wrong with him.

The RAF sent a driver and a doctor to collect them and they were brought back to England where MacCarthy was admitted to hospital. They tried to diagnose what was wrong with him but it remained a mystery. He began to have fits more regularly. They would usually pass quickly but he was worried and was convinced they had something to do with the beatings to the head he had received whilst a prisoner of war. Perhaps the memories stirred up in Dachau had aggravated his condition.

When he was eventually discharged from hospital, Kathleen and Aidan decided it was time to buy a house. They had been living in RAF accommodation for years, moving from one house to another and now Kathleen wondered what she would do if he died. What about the girls? Where would she go? They bought a four-bedroomed detached house in Northwood, North London, close to the joint military headquarters. MacCarthy made sure to celebrate his Beara roots, naming their new house 'Dunboy' after the famous castle a few miles west of Castletownbere.

Over the following two years he had a number of fits on the train while on his way to work. It was a huge worry for Kathleen and the doctors still could not figure out what was wrong with him. One day a friend and RAF consultant was walking along a hospital corridor behind MacCarthy and noticed that his walk was not quite right. He had problems moving his hands contra-ways to his feet.[25] The consultant turned to Kathleen and said: 'I know what it is, it's a brain tumour.' MacCarthy was immediately brought to Queen's Square Hospital in London, which specialised in neurosurgery.

Kathleen went to visit him every day and was told by the specialist: 'if it's deep rooted and we can't get at it that's the end but if it's a benign tumour in the brain lining we're all right.' At the hospital Kathleen met a fellow Galway woman. She was a doctor and Kathleen asked her to call and tell her he was alive as soon as the operation was over. She waited anxiously at home and, when eventually the phone rang, was told 'yes, he's out, the operation is over and he's in the recovery room. He must be all right because he's asking questions.' That was all she needed to know. She brought the children in to see him and a few weeks later he was well enough to go home. The tumour turned out be benign, which confirmed MacCarthy's suspicion that the daily beatings to the head with rifle butts had caused bleeding in his brain which had led to the tumour.

MacCarthy's doctors were aware of what he had been through during the war and they advised him to write down his memories. This would exercise his brain and aid his recovery. They also believed it would be therapeutic and might help to get rid of his recurring nightmares. And so, twenty-five years after end of the war, he started to engage once again with the experiences that in many ways he would have preferred to have left buried forever.[26]

Some years later he allowed a doctor friend to read the memoir. His friend, who was also a poet, insisted that the memoir should be published and brought the manuscript to his publishers. MacCarthy's memoir, *A Doctor's War* was eventually published in 1979. When his family read it they were shocked. It was the first time that they understood the true extent of what he had been through. He had never spoken about the details of his experiences up to that point. His siblings even thought that some of his war stories had been made up. Now they read for first time the true horror of his captivity at the hands of the Imperial Japanese Army.

When Kathleen read the book she was very upset; she had been the only person who knew how badly he had been affected by his captivity. She had lived with the nightmares that haunted her husband for so many years and could see the physical scars. She had never asked him to discuss what he had gone through because it would bring the nightmares back. She had always felt it was best to leave it all in the past.

When Nicola and Adrienne read the book they found it hard to believe that any of it could have happened, let alone to their father.[27] Now his secrets were finally out in the open and he began to discuss his captivity with them. Sometimes this would be triggered by innocuous events such as if Nicola or Adrienne were bitten by a mosquito he would recall a similar experience from captivity in Java.

In the early 1970s the Troubles in Ireland were entering their darkest days and the Provisional IRA bombing campaign in Britain was under way. MacCarthy was warned against returning to Ireland on holidays by the RAF because he would be a potential target. Being unable to return to Castletownbere for a number of years broke his heart. Many years later his daughters found out that their mother used to search under the car with a mirror before he went to work each morning, in case a bomb had been planted during the night.[28]

Aidan MacCarthy at the Central Medical Establishment in London, 1950s.

Aidan MacCarthy laying wreath at the Cenotaph in Manchester, 1960s.

Aidan MacCarthy with his samurai sword in the garden of his Northwood home, London, in the 1980s.

Aidan MacCarthy's medals (l–r): OBE, George Medal, 1939–1945 Star, Pacific Star, War Medal 1939–45, and Knight's Cross of the Order of St Sylvester. (The bottom row is the dress version of the medals.) BARRY MURPHY.

In 1971, MacCarthy retired from the RAF on his fifty-eighth birthday having attained the rank of Air Commodore – the highest rank attainable by non-combat officers.

He had spent thirty-one years in the service and, after retiring, he continued working as a civilian doctor at the Central Medical Establishment in London. Part of his work there involved medically assessing applicants to the air force. This meant that he was able to keep in contact with all of his former colleagues and stay connected with his wider circle of friends.[29]

Just a few months after MacCarthy retired, Emperor Hirohito controversially made his first state visit to Britain. Hirohito was greeted by silent crowds. Former POWs lined the route and turned their backs to him when the state procession made its way along the Mall towards Buckingham Palace. As MacCarthy watched the visit on television, he was visibly upset by the fact that Hirohito was afforded such respect without atoning for the suffering of the prisoners at the hands of his soldiers during the war. By the end of 1958, every war criminal in Japan who had not been executed had been granted amnesty and was released.[30] To add insult to so many injuries, Hirohito was presented with an award by Prince Phillip.

Throughout MacCarthy's career, his daughter Adrienne had seen how much her father enjoyed his work helping and curing people. She decided to follow him into the medical profession. She moved out of home and began studying nursing at Middlesex University Hospital. Kathleen still insisted on washing Adrienne's clothes and, because he was working nearby, MacCarthy would occasionally collect a suitcase from their daughter. One day, as he was making his way down Baker Street, he was stopped by a policeman. Because he was Irish the policeman wanted to know what he was carrying in the suitcase. He had to open it on the side of the street and show that it was full of women's underwear. He nearly died with embarrassment but considered it worth it for the story he was able to tell afterwards.

At different times through the 1950s, 1960s and 1970s Aidan's siblings Michael, Jim and Eileen ran the family pub in Castletownbere. When Michael and Eileen died, Jim was the last of them to run the business. He was a gentle west Cork bachelor who doted on his many nieces and nephews. He would often take them to the cinema and feed them as much ice cream and soft drinks as they wanted. He was popular in Castletownbere and there was a bend in the road on the approach to the town that was known as 'Jim's Corner' after he had driven his car into the wall and broken nearly every bone in his body.

When Jim died in 1978, Aidan considered selling the business because there was no one in the family to run it. Adrienne persuaded her father to hold onto it until she finished her training as a nurse and said she would try her hand at running it for six months. When she moved over in 1979 at the age of twenty-two, MacCarthy was delighted. He now had an excuse to travel home three or four times annually.[31]

Nicola moved to Castletownbere in 1991 following a serious accident when she was almost killed in a bus crash in Kenya. She set up a restaurant a few doors up the street from the pub. Aidan swelled with pride as he and Kathleen stood across the street from the family business started by his grandfather and both of them became emotional.

In later life he had problems with cataracts. It was painful but he never complained. He was always very positive and, if he felt down, he hid it well. He loved sports and spent a lot of his time watching football, racing, rugby or American football. At the house in Northwood, near London, he had a little library and loved to read, especially fiction. His nephew Brian recalled that at no point did he ever hear MacCarthy show any self-pity or anger.[32]

At the age of seventy-nine, MacCarthy was diagnosed with an aortic aneurism, a blister on the artery coming out of the heart. He described it as a ticking time bomb but decided not to undergo surgery as it was a risky procedure at his age. Instead, he diligently took aspirin and did his exercises every morning. He finally decided to retire fully from his work for the air force at the age of eighty.

Towards the end of his life, it seemed that the publishing of the book had indeed begun the process by which he was able to talk more openly about his experiences. He said he remembered his captivity as if it was a bad dream.[33] He felt that he had a duty to tell people his story because it might help them to form an opinion about national hatred and atomic bombs. The fiftieth anniversary of the dropping of the bomb in 1995 reaffirmed this, and his attitude was that if you have something important to tell people you should say it.[34] Around that time he recorded several interviews, including one with RTÉ radio in which he spoke frankly and often with humour about his experiences during the war. On 2 October 1995 he spoke at an event organised by the Beara Historical Society. For over an hour he gave an account of his experiences as a prisoner of war to a packed audience in Castletownbere. He spoke with incredible honesty and seemed to have arrived at a stage where the demons that haunted his past, particularly in the years immediately after the war, had finally been put to rest.

The following morning he left for London. A few days later, on Monday 9 October, he was going about his usual routine. He had studied the form in the morning newspapers before going to the bookies where he had an account. After lunch he spent the afternoon in the lounge watching television.

Kathleen was pottering around when, shortly before 4 p.m., she noticed his hand hanging by the side of the armchair. He had had a stroke and was unconscious.

She called an ambulance. In the midst of this, the phone rang: it was RTÉ calling to say that the interview would be broadcast the following week. Kathleen explained that he was being brought to hospital in an ambulance. They offered to cancel the broadcast but she insisted they go ahead with it. The ambulance arrived and brought Aidan to the nearby Mount Vernon Hospital where the doctors confirmed that he had had a massive stroke. The bleeding in his brain was caused by high blood pressure due to his weight and age. Kathleen stayed with him and during the night the doctor called her aside and told her there was very little hope. She asked, 'Should I ring Ireland?' The doctor replied, 'Yes, ring home.' Adrienne and Nicola travelled from Castletownbere and two days later on 11 October 1995, Dr Aidan MacCarthy OBE, GM, MB, BCH, BAL, Knight of St Sylvester, Air Commodore RAF (retired) and *hibakusha*, died.

He had insisted on being buried in Castletownbere. On the following Tuesday, a large crowd gathered at Cork Airport to meet his funeral cortège and accompany him on his last journey home to west Cork. In Castletownbere, another large crowd was gathered on the main street outside the Church of the Sacred Heart. His remains were carried into the church where so many decades previously he had served as an altar boy. The following morning, his dear friend of many years, Father Sean O'Shea, celebrated his requiem Mass. On leaving the church the coffin was carried shoulder high and led by a lone piper to MacCarthy's Bar – the place where he was born over eighty-two years previously and which had been his sanctuary throughout his captivity. He was buried at Droum cemetery overlooking the harbour.

Following the burial, the mourners gathered at the local Cametringane Hotel for refreshments. Unexpectedly, MacCarthy's distinct voice was heard in the reception room. The mourners fell silent and listened intently. RTÉ was broadcasting his radio interview and MacCarthy was speaking at his own funeral, telling his war story. Some of the older people found the experience upsetting. As the interview drew to a close, the interviewer asked what had given him the strength to survive his experiences. MacCarthy replied that it was a combination of 'my Irish Catholic heritage, my family background, my Jesuit training in Clongowes and lots and lots of luck.' With that the mourners stood and applauded.

Epilogue

I first heard the story of Aidan MacCarthy in 1999. I had just finished university and was helping out at my maternal grandmother, Margaret O'Sullivan's bar, The Rendevous, in the suburbs of Cork city for a few months. It was an old fashioned suburban bar that my grandparents had owned for many years. My grandmother was selling the business and my role was just to keep the place ticking over until the sale was completed. I used to enjoy the quiet afternoons when a few regular customers, mostly retired, would come in and sit at the bar counter and there was time to have a conversation with them. There was one customer in particular who had been in the RAF and we used to have interesting conversations about history and politics. He told me a story about a doctor from west Cork who had been a prisoner of the Japanese during the Second World War and had survived the atomic bomb attack on Nagasaki. He mentioned that this doctor had a connection to a MacCarthy's Bar in Castletownbere.

A few months later, while driving around the Beara Peninsula, I ended up in the town. Seeing the name 'MacCarthy' above the door, I entered and can remember asking the woman behind the counter if I was in the right place – there could have been more than one bar in the town with the same name. She smiled and replied, 'Yes, that was my father', pointed to a framed newspaper article on the wall, and told me to read it. This was the first time I met Adrienne MacCarthy and also the first time I read an account of her father's incredible story of survival. By the time I had finished reading, Adrienne had placed the samurai sword on the bar counter.

It was a strange sight to see a Japanese sword in a pub in rural west Cork. The first question was: how did it get there? Adrienne told me it had been given to her father at the end of the Second World War. In the moments following the Japanese surrender the former prisoners were intent on killing the camp commandant. Her father had protected the Japanese officer, saved his life and, in gratitude, was given the sword. This was the story her father had told her. Adrienne told me how the ashes of the ancestors of the officer were embedded in the sword handle. There was also a rumour that it was still radioactive from the atomic bomb that had been dropped on Nagasaki.

As a piece of craftsmanship the sword is mesmerising: over three feet in length, perfectly balanced, intricately decorated and still razor sharp, even though it is decades since it was last sharpened.

The origin of the sword was known, but only in the form of an outline of the events following the Japanese surrender. There were very few details. It was clear that the sword meant a lot to Adrienne as a symbol of what her father had endured. But the sword also raised the possibility that somewhere in Japan there was a family who, to their dying shame, had lost their ancestral sword because their father or grandfather had given it away. Would they like to know where it was?

I got a copy of Aidan's memoir *A Doctor's War* and read it over two nights. It is a fascinating and engrossing account of his story, in his own words. The problem is that he often uses so few words to describe his experiences. What strikes you when reading his book is that he sometimes outlines in one paragraph

The interior of MacCarthy's Bar. A photograph of Aidan MacCarthy is displayed behind the counter. BOB JACKSON

an event upon which someone else would base an entire book or life story. Because of his genuine, self-effacing modesty, his memoir is sometimes short on detail. You know that there is a lot more to the story that he is not telling. His account gives a vivid account of how he survived the war and he describes, almost casually, one near-death experience after another. Yet his character comes through more in what he does not say rather than what he does.

His account of the atomic bomb attack and its aftermath is just four pages in length, slightly over 1,000 words. Aidan describes himself as being 'lucky enough' to be awarded the George Medal for rescuing the crew of the bomber that crashed in England early in the war. The official RAF accounts of the same event provide a more detailed description of an almost superhuman act of bravery.

It is, quite simply, the best story I have ever heard. I told the story for years and people would usually comment that they could not understand why they had never heard of him before. One thing that always struck me was that people would remember the details, many years later.

Maybe part of the reason the story was not widely known is because, as an Irish person serving with British forces, the legacy of the Troubles complicated the relationship between such stories and public discourse in Ireland. For many decades, accounts of Irish people serving in the First and Second World Wars were taboo.

It is a story that deserved to be told and, in 2010, Gary Lennon and I began work on making a documentary about Aidan's story. We started by interviewing his daughters Adrienne and Nicola and his widow, Kathleen, in July of that year. Our intention was to tell his story and also to find the Japanese family of the officer who had given Aidan the sword. We hoped that bringing the two families together would reveal the full story behind how such an important artefact had ended up in a bar in west Cork. It would also reconnect a Japanese family with the ashes of their ancestors. But where do you start? We did not know the officer's name nor whether he had any surviving descendants.

Kathleen was ninety-three years old when we interviewed her in July 2010. The interview was in the MacCarthy family home above the bar. Afterwards, as we were packing away the lights and camera equipment, Kathleen casually mentioned that when Aidan was given the sword, the Japanese officer also gave him a portrait photograph. The photo was somewhere in their possession. She did not know where it was but told us that if we could find this photo it would help us find the person who had given Aidan the sword. This began a search that went on for years.

By developing contacts with a network of prisoner-of-war organisations, researchers, retired service personnel and institutions around the world, a clearer picture of Aidan's war story slowly began to emerge. There were a number of sources to work with: his memoirs, radio interviews, newspaper articles, military archives, books, interviews with his family, people who knew him and so on.

It would have been very useful to find someone who knew him in the camps, but the chances of that reduced as the years went by. At one stage, I made contact with an Australian former POW called Allan Chick who had been on the *Tamahoku Maru*. He had also been in Camp 14B when the bomb was dropped. In March 2012, I drove north from Melbourne, Australia, for about four hours to interview him at a nursing home in Gippsland, Victoria. I showed Allan photographs of Aidan and played recordings of his voice, but he did not remember him. He was ninety-two and too much time had passed.

In parallel with researching Aidan's story, the search to find the family of the Japanese officer who gave him the sword proved more difficult. The only thing we had to go on was that he was a Japanese POW camp commandant who had gifted his sword to an Allied POW almost seventy years earlier. We were looking for a person or family in a country with a population of around 130 million, without the certainty that the person we were looking for even existed (as it was possible that the family had died out). It was like searching for the proverbial needle in a haystack.

There were two approaches to this search. One was to research the names of the Japanese officers at the camp in Nagasaki and try to make contact with their relatives and thereby rule them in or out of the search.

The other approach was to find the photograph mentioned by Kathleen. We pestered Nicola and Adrienne for three years, phoning every few weeks to give an update on how the project was going, always asking if there was any sign of the photo. Did they want help in searching for it? Did they need help moving boxes down from an attic? The family had moved house many times and they had countless boxes and cases full of papers, documents, photos, old bills – even the receipt, telegrams and menus from Aidan and Kathleen's wedding in 1948. The chances of finding a photograph given to their father almost seven decades previously were slim.

At one stage a Japanese sword expert in Tokyo, Paul Martin, mentioned in an email that on the tang of the sword – the metal of the blade under the handle – sword smiths would often engrave the name of the person who made it. More importantly, they would sometimes engrave the name of the person for whom it had been made. Martin offered to help me through the process, via Skype, in order to remove the handle and reveal the tang. He told me I needed to have a chopstick, a wooden mallet and a dry cloth. I drove to Castletownbere early one Saturday morning with a normal hammer, a pencil and a towel. Adrienne kindly opened the pub, and showed me up into the living room upstairs above the bar. When the Skype call was up and running I showed Martin my hammer and pencil. He told me I needed the correct tools or else he wouldn't continue so I asked him to give me ten minutes. Luckily the owner of a nearby Chinese restaurant opened the door and gave me a pair of wooden chopsticks, and after a detour to the local hardware shop I had a wooden mallet. With the Skype connection up and running again, Martin showed me how to remove the bamboo peg – slowly and with infinite care – which held the handle in place. It took a long time to remove the peg but eventually

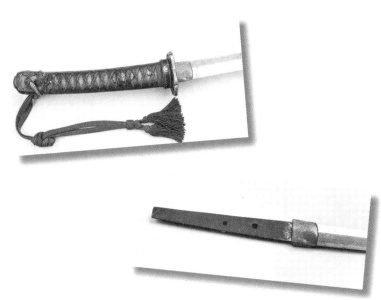

(*Left*): The Second World War-era military handle is decorated with sharkskin, leather, metal ornaments and cord. The bamboo peg holding the handle in place is visible near the hilt. (*Right*): The sword with handle removed. The tang was shortened when Kusuno joined the military, suggesting it may have originally been a two-handed sword. Two holes for bamboo pegs on the original handle are also visible. BARRY MURPHY

the handle slid off the tang for the first time in many decades. As soon as I held it up to the screen Martin said the sword was possibly hundreds of years old. There were two holes in the metal for the two pegs of its original handle and the length of the tang had been cut. It had been shortened to accommodate the standard-issue Second World War handle and ornaments. This indicated that the blade was possibly a much older, two-handed design. Unfortunately, there was no visible engraving on the tang so it did not bring us any closer to confirming who previously owned the sword.

Paul Martin also confirmed that the handle was of Second World War origin and that it was made of sharkskin, wood and leather with metal ornaments. The design is distinctly Japanese, with twenty cherry blossom motifs on the handle alone. He also confirmed that the story about the ancestral ashes of the previous owner being embedded in the handle was most likely untrue.

In order to confirm whether the sword was radioactive I borrowed a Geiger counter from the physics department at the college where I work and drove to Castletownbere early on another Saturday morning. A physics lecturer colleague had told me that it was unlikely the sword would be radioactive after so many years unless a particle of plutonium had lodged somewhere in the handle. As I passed the sensor over the blade and handle it made a distinctive random clicking sound. As expected, the meter reading indicated there was no radiation. Interestingly, Adrienne and Nicola's pet pugs turned out to be more radioactive than the sword!

The search for the original owner of the sword continued over the years, with countless emails, letters and phone calls. By liaising with organisations in the US and Japan it was possible to identify the names of the Japanese officers at Camp 14B in Nagasaki. The American military had recorded the name and rank of every POW camp officer and guard. Volunteers at the Japanese POW Research Organisation were extremely helpful in identifying which of these officers would have been entitled to carry a sword. They also put us in contact with the family of the Japanese camp doctor at Camp 14B, a Dr Danno. We interviewed his daughter at her home near Nagasaki in 2012. She was eighty-three years old at the time, and told us that her father had returned from the war, telling the family that he had given his sword 'to an Allied POW doctor'.[1] We thought we had struck gold. Dr Danno was surely the officer we were looking for.

Funding for the production was always an issue. We managed to get some development funding from the Irish Film Board to get the project off the ground. Eventually, having been refused by various funding bodies numerous times, in April 2013 the Broadcasting Authority of Ireland gave it the green light. This meant that a 48-minute version of the documentary would be broadcast on TV3, in Ireland, later that year. It also meant that we could return to Japan with Nicola MacCarthy to meet the family of the person we believed had given her father the sword. We were due to travel in July but Ms Danno became ill so we had to postpone the trip until August. There was an upside to this because it meant we would be in Nagasaki on 9 August – the sixty-eighth anniversary of the dropping of the bomb.

Then, out of the blue, on the morning of 18 July 2013, I got an emotional phone call from Nicola. She had found the photograph given to her father by the POW camp commandant. She had been moving some furniture when a suitcase full of old books had fallen from the top of a wardrobe. Nicola had checked the case previously but had ruled it out because it seemed to contain only old books. When it hit the ground the books fell out and an old photograph album was among them. Its contents spilled onto the floor. There were original documents, statements, newspaper clippings and photos that her father had collected during the war. In amongst these was a photo of a Japanese officer, holding the sword. I drove straight to Castletownbere to Nicola's house, and there it was on her dining room table: a portrait of an austere-looking Japanese officer holding the same sword that her father brought home from the war, the sword in MacCarthy's Bar. This was the missing piece of the puzzle.

Nicola was convinced that Kathleen, who had died a few months previously, and her father had played a role in locating it. She had spent a number of hours a day for many months going through the multitude of boxes and bags of documents that the family had gathered up over the years. The family are self-confessed hoarders and had lived in twenty-one houses. Up to that point Nicola had found nothing and had already given up on finding it.

The fact that Aidan kept the photo for the rest of his life speaks volumes. Had he held any animosity towards Kusuno, he would surely have discarded it on the long journey home or in the intervening years. He had gathered up a treasure trove of documents during his time in the camps, preserved them and made sure they were all kept together. The family had moved house so many times yet this collection had never been lost. For a very long time, he had been unable to discuss his captivity publicly, yet privately he kept this collection as a memorial. His daughters had never seen or heard of this collection before and Kathleen may have been the only other person who knew anything about it.

On the reverse side of the photograph was an inscription in Japanese. I took a photo of this and sent it to our translator in Japan. Allowing for time differences I had to wait until the following morning to get the translation via email. I nearly fell off the chair when, at about 7 a.m., I read what was written on the back of the photo:

> To my dear friend Dr MacCarthy, this is with my parting gift to you on this day the arrival of the peace, August 1945. Kusuno

This confirmed that the sword was given as a gift and had not been taken or surrendered – a particularly important point from a Japanese perspective. It also meant that with the photo and the Kusuno family name, it might be possible to find the officer's family, if they existed.

US military records confirmed that 2nd Lieutenant Isao Kusuno was camp commandant of a POW camp from May to September 1945. However, it was not Camp 14B in Nagasaki but Camp 26 at Keisen about a hundred miles to the north.

In Aidan's collection was another document that placed him at Camp 26. His first typed order when he took over the camp is headed 'No. 26 Camp orders No. 1. Issued 3rd September 1945'. This was when the war formally came to an end after the official surrender was signed on board the USS *Missouri* in Tokyo Bay on 2 September.

It meant that we were looking for descendants of Isao Kusuno and not the family of Dr Danno.

All of this happened very quickly. We flew to Nagasaki two weeks later on 7 August 2013. With the photo and the family name we were able to get press and local TV coverage in Japan to help with the search. There was a lot of excitement and local interest when we arrived in Nagasaki on 8 August. A TV news crew covered the story and articles were printed in local and national newspapers.

On the morning of the anniversary of the dropping of the bomb, 9 August, we brought Nicola to visit the site of Camp 14B in Nagasaki where her father had survived the explosion exactly sixty-eight years previously. The Mitsubishi factory was rebuilt after the war and is still operating. Next to it is a patch of grass behind a wire fence where the POW camp and bomb shelter had once been. It was an emotional experience for Nicola because the area would have looked very similar when the bomb was dropped. The site of the camp, surrounded by buildings, was between the railway track and the factory just as her father had described. The stifling August humidity of southern Japan that we experienced would have been almost identical on that infamous morning.

Shortly after, we attended the public ceremony at the nearby Nagasaki Peace Park, close to the epicentre of the bomb. The ceremony marks the exact moment the bomb detonated at 11.02 a.m. The crowd fell silent and the sound of an air-raid siren echoing up the Urakami valley was eerily reminiscent of how it would have been in 1945. Then one of the original bells of the Urakami Cathedral began to ring, reverberating across the valley just as it had before the bomb was dropped. At the end of the moving ceremony, Nicola laid a wreath in honour of her father and of the thousands of people killed by the bomb.

Later that evening we drove about four hours north to Keisen and the following morning met the local POW Camp 26 research group. They showed us around the site of the former labour camp, pointing out the rice paddy fields where the American B-29s had dropped supplies following the Japanese surrender. At around 11 a.m. our translator received a call from one of the newspapers that had printed an article the previous day about our search. The grandson of Isao Kusuno had made contact.

About an hour later we sat in the rental car waiting for his call to come through. There were six of us in the people carrier and the mobile phone was set to speakerphone. We had the camera and microphones ready to record. Eventually the phone rang. We turned off the air conditioning and kept the windows closed to reduce noise. The translator answered and the conversation, in Japanese, began. It was 40 degrees Celsius outside and quickly began to get a lot hotter inside the car. You could tell by the tone of the conversation it was all very positive. But it went on for over twenty minutes. As we sweated, we were all thinking the same thing: what on earth are they talking about?

West Japan Daily (top) and *Asahi Shimbun* newspaper cuttings reporting Gambit Pictures Ltd's search for Lieutenant Kusuno's family. BOB JACKSON

As soon as the conversation ended we spilled out of the car to get some air. The translator confirmed that it had been Kusuno's grandson, Satoshi Kusuno, on the phone. He had seen the article the previous day and had agreed to meet us that evening at his grandfather's grave, which was equidistant between him and Keisen, where we were at the time. We were under pressure to get there on time as we knew we would have only about thirty minutes of daylight. At around 7 p.m. we arrived at the cemetery in Kitakyushu where, finally, the MacCarthy and Kusuno families met. This brought to an end a search that had gone on for many years. Satoshi Kusuno was there with his mother, Mitzuko, and his sister, Kaori. They brought photos of their grandfather and were very touched by the fact that Nicola's father had taken such good care of his photo of their grandfather. They were also surprised to see the inscription he had written. During the conversation Satoshi came to the realisation that, had Nicola's father not saved his grandfather, he himself would not be alive.

It turned out that the Kusunos were unaware that their grandfather had even had a sword. Satoshi made the point that because Japan had lost the war, his grandfather and father never spoke about it afterwards. In his words, they took all of their memories of the period with them to the grave. At the end of the meeting Nicola invited the Kusuno family to Castletownbere to see the sword.

In November 2014, after over four years of production, the feature-film version of the documentary *A Doctor's Sword* premiered to a full house at the Cork Film Festival. It was completed with funding from UCC, Cork City Council, Cork County Council Arts Office and the Irish Film Board. It had sold out over a week in advance and it seemed as if the entire population of the Beara Peninsula had travelled to see it. To

Nicola MacCarthy with Satoshi Kusuno at the graveside of Isao Kusuno, Kitakyushu, 10 August 2013. GAMBIT PICTURES LTD

finally see Aidan's story and the search for the sword on the big screen was a very emotional experience for all involved. The response the film received led to a distributor (Wildcard) picking up the film and it was released in Irish cinemas in August 2015, on the seventieth anniversary of the dropping of the atomic bombs.[2] Surpassing all expectations, the film remained in cinemas for seven weeks and was later nominated for an Irish Film & Television Award in 2016, in the best documentary category. As a project that had been on a knife-edge for so many years it was an incredible honour that it received such acclaim.

Similar to Aidan's personal story, luck was a huge factor throughout.

* * *

Those who knew Aidan always use similar adjectives to describe him: kind, decent, warm and affectionate. He was loved for his humour and sense of fun.[3] His beloved wife, Kathleen, remembered the small details of his generosity, like the way he used to bring food and tablets to an Irish newspaperman on Baker Street in London. He looked after him until he died.

His nephew Brian described him as a man born with a tough, strong personality, a quiet unassuming confidence without a hint of arrogance. His cousin mentioned that he had an intense look on his face that frightened some people.[4] For such a man to be held captive and powerless at the hands of others would have stirred up deep feelings of animosity. But he forgave his captors and never allowed hatred to consume him. Others were less fortunate and were destroyed by what they experienced, 'but they couldn't break him'.[5]

In the radio interview broadcast at his funeral, Aidan was asked if he felt he had suffered any long-term effects. He listed a catalogue of injuries: four operations on his right elbow to repair the damage inflicted in Java when his elbow was smashed, a brain tumour, skin cancer and throat cancer. He also had a spot on his left hip that used to become infected now and again, 'as though to remind me of past horrors … but, apart from that, no'.[6] This gives an insight into the positive nature of his personality, which was also mentioned by his nephew, Brian, who never saw him show any self-pity, anger or sadness.

The week before he died, Aidan told the Beara Historical Society that he regarded himself as lucky.[7] He had many reasons to believe this (although it could be argued either way whether he was extremely lucky or extremely unlucky that he chose the side of the coin that led to him joining the RAF). He was lucky that he survived Dunkirk, was sent to Bandung POW camp instead of another, was woken by a rat before the torpedo struck, was not dumped at sea by the Japanese whalers, was in the bomb shelter when the atomic bomb struck, was not closer to the bomb, the list goes on and on ... Had the *Tamahoku Maru* not been torpedoed he could have ended up at the intended destination of Kure Harbour near Hiroshima and been sent to a POW camp in the city. His survival had hung by a thread for so many years and had luck not been on his side on just one of these occasions he would never have made it home. He would have joined the many thousands of others now forgotten in unmarked graves in the jungles of South-East Asia, cremated in Japan or somewhere on the seabed in a sunken hell ship. His story and his legacy would have been lost, and he would have become another statistic among the anonymous millions who died in the war. The odds of surviving even one of these episodes were slim but to have prevailed through so many in succession is little short of a miracle.

Remarkably, Aidan is one of the few people to have survived the two events which bookend the Second World War: he was at the evacuation of Dunkirk and was in the POW camp closest to the epicentre of the atomic bomb which destroyed Nagasaki.[8] In both of these infamous events he was crouching in a hole, praying that his life would be spared.

When asked if he felt the dropping of the atomic bomb was justified, his response was consistent: he felt he was the wrong person to ask because it had saved his life. He did not like the atomic bomb and considered it a horrible weapon, and having witnessed its effects wished it had never been invented.[9] But he was also very glad the Americans had it and used it at the time because otherwise he would not have survived. He acknowledged that selfishness for one's own survival has an influence on one's opinion.[10] Nobody knows how history would have transpired had the bombs not been dropped. Maybe the Japanese would have surrendered. Maybe an Allied invasion would have led to even greater loss of life. We will never know.

After Aidan's death Kathleen moved to Castletownbere where she lived in the apartment above MacCarthy's Bar. She kept up the tradition of Aidan's mother and continued recording details of the family's progress in the same notebook. She also maintained the MacCarthy tradition of always having an open house for visitors, especially for those in the town who had no one to share Christmas with. She passed away in April 2013 at the age of ninety-seven. Her humour and wit were still razor sharp right up until the time she died. Incredibly, she had only ever been admitted to hospital twice, on each occasion to give birth to a daughter.

Aidan's survival is tied to the lives of so many others and it is impossible to calculate how many people are alive today due to his intervention. Satoshi Kusuno, grandson of Isao Kusuno, counted himself among them. On reading the text of the message Isao Kusuno wrote on the back of the photo, Japanese sword expert Tomoyuki Ohmura believed Kusuno gifted his sword in gratitude for the many Japanese lives Aidan saved in the aftermath of the bomb.[11] Even as a young man he saved members of his family from drowning with his quick thinking and decisive action. The descendants of the crew that crashed at Honington owe their existence to his bravery, French civilians during the early months of the war, and the daughter of the police superintendent in Fukuoka and her children are alive today because he went out of his way to cure her pneumonia. When he was in his sixties a neighbour in Northwood in London, Jim Mitchell, was drilling a hole in a wooden fence and hit an electrical cable. Mitchell's son ran to the MacCarthys and Adrienne, who was training to be a nurse, went to help. She found their neighbour was stuck to the fence and was turning

Dr Aidan MacCarthy, aged eighty-two.

HRH Prince Henry of Wales KCVO unveils the plaque naming the Aidan MacCarthy Medical Centre on 20 July 2017, with Wing Commander Kurt von Bussmann, Senior Medical Officer, RAF Honington (right). RAF HONINGTON

purple. She tried to check his pulse but was blown back by the electricity. When Aidan arrived she told him not to touch him so Aidan picked up a wooden plank, knocked him clear of the electrical cable, and saved his life.

The high regard in which Dr Aidan MacCarthy is still held by the RAF is demonstrated by the fact that a new medical facility, opened in 2017 at RAF Honington, is named after him.

It is obviously a doctor's duty to preserve life, which he did throughout his professional career and was publicly honoured for his work in the camps, but it is the extra lengths he went to, time and again, that stand out. He did this with a self-effacing modesty that he attributed to being a Beara man.[12] It is a fitting tribute to an incredible survivor of the Second Word War that he should be remembered not for the lives he took, but for those he saved. A war hero, in the truest sense.

BOB JACKSON

Acknowledgments

This book would not have been possible were it not for the generosity and hard work of a huge number of people. I will attempt to include everyone who assisted in this endeavour and I hope I have not omitted anyone in error.

I would like to first of all thank my wonderful wife, Stephanie, for many years of patience, support, advice and understanding. Without your contribution this book would have never been completed.

Adrienne and Nicola MacCarthy for their incredible generosity and understanding throughout this lengthy process.

My parents, Mairead and Ray, and brother David.

Kathleen MacCarthy, Deirdre O'Brien and Brian O'Brien. All at The Collins Press. Paddy and Doreen Tobin, Fachtna O'Donovan, Teddy Black, Cicely Glason, Ger and Maura McCarthy, Jane Hollingdale, Fr Sean O'Shea, Carol Tobin. Margaret Doyle and Michael Sheil (Clongowes Wood College).

Yvonne McGuinness, Cillian Murphy, Catherine Moylan, Conor Buttimer, Claire & Conor Howell, Des Bishop, Cathal Murray, John Ahern, Ailbhe Keogan, Michael Kelly, Jimmy Deenihan.

Catriona Mulcahy (UCC Archives), Michael Holland, Anne Bradford and Helen O'Donovan (Records Administration office, UCC).

Gary Lennon, Ronan Coyle, George Doyle, Brian Walsh (RTÉ).

Pat Doherty, Siobhán O'Callaghan, Phyl Guerin, Catherine Murray and all at the Institute of Technology Tralee.

Patrick O'Neill, Suzanne Murray and the staff at Wildcard Distribution.

Ron Taylor (FEPOW Community), Tony Coombs, Kurt Von Bussmann (RAF), Gus Cabre (RAF), Tracey Allen (RAF News), Julian Ryall, Hilary Whyte, Jan Thompson, Meg Parkes and Geoff Gill (Liverpool School of Tropical Medicine), Lesley Clark (Java Journal), Pam Stubbs, Margaret Martin.

Taeko Sasamoto and Toru Fukubayashi (POW Research Network Japan), Tomoyuki Ohmura, Wes Injerd (Mansell. com), Henriette van Raalte, Georgina van der Kuil, Tim van der Kuil, Boudewyn van Oort, Paul Niessen.

Pádraig Óg Ó Ruairc, David and Ann Power, Mairead Treanor and Aidan Murphy (Met Éireann), Gordon Leigh (RAF Museum, Hendon), Sebastian Cox (RAF Air Historical Branch), Jack Heyn, Bill Swain (USAF 3rd Bomber Group historian), Professor Richard Overy (University of Exeter), William Chorley.

Endnotes

Preface

1 Dr Aidan MacCarthy, *A Doctor's War*, p. 82, The Collins Press, Cork, 2005.
2 *Ibid.*

1. Home

1 Dr Aidan MacCarthy, Beara Historical Society lecture, October 1994.
2 Gerdie Harrington, *Beara Down Memory Lane*, p. 27, Beara Historical Society, Castletownbere, 2007.
3 *Ibid.*, p. 44.
4 www.irishtimes.com/news/royal-visits-mark-20th-century-dawn-1. 572637, accessed 14 July 2015.
5 D.F. changed the spelling of the family surname to MacCarthy some time after 1911 – most likely in the late 1920s.
6 Author interview with Fr Sean O'Shea, Castletownbere, August 2015.
7 Author interview with Cicely Glason (Dr MacCarthy's cousin), March 2016.
8 Author interview with Fr Sean O'Shea, Castletownbere, November 2015.
9 John Ware, 'Bantry Bay in the First World War', *History Ireland*, November–December 2014, p. 31.
10 MacCarthy, Beara Historical Society lecture, October 1994.
11 Harrington, *op. cit.*, p. 47.
12 Ware, *op. cit.*, p. 32.
13 MacCarthy, Beara Historical Society lecture, October 1994.
14 *Ibid.*
15 *A Doctor's Sword* documentary interview, Gambit Pictures Ltd, July 2013.
16 Author interview with Brian O'Brien (Dr MacCarthy's nephew), January 2016.
17 *The Irish Times*, 31 March 1921.
18 Author interview with Deirdre O'Brien (Dr MacCarthy's niece), August 2015.
19 *The Southern Star*, Sandra Mac Liammóir interview, 4 November 1995.

20 Author interview with Brian O'Brien, January 2016.
21 Author interview with Fr Sean O'Shea, November 2015.
22 MacCarthy, Beara Historical Society lecture, October 1994.
23 *Ibid.*
24 Author interview with Deirdre O'Brien, August 2015.
25 *Ibid.*
26 Clongowes Wood College, Margaret Doyle, archivist, via email, 3 March 2016.
27 University College Cork, Records Office, March 2016.
28 *Cork Examiner*, 9 September 1932, p. 14.
29 *Cork Examiner*, 17 September 1932, p. 5.
30 *Ibid.*
31 *Cork Examiner*, 12 October 1946.
32 Author interview with Deirdre O'Brien, August 2015.
33 *A Doctor's Sword* documentary interview, Gambit Pictures Ltd, July 2013.
34 University College Cork, Records Office, March 2016.
35 MacCarthy, Beara Historical Society lecture, October 1994.
36 Dr Aidan MacCarthy interview, C103FM County Sound, 2 October 1995.
37 *Ibid.*
38 University College Cork, Records Office, March 2019.

2. War in Europe
1 Dr Aidan MacCarthy, Beara Historical Society lecture, 2 October 1995.
2 *Ibid.*
3 *Away to War*, RTÉ Radio interview with Dr Aidan MacCarthy, October 1995.
4 *Ibid.*
5 *The London Gazette*, 26 September 1939.
6 Antony Beevor, *The Second World War*, p. 33, Little, Brown & Company, New York City, 2014.
7 *Ibid.*, p. 49.
8 Dr Aidan MacCarthy, *A Doctor's War*, p. 15, The Collins Press, Cork, 2005.
9 *Ibid.*, p. 16.
10 *Away to War*, RTÉ Radio, October 1995.
11 MacCarthy, *op. cit.*, p. 16.
12 *Ibid.*, p. 20.
13 *Ibid.*, p. 22.
14 *Ibid.*, p. 23.
15 *Ibid.*, p. 17.
16 *Ibid.*, p. 25.

17 *Ibid.*, p. 25.
18 *Ibid.*, p. 26.
19 MacCarthy, Beara Historical Society lecture, 2 October 1995.
20 *Away to War*, RTÉ Radio, October 1995.
21 *Ibid.*
22 MacCarthy, Beara Historical Society lecture, 2 October 1995.
23 MacCarthy, *op.cit.*, p. 27.
24 *Ibid.*, p. 27.
25 Beevor, *The Second World War*, p. 139.

3. Bomber Command

1   Professor Richard Overy, University of Exeter, email April 2016.
2   Dr Aidan MacCarthy, Beara Historical Society lecture, 2 October 1995.
3   *Away to War*, RTÉ Radio interview with Dr Aidan MacCarthy, October 1995.
4   *Ibid.*
5   *Ibid.*
6   Dr Aidan MacCarthy, *A Doctor's War*, p. 36, The Collins Press, Cork, 2005.
7   RAF Awards No. 259, RAF Cosford.
8   MacCarthy, Beara Historical Society lecture, 2 October 1995.
9   RAF Awards No. 259, RAF Cosford.
10 *Cork Examiner*, *c.*1979.
11 MacCarthy, Beara Historical Society lecture, 2 October 1995; *Away to War*, RTÉ Radio, October 1995.
12 *Away to War*, RTÉ Radio, October 1995.
13 MacCarthy, *op. cit.*, p. 36.
14 MacCarthy, Beara Historical Society lecture, 2 October 1995.
15 *Ibid.*
16 *Away to War*, RTÉ Radio, October 1995.
17 Dr Aidan MacCarthy interview, C103FM County Sound, 2 October 1995.
18 Antony Beevor, *The Second World War*, p. 189, Little, Brown & Company, New York City, 2014.
19 Hitler's War in the East was referred to as 'Rassenkrieg' or 'race war'. The Nazis regarded the Slavic Russians as an inferior race. The Soviets responded in kind with equal disregard for human life or suffering.
20 Beevor, *op. cit.*, p. 294.
21 John Ware, 'Bantry Bay in the First World War', *History Ireland*, November–December 2014, p. 33.
22 Beevor, *op. cit.*, p. 297.
23 Cameron Forbes, *Hellfire*, p. 81, Pan Macmillan Australia, Sydney, 2005.

4. War in the East

1   Cameron Forbes, *Hellfire*, p. 18, Pan Macmillan Australia, Sydney, 2005.

2   Lord Russell of Liverpool, *The Knights of Bushido*, p. 2, Skyhorse Publishing, New York City, 2008.

3   Forbes, *op. cit.*, p. 34.

4   Russell, *op. cit.*, p. 55.

5   Imperial Rescript to Soldiers and Sailors, 1882.

6   Louis Allen & Jean Wilson, *Lafcadio Hearn, Japan's Great Interpreter: a New Anthology of His Writings 1894–1904*, p. 212, Routledge, Abingdon-on-Thames, 1995.

7   Richard J. Smethurst, *A Social Basis for Prewar Japanese Militarism*, p. 9, University of California Press, Berkeley, 1974.

8   Laura Hillenbrand, *Unbroken*, p. 43, Random House, New York City, 2010.

9   Russell, *op. cit.*, p. xvii.

10 Forbes, *op. cit.*, p. 31.

11 Russell, *op. cit.*, p. 1.

12 Forbes, *op. cit.*, p. 44.

13 *Ibid.*, p. 16.

14 *Ibid.*, p. 20.

15 *Ibid.*, p. 44.

16 *Ibid.*

17 *Ibid.*, p. 45. This was similar to Hitler's elimination of opposition after being named Chancellor in January 1933.

18 One example was the 'Three Alls Policy': Kill All, Burn All, Loot All. Another was a competition between officers to be the first to behead 100 prisoners. Officers Toshiaki Mukai and Tsuyoshi Noda's exploits were followed by the *Tokyo Nichi Nichi Shimbun* newspaper like a golf competition. Although the events have been denied since, it is significant that in 2003 the families of the two officers took a defamation case against several newspapers that covered the 'contest' in 1937. In 2005 a Tokyo district court dismissed the case on the basis that the 'contest' did occur and although the original newspaper articles contained some errors, the officers admitted that they had raced to behead 100 people – http://web.international.ucla.edu/institute/article/28873, accessed 5 March 2016.

19 Hillenbrand, *op. cit.*, p. 43.

20 Forbes, *op. cit.*, p. 36.

21 http://www.ioc.u-tokyo.ac.jp/~worldjpn/documents/texts/docs/19411208.O1E.html, accessed 15 February 2016.

22 Stanley Sandler, *World War II in the Pacific*, p. 85, Garland Publishing Inc, New York & London, 2001.

23 Dr Aidan MacCarthy, *A Doctor's War*, p. 41, The Collins Press, Cork, 2005.
24 Dr Aidan MacCarthy, Beara Historical Society lecture, 2 October 1995.
25 MacCarthy, *op. cit.*, p. 42.
26 Antony Beevor, *The Second World War*, p. 172, Little, Brown & Company, New York City, 2014.
27 Dr Aidan MacCarthy interview, C103FM County Sound, 2 October 1995.
28 MacCarthy, *op. cit.*, p. 42.
29 MacCarthy, Beara Historical Society lecture, 2 October 1995.
30 *Ibid.*
31 MacCarthy, *op. cit.*, p. 44.
32 MacCarthy, Beara Historical Society lecture, 2 October 1995.
33 MacCarthy, *op. cit.*, p. 45.
34 *Ibid.*, p. 47.
35 *Ibid.*, p. 47.
36 MacCarthy interview, C103FM County Sound.
37 *Away to War*, RTÉ Radio interview with Dr Aidan MacCarthy, October 1995.
38 MacCarthy, *op. cit.*, p. 50.
39 Russell, *op. cit.*, p. 56.

5. The Shadow of the Rising Sun

1   Dr Aidan MacCarthy interview, C103FM County Sound, 2 October 1995.
2   *Ibid.*
3   MacCarthy family archive, newspaper cutting, 1946.
4   *Away to War*, RTÉ Radio interview with Dr Aidan MacCarthy, October 1995.
5   Dr Aidan MacCarthy, *A Doctor's War*, p. 55, The Collins Press, Cork, 2005.
6   Meg Parkes & Geoff Gill, *Captive Memories*, p. 103, Carnegie Publishing, Lancaster, 2015.
7   Dr Aidan MacCarthy, Beara Historical Society lecture, 2 October 1995.
8   *Away to War*, RTÉ Radio, October 1995.
9   *Ibid.*
10 MacCarthy interview, C103FM County Sound.
11 *Ibid.*
12 Les & Pam Stubbs, *Unsung Heroes of the Royal Air Force*, p. 67, Tucann Books, Lincoln, 2011.
13 Robert Widders, *The Emperor's Irish Slaves*, p. 44, The History Press Ireland, Dublin, 2012.
14 MacCarthy, *op. cit.*, p. 57.
15 *Away to War*, RTÉ Radio, October 1995.

16 Ken Adams, *Healing in Hell*, p. 65, Pen & Sword, Barnsley, 2011.
17 MacCarthy, *op. cit.*, p. 67.
18 Stubbs, *op. cit.*, p. 28.
19 Liverpool School of Tropical Medicine https://soundcloud.com/mosaic science/prisoners-of-war, accessed 7 January 2016.
20 MacCarthy, *op. cit.*, p. 61.
21 Liberation Questionnaire: WO 344/389, UK National Archives, Kew.
22 MacCarthy, *op. cit.*, p. 61.
23 Parkes & Gill, *op. cit.*, p. 29.
24 Geoff Gill and Meg Parkes, Liverpool School of Tropical Medicine, via email, 6 March 2016.
25 Interview with Tom Pledger (Australian fomer POW) – https://www.youtube.com/watch?v=38TY2O gx2wA, accessed 23 January 2016.
26 MacCarthy, *op. cit.*, p. 108.
27 https://soundcloud.com/mosaicscience/prisoners-of-war, accessed 26 January 2016.
28 Adams, *op. cit.*, p. 65.
29 Stubbs, *op. cit.*, p. 30.
30 Adams, *op. cit.*, p. 65.
31 Liverpool School of Tropical Medicine https://soundcloud.com/ mosaicscience/prisoners-of-war, accessed 11 January 2016.
32 Parkes & Gill, *op. cit.*, p. 29.
33 MacCarthy, *op. cit.*, p. 72.
34 *Ibid.*, p. 63.
35 *Ibid.*
36 *Ibid.*, p. 75.
37 *Ibid.*, p. 64.
38 *Ibid.*, p. 68.
39 MacCarthy, Beara Historical Society lecture, 2 October 1995.
40 MacCarthy, *op. cit.*, p. 69.
41 *Ibid.*
42 *Ibid.*, p. 65.
43 Telephone interview with Cicely Glason (Dr MacCarthy's cousin), March 2016.
44 MacCarthy, *op. cit.*, p. 159.
45 *Away to War*, RTÉ Radio, October 1995.
46 MacCarthy, *op. cit.*, p. 70.
47 *Ibid.*, p. 71.
48 *Ibid.*
49 *Away to War*, RTÉ Radio, October 1995.

50 MacCarthy, *op. cit.*, p. 73.

51 *Ibid.*, p. 74.

52 *Ibid.*, p. 72.

53 *Ibid.*, p. 75.

54 Liberation Questionnaire: WO 344/389, UK National Archives, Kew.

6. Voyage to Hell

1 Dr Aidan MacCarthy, *A Doctor's War*, p. 81, The Collins Press, Cork, 2005.

2 *Ibid.*, p. 82.

3 *Ibid.*

4 *Ibid.*

5 http://theskylookeddown.blogspot.ie/2009/01/6-destination-railroad. html, accessed 4 August 2015.

6 *Ibid.*, accessed 3 August 2015.

7 MacCarthy, *op. cit.*, p. 83.

8 http://theskylookeddown.blogspot.ie/2009/01/6-destination-railroad. html, accessed 7 August 2015.

9 *Ibid.*, accessed 6 August 2015.

10 Henriette van Raalte (survivor of Tjideng Camp), via email, 19 July 2015.

11 MacCarthy, *op. cit.*, p. 83.

12 Robert Widders, *The Emperor's Irish Slaves*, p. 129, The History Press Ireland, Dublin, 2012. See also MacCarthy, *op. cit.*, p. 84.

13 Meg Parkes & Geoff Gill, *Captive Memories*, p. 105, Carnegie Publishing, Lancaster, 2015.

14 MacCarthy, *op. cit*, p. 84.

15 Amy Rozenberg, *Lost and Found Worlds*, p. 66, Trafford Publishing, Bloomington, 2012.

16 *Ibid.*, p. 67.

17 Louisa Priesman-Bogaardt. *Dark Skies Over Paradise*, p. 68, Trafford Publishing, Bloomington, 2006.

18 *Ibid.*, p. 69.

19 MacCarthy, *op. cit.*, p. 84.

20 Taeko Sasamoto, POW Research Organisation, Japan, *A Doctor's Sword* documentary interview, Gambit Pictures Ltd, August 2013.

21 Joseph, Jennifer, 'POWs Left in the Cold: Compensation Eludes American WWII Slave Labourers for Japanese Companies', *Pepperdine Law Review*, Malibu (California), 2001, p. 209.

22 MacCarthy, *op. cit.*, p. 85.

23 Liverpool School of Tropical Medicine https://soundcloud.com/mosaic science/prisoners-of-war, accessed 11 January 2016.

24 MacCarthy, *op. cit.*, p. 85.
25 http://www.mansell.com/pow_resources/camplists/fukuoka/fuk-14-nagasaki/tamahoku_maru.html, accessed March 2016.
26 Les & Pam Stubbs, *Unsung Heroes of the Royal Air Force*, p. 68, Tucann Books, Lincoln, 2011.
27 Widders, *op. cit.*, p. 132.
28 http://www.mansell.com/pow_resources/camplists/fukuoka/fuk-14-nagasaki/tamahoku_maru.html, accessed 21 October 2015.
29 *Ibid.*, accessed 22 October 2015.
30 MacCarthy, *op. cit.*, p. 87.
31 *Ibid.*
32 http://www.mansell.com/pow_resources/camplists/fukuoka/fuk-14-nagasaki/tamahoku_maru.html, accessed 22 October 2015.
33 Stubbs, *op. cit.*, p. 49.
34 http://www.mansell.com/pow_resources/camplists/fukuoka/fuk-14-nagasaki/tamahoku_maru.html, accessed 23 October 2015.
35 Dr Aidan MacCarthy, Beara Historical Society lecture, 2 October 1995.
36 http://www.mansell.com/pow_resources/camplists/fukuoka/fuk-14-nagasaki/tamahoku_maru.html, accessed 25 October 2015.
37 *The Irish Times*, 25 October 1995, p. 13.
38 Alistair Urquhart, *The Forgotten Highlander*, p. 224, Abacus, London, 2011.
39 MacCarthy, Beara Historical Society lecture, 2 October 1995.
40 MacCarthy, *op. cit.*, p. 89.
41 http://www.mansell.com/pow_resources/camplists/fukuoka/fuk-14-nagasaki/tamahoku_maru.html, accessed 25 October 2015.
42 MacCarthy, *op. cit.*, p. 89.
43 *Ibid.*, p. 90.
44 http://www.mansell.com/pow_resources/camplists/fukuoka/fuk-14-nagasaki/tamahoku_maru.html, accessed 24 October 2015.
45 *Ibid.*, accessed 25 October 2015.
46 *Ibid.*
47 MacCarthy, Beara Historical Society lecture, 2 October 1995.
48 MacCarthy, *op. cit.*, p. 90.
49 *Ibid.*
50 MacCarthy, Beara Historical Society lecture, 2 October 1995.
51 MacCarthy, *op. cit.*, p. 90.
52 *Ibid.*, p. 91.
53 *Ibid.*
54 *Ibid.*

7. An Unlikely Saviour

1 Richard O'Kane, *Clear the Bridge*, p. 205, Presidio Press, Novato, 1996.
2 Cameron Forbes, *Hellfire*, p. 383, Pan Macmillan Australia, Sydney, 2005.
3 O'Kane, *op. cit.*, p. 222.
4 Forbes, *op. cit.*, p. 382.
5 *Ibid.*, p. 383.
6 *Away to War*, RTÉ Radio interview with Dr Aidan MacCarthy, October 1995.
7 http://www.mansell.com/pow_resources/camplists/fukuoka/fuk-14-nagasaki/tamahoku_maru.html, accessed 26 October 2015.
8 http://www.australian-pow-ww2.com/tamahoko_maru_27.html, accessed 27 October 2015
9 *Away to War*, RTÉ Radio, October 1995.
10 *Ibid.*
11 http://www.mansell.com/pow_resources/camplists/fukuoka/fuk-14-nagasaki/tamahoku_maru.html, accessed 24 October 2015.
12 *Away to War*, RTÉ Radio, October 1995.
13 *The Southern Star*, Sandra Mac Liammóir interview, 4 November 1995, p. 9.
14 Dr Aidan MacCarthy, Beara Historical Society lecture, 2 October 1995.
15 *Away to War*, RTÉ Radio, October 1995.
16 Dr Aidan MacCarthy, *A Doctor's War*, p. 98, The Collins Press, Cork, 2005.
17 *Away to War*, RTÉ Radio, October 1995.
18 MacCarthy, *op. cit.*, p. 97.
19 *Ibid.*
20 Forbes, *op. cit.*, p. 378.
21 *Ibid.*, p. 99.
22 MacCarthy, Beara Historical Society lecture, 2 October 1995.
23 *Away to War*, RTÉ Radio, October 1995.
24 MacCarthy, Beara Historical Society lecture, 2 October 1995.
25 *Effects of Atomic Bomb on Hiroshima & Nagasaki*, US Strategic Bombing Survey, Washington, 19 June 1946 (Motion Picture).
26 *Away to War*, RTÉ Radio, October 1995.
27 Les and Pam Stubbs, *Unsung Heroes of the Royal Air Force*, p. 45, Tucann Books, Lincoln, 2011.
28 MacCarthy, *op. cit.*, p. 100.
29 *Away to War*, RTÉ Radio, October 1995.
30 MacCarthy, Beara Historical Society lecture, 2 October 1995.
31 MacCarthy, *op. cit.*, p. 104.
32 *Ibid.*, p. 103.

33 MacCarthy, Beara Historical Society lecture, 2 October 1995.
34 MacCarthy, *op. cit.*, p. 107.
35 MacCarthy, Beara Historical Society lecture, 2 October 1995.
36 MacCarthy, *op. cit.*, p. 103.
37 MacCarthy, Beara Historical Society lecture, 2 October 1995.
38 MacCarthy, *op. cit.*, p. 123.

8. A Slave in Nagasaki
1   Dr Aidan MacCarthy, *A Doctor's War*, p. 107, The Collins Press, Cork, 2005.
2   *Away to War*, RTÉ Radio interview with Dr Aidan MacCarthy, October 1995.
3   MacCarthy, *op. cit.*, p. 109.
4   *Ibid.*
5   *Ibid.*, p. 120.
6   *Ibid.*
7   *Effects of Atomic Bomb on Hiroshima & Nagasaki*, US Strategic Bombing Survey, Washington, 19 June 1946 (Motion Picture).
8   MacCarthy, *op. cit.*, p. 112.
9   *Ibid.*, p. 119.
10 Dr Aidan MacCarthy, Beara Historical Society lecture, 2 October 1995.
11 MacCarthy, *op. cit.*, p. 108.
12 *Ibid.*, p. 103.
13 *Ibid.*, p. 121.
14 *Ibid.*, p. 108.
15 MacCarthy, POW camp diary entry, December 1944.
16 *Effects of Atomic Bomb on Hiroshima & Nagasaki*, US Strategic Bombing Survey, Washington, 19 June 1946 (Motion Picture).
17 MacCarthy, *op. cit.*, p. 123.
18 *Ibid.*, p. 122.
19 *Ibid.*

9. Final Reserves
1. Dr Aidan MacCarthy, POW Camp diary entry, December 1944.
2   Dr Aidan MacCarthy, *A Doctor's War*, p. 112, The Collins Press, Cork, 2005.
3   http://apjjf.org/-William-Underwood/1823/article.html, accessed 17 February 2016.
4   Meg Parkes & Geoff Gill, *Captive Memories*, p. 29, Carnegie Publishing, Lancaster, 2015.

Endnotes

5   MacCarthy, *op. cit.*, p. 114.

6   *Ibid.*, p. 113.

7   *Ibid.*, p. 117.

8   *Ibid.*, p. 118.

9   Dr Aidan MacCarthy, Beara Historical Society lecture, 2 October 1995.

10 MacCarthy, *op. cit.*, p. 122.

11 *Ibid.*, p. 124.

12 *Ibid.*, p. 110.

13 *Ibid*.

14 *Ibid.*, p. 111.

15 *Ibid*.

16 http://www.flyingbombsandrockets.com/V1_summary_se1.html, accessed 9 January 2016.

17 MacCarthy, *op. cit.*, p. 118.

18 Dr Aidan MacCarthy interview, C103FM County Sound, 2 October 1995.

19 MacCarthy, *op. cit.*, p. 119.

20 Takashi Nagai, *The Bells of Nagasaki*, p. ix, Kodansha International, Tokyo, 1994.

21 http://atomicbombmuseum.org/2_manhattan.shtml, accessed 12 December 2015.

22 MacCarthy, *op. cit.*, p. 124.

23 United States Strategic Bombing Survey, Summary Report (Pacific War) (Washington: US GPO, 1946), Vol 1, p. 16.

24 MacCarthy interview, C103FM County Sound.

25 MacCarthy, Beara Historical Society lecture, 2 October 1995.

26 MacCarthy, *op. cit.*, p. 124.

27 MacCarthy, Beara Historical Society lecture, 2 October 1995.

28 http://www.mansell.com/pow_resources/Formosa/doc2701-trans.html, accessed 27 December 2015.

29 http://www.telegraph.co.uk/comment/letters/3595568/One-Hundred-Million-Souls-for-the-Emperor.html, accessed 11 March 2016.

30 Les & Pam Stubbs, *Unsung Heroes of the Royal Air Force*, p. 70, Tucann Books, Lincoln, 2011.

31 http://www.historynet.com/american-prisoners-of-war-massacre-at-palawan.htm, accessed 25 November 2015.

32 Laura Hillenbrand, *Unbroken*, p. 293, Random House, New York City, 2010.

33 Takashi Nagai, *The Bells of Nagasaki*, p. 101, Kodansha International, Tokyo, 1994; http://www.peace-museum.pref.okinawa.jp/english/index.html

34 Nagai, *op. cit.*, p. ix.

35 '*Truman informs the nation that an atomic weapon has been detonated in Japan, August 6, 1945*' – http://www.pbs.org/wgbh/americanexperience/features/primary-resources/truman-hiroshima/, accessed 25 February 2016.

36 MacCarthy, *op. cit.*, p. 108.

37 John Fletcher-Cooke, *The Emperor's Quest*, Leo Cooper, Barnsley, 1994, p. 127.

38 http://avalon.law.yale.edu/20th_century/mp07.asp, accessed 26 October 2015.

39 Wesley Craven & James Cate, *The Pacific: Matterhorn to Nagasaki – The Army Air Forces in World War II. Volume V*, p. 719, Office of Air Force History, Washington, 1983.

40 William L. Laurence, *Eye Witness Account Atomic Bomb Mission Over Nagasaki*, US War Department Bureau of Public Relations, http://www.atomic archive.com/Docs/Hiroshima/Nagasaki.shtml, accessed 7 January 2016.

41 *Effects of Atomic Bomb on Hiroshima & Nagasaki*, US Strategic Bombing Survey, Washington, 19 June 1946 (Motion Picture).

42 Nagai, *op. cit.*, p. 1.

43 http://avalon.law.yale.edu/20th_century/mp07.asp, accessed 25 October 2015.

44 http://www.historylearningsite.co.uk/world-war-two/the-pacific-war-1941-to-1945/the-bombing-of-nagasaki/, accessed 26 October 2015.

45 http://www.nytimes.com/1995/08/07/world/kokura-japan-bypassed-by-a-bomb.html, accessed 17 February 2016.

46 Nagai, *op. cit.*, p. 26.

47 MacCarthy interview, C103FM County Sound.

48 Nagai, *op. cit.*, p. 6.

49 *Away to War*, RTÉ Radio interview with Dr Aidan MacCarthy, October 1995.

10. 'The End of the World'

1 *Away to War*, RTÉ Radio interview with Dr Aidan MacCarthy, October 1995.

2 *Effects of Atomic Bomb on Hiroshima & Nagasaki*, US Strategic Bombing Survey, Washington, 19 June 1946 (Motion Picture).

3 http://atomicbombmuseum.org/2_firstbombs.shtml, accessed 22 March 2016.

4 Dr Aidan MacCarthy, *A Doctor's War*, The Collins Press, Cork, 2005, p. 125.

5 *Effects of Atomic Bomb on Hiroshima & Nagasaki*, US Strategic Bombing Survey (Motion Picture).

6   http://atomicbombmuseum.org/3_radioactivity.shtml, accessed 22 March 2016.

7   www.aasc.ucla.edu, accessed 27 October 2015.

8   Takashi Nagai, *The Bells of Nagasaki*, p. 55, Kodansha International, Tokyo, 1994.

9   MacCarthy, *op. cit.*, p. 125.

10 http://www.atomicarchive.com/Docs/Hiroshima/Nagasaki.shtml, accessed 23 March 2016.

11 'Atom Bomb Effects', *LIFE Magazine*, 11 March 1946.

12 *Ibid.*

13 Nagai, *op. cit.*, p. 28.

14 William L. Laurence, *Eye Witness Account Atomic Bomb Mission Over Nagasaki*, US War Department Bureau of Public Relations, http://www. atomicarchive.com/Docs/Hiroshima/Nagasaki.shtml, accessed 7 January 2016.

15 *Ibid.*

16 http://www.bbc.co.uk/history/ww2peopleswar/timeline/factfiles/ nonflash/a6652262.shtml, accessed 28 October 2015. Leonard Cheshire went on to found the Leonard Cheshire Foundation. Its facilities are often referred to as Cheshire Homes.

17 Nagai, *op. cit.*, p. 65.

18 F.J. Johnson, Australian POW, *www.atomicbombmuseum.org*, accessed 31 March 2016.

19 MacCarthy, Beara Historical Society lecture, 2 October 1995.

20 *Away to War*, RTÉ Radio, October 1995.

21 MacCarthy, *op. cit.*, p. 126.

22 *Away to War*, RTÉ Radio, October 1995.

23 MacCarthy, *op. cit.*, p. 126.

24 *Away to War*, RTÉ Radio, October 1995.

25 MacCarthy, *op. cit.*, p. 130.

26 Nagai, *op. cit.*, p. 23.

27 MacCarthy, *op. cit.*, p. 129.

28 Nagai, *op. cit.*, p. 12.

29 Nagasaki Atomic Bomb Museum, http://nagasakipeace.jp/japanese/ atomic/record/scene/1102.html, accessed 3 March 2016.

30 *Effects of Atomic Bomb on Hiroshima & Nagasaki,* US Strategic Bombing Survey (Motion Picture).

31 MacCarthy, Beara Historical Society lecture, 2 October 1995.

32 MacCarthy interview, C103FM County Sound.

33 *Away to War*, RTÉ Radio, October 1995.

34 Nagai, *op. cit*., p. 70.

35 MacCarthy, Beara Historical Society lecture, 2 October 1995.

36 *Effects of Atomic Bomb on Hiroshima & Nagasaki*, US Strategic Bombing Survey (Motion Picture).

37 MacCarthy, Beara Historical Society lecture, 2 October 1995.

38 *Ibid*.

39 *Away to War*, RTÉ Radio, October 1995.

40 http://atomicbombmuseum.org/3_radioactivity.shtml, accessed 5 March 2016.

41 MacCarthy, Beara Historical Society lecture, 2 October 1995.

42 http://www.hiroshima-spirit.jp/en/museum/morgue_w17.html, accessed 10 March 2016.

43 http://atomicbombmuseum.org/3_radioactivity.shtml, accessed 9 March 2016.

44 http://www.atomicarchive.com/Docs/MED/med_chp. 22.shtml

45 Nagai, *op. cit*., p. 61.

46 Nagai, *op. cit*., p. 73.

47 *Away to War*, RTÉ Radio, October 1995.

48 http://atomicbombmuseum.org/1_overview.shtml, accessed 9 March 2016.

49 MacCarthy, Beara Historical Society lecture, 2 October 1995.

50 Nagai, *op. cit*., p. 88.

51 http://atomicbombmuseum.org/3_radioactivity.shtml, accessed 10 March 2016.

52 It is worth noting that among the dead were 8,000 of the city's Catholic community, an unusually high number of Catholics for a Japanese city. See Nagai, *op. cit*., p. 106.

53 Nagai, *op. cit*., p. 67.

54 MacCarthy, *op. cit*., p. 131.

55 *Away to War*, RTÉ Radio, October 1995.

56 *Ibid*.

57 MacCarthy, *op. cit*., p. 132.

58 MacCarthy, Beara Historical Society lecture, 2 October 1995.

59 *Away to War*, RTÉ Radio, October 1995.

60 Nagai, *op. cit*., p. 79.

11. Liberation

1 *Away to War*, RTÉ Radio interview with Dr Aidan MacCarthy, October 1995.

2 Dr Aidan MacCarthy, *A Doctor's War*, p. 133, The Collins Press, Cork, 2005.

Endnotes

3   Dr Aidan MacCarthy, Beara Historical Society lecture, 2 October 1995.
4   *A Doctor's Sword* documentary interview, Gambit Pictures Ltd, July 2012.
5   Meg Parkes & Geoff Gill, *Captive Memories*, p. 29, Carnegie Publishing, Lancaster, 2015.
6   MacCarthy, Beara Historical Society lecture, 2 October 1995.
7   Takashi Nagai, *The Bells of Nagasaki*, p. 78, Kodansha International, Tokyo, 1994.
8   *Ibid.*, p. 103.
9   *Away to War*, RTÉ Radio, October 1995.
10   *Ibid.*
11   MacCarthy, *op. cit.*, p. 133.
12   *Ibid.* p. 139.
13   MacCarthy, Beara Historical Society lecture, 2 October 1995.
14   MacCarthy, *op. cit.*, p. 140.
15   MacCarthy, Beara Historical Society lecture, 2 October 1995.
16   *Ibid.*
17   *Ibid.*
18   MacCarthy, *op. cit.*, p. 137.
19   *Ibid.*, p. 142.
20   *Ibid.*, p. 141.
21   MacCarthy, Beara Historical Society lecture, 2 October 1995.
22   MacCarthy, *op. cit.*, p. 151.
23   MacCarthy, Beara Historical Society lecture, 2 October 1995.
24   *Ibid.*
25   Gerdie Harrington, *Beara Down Memory Lane*, p. 46, Beara Historical Society, Castletownbere, 2007.
26   MacCarthy, *op. cit.*, p. 154.
27   *Ibid.*, p. 156.
28   *Ibid.*, p. 157.

12. Post-War Life

1   Dr Aidan MacCarthy, *A Doctor's War*, p. 159, The Collins Press, Cork, 2005.
2   *Ibid.*, p. 158.
3   Liberation Questionnaire: WO 344/389, UK National Archives, Kew.
4   Laura Hillenbrand, *Unbroken*, p. 349, Random House, New York City, 2010.
5   *Ibid.*, p. 346.
6   *Ibid.*, p. 347.
7   *Ibid.*, p. 390.
8   Dr Aidan MacCarthy interview, C103FM County Sound, 2 October 1995.

279

9   Author interview with Deirdre O'Brien (Dr MacCarthy's niece), August 2015.

10 *Away to War*, RTÉ Radio interview with Dr Aidan MacCarthy, October 1995.

11 MacCarthy, *op. cit.*, p. 145.

12 *Ibid.*, p. 142.

13 Amy Rozenberg, *Lost and Found Worlds*, p. 68, Trafford Publishing, Bloomington, 2012.

14 http://www.boudewynvanoort.com/1946/02/sone-tribunal/, accessed 28 March 2016.

15 Immediately after the war ended there was worldwide outcry for punishment of the Japanese who had murdered and abused prisoners of war. The war-crimes trials began but new political realities quickly emerged, as the American occupation force oversaw the transition to democracy, the Cold War was beginning. As the fear of communism began to spread in Asia, American leaders saw the necessity of a future alliance with Japan.

    These war-crimes trials became intensely unpopular in Japan and over time the need for justice became secondary to America's security. Within three to four years of the end of the war, the trials of war criminals ceased. The Korean War began in 1950 and this revived the Japanese economy as UN forces used Japan as a logistics and supply hub for the war. In 1951 the Allies and Japan signed the Treaty for Peace ending the occupation. This treaty also waived the right of former POWs and their families to seek compensation from Japan and the companies that had enslaved them (see Laura Hillenbrand, *Unbroken*, p. 390).

16 Author interview with Deirdre O'Brien, August 2015.

17 Dr Aidan MacCarthy, Beara Historical Society lecture, 2 October 1995.

18 Author interview with Brian O'Brien (Dr MacCarthy's nephew), January 2016.

19 *A Doctor's Sword* documentary interview, Gambit Pictures Ltd, July 2013.

20 Author interview with Brian O'Brien, January 2016.

21 *A Doctor's Sword* documentary interview, Gambit Pictures Ltd, July 2013.

22 *Ibid.*

23 *A Doctor's Sword* documentary interview, Gambit Pictures Ltd, July 2010

24 *A Doctor's Sword* documentary interview, Gambit Pictures Ltd, July 2013.

25 Author interview with Brian O'Brien, January 2016.

26 *Cork Examiner*, *c.*1979.

27 *A Doctor's Sword* documentary interview, Gambit Pictures Ltd, July 2010.

28 *Ibid.*

29 *Ibid.*
30 This contrasts with the situation in Germany where even today former Nazis in their nineties are put on trial and convicted.
31 *A Doctor's Sword* documentary interview, Gambit Pictures Ltd, July 2010.
32 Author interview with Brian O'Brien, January 2016.
33 MacCarthy interview, C103FM County Sound.
34 MacCarthy, Beara Historical Society lecture, 2 October 1995.

Epilogue

1 *A Doctor's Sword* documentary interview, Gambit Pictures Ltd, July 2012.
2 The feature film was completed with funding from Aidan's alma mater University College Cork, Cork City Council, Cork County Council Arts Office and the Irish Film Board.
3 When Aidan's nephew Brian was visiting Northwood one summer afternoon. Aidan told him to grab the ladder as he carried a bucket and bags. He was looking after a neighbour's house and he had a key. They spent the afternoon stealing the neighbour's apples and brought them back to Kathleen to make apple pies. He reckoned they wouldn't be missed.
4 Telephone interview with Cicely Glason (Dr MacCarthy's cousin), March 2016.
5 Interview with Brian O'Brien (Dr MacCarthy's nephew), January 2016.
6 *Away to War*, RTÉ Radio interview with Dr Aidan MacCarthy, October 1995.
7 Dr Aidan MacCarthy, Beara Historical Society lecture, 2 October 1995.
8 There are others who survived Dunkirk and were close to Nagasaki city when the atomic bomb was dropped (e.g. Alistair Urquhart). Dr Aidan MacCarthy was just over a mile from the epicentre of the atomic bomb.
9 Dr Aidan MacCarthy interview, C103FM County Sound, 2 October 1995.
10 Dr Aidan MacCarthy, Beara Historical Society lecture, 2 October 1995.
11 *A Doctor's Sword* documentary interview, Gambit Pictures Ltd, July 2013.
12 MacCarthy, Beara Historical Society lecture, 2 October 1995.

Bibliography

Adams, Ken, *Healing in Hell*, Pen & Sword, Barnsley, 2011

Allen, Louis & Wilson, Jean, *Lafcadio Hearn: Japan's Great Interpreter: A New Anthology of His Writings 1894–1904*, Routledge, Abingdon-on-Thames, 1995

Beevor, Antony, *The Second World War*, Little, Brown & Company, New York City, 2014

Craven, Wesley & Cate, James, *The Pacific: Matterhorn to Nagasaki – The Army Air Forces in World War II. Volume V*, University of Chicago Press, Chicago, 1953

Fletcher-Cooke, John, *The Emperor's Guest*, Leo Cooper (publisher), Barnsley, 1994

Forbes, Cameron, *Hellfire*, Pan Macmillan Australia, Sydney, 2005

Gill, Geoff & Parkes, Meg, *Captive Memories*, Carnegie Publishing, Lancaster, 2015

Goetz Holmes, Linda, *Unjust Enrichment*, Stackpole Books, Mechanicsburg, 2000

Harrington, Gerdie, *Beara Down Memory Lane*, Beara Historical Society, Castletownbere, 2007

Hillenbrand, Laura, *Unbroken*, Random House, New York City, 2010

Lamont-Brown, Raymond, *Ships from Hell: Japanese War Crimes on the High Seas*, Sutton Publishing Ltd, Gloucestershire, 2002

MacCarthy, Aidan, *A Doctor's War*, The Collins Press, Cork, 2005

Martin, Margaret (ed.), *Prisoners in Java: Accounts by Allied Prisoners of War in the Far East (1942–1945) Captured in Java*, Hamwic, Southampton, 2007

McGowran, Tom, *Beyond the Bamboo Screen: Scottish Prisoners of War Under the Japanese*, Cualann Press, Dunfermline, 1999

Nagai, Takashi, *The Bells of Nagasaki*, Kodansha International, Tokyo, 1994

O'Kane, Richard, *Clear the Bridge*, Presidio Press, Novato, 1996

Priesman-Bogaardt, Louisa, *Dark Skies Over Paradise*, Trafford Publishing, Bloomington, 2006

283

Rozenberg, Amy, *Lost and Found Worlds*, Trafford Publishing, Bloomington, 2012

Russell, Edward Frederick Langley, Lord Russell of Liverpool, *The Knights of Bushido*, Skyhorse Publishing, New York City, 2008

Sandler, Stanley, *World War II in the Pacific*, Garland Publishing Inc, New York & London, 2001

Smethurst, Richard J., *A Social Basis for Prewar Japanese Militarism: The Army & the Rural Community*, University of California Press, Berkeley, 1974

Stubbs, Les & Pam, *Unsung Heroes of the Royal Air Force*, Tucann Books, Lincoln, 2011

Urquhart, Alistair, *The Forgotten Highlander*, Abacus, London, 2011

Widders, Robert, *The Emperor's Irish Slaves*, The History Press Ireland, Dublin, 2012

Wigmore, Lionel, *The Japanese Thrust*, Australian War Memorial, Canberra, 1968

Williams, Ronald & Frank, *The Jungle Journal: Prisoners of the Japanese in Java 1942–45*, The History Press, Gloucestershire, 2013.

Newspapers and periodicals

History Ireland
The Cork Examiner
The Irish Times
The London Gazette
The Southern Star

Journals

'Atom Bomb Effects', *LIFE Magazine*, 11 March 1946

Joseph, Jennifer, 'POWs Left in the Cold: Compensation Eludes American WWII Slave Labourers for Japanese Companies', *Pepperdine Law Review*, Malibu (California), 29 December 2001

Laurence, William L., 'Eye Witness Account Atomic Bomb Mission Over Nagasaki', US War Department Bureau of Public Relations, 9 September 1945

Linton, Suzannah, 'Rediscovering the War Crimes Trials in Hong Kong, 1946–48', *Melbourne Journal of International Law*, May 2012

Organisations

Clongowes Wood College Archive Office, County Kildare, Ireland
University College Cork, Records Office, Cork, Ireland
University College Cork, Archives, Cork, Ireland

Bibliography

RAF Museum, Cosford, UK
POW Research Organisation, Japan
Liverpool School of Tropical Medicine, UK
Imperial War Museum, London, UK
UK National Archives, Kew, London, UK

Other Sources

A Doctor's Sword documentary interviews, Gary Lennon, Gambit Pictures Ltd,
    July 2010, August 2013, August 2014
C103FM County Sound
Effects of Atomic Bomb on Hiroshima & Nagasaki, US Strategic Bombing Survey
    (Motion Picture)
Telephone interview with Cicely Glason (Aidan MacCarthy's cousin), March
    2016
Dr Aidan MacCarthy, *Beara Historical Society lecture*, October 1994
Dr Aidan MacCarthy, *Beara Historical Society lecture*, 2 October 1995
Dr Aidan MacCarthy, POW camp diary
Dr Aidan MacCarthy, personal archive
Interview with Deirdre O'Brien (Aidan MacCarthy's niece), August 2015
Interview with Brian O'Brien (Aidan MacCarthy's nephew), January 2016
Interviews with Fr Sean O'Shea, Castletownbere, August and November, 2015
Professor Richard Overy, University of Exeter (email, 1 April 2016)
Geoff Gill and Meg Parkes, Liverpool School of Tropical Medicine (email, 6
    March 2016)
Henriette van Raalte (Tjideng survivor), (email, 19 July 2015)
RTÉ Radio Interview, Brian Walsh, Away to War, RTÉ Radio, October 1995
United States Strategic Bombing Survey, Summary Report (Pacific War)
    (Washington: US GPO, 1946), Vol 1, p. 16

Websites

www.aasc.ucla.edu
www.atomicarchive.com
http://atomicbombmuseum.org
www.boudewynvanoort.com
www.flyingbombsandrockets.com
www.hiroshima-spirit.jp
www.historylearningsite.co.uk
www.ioc.u.tokyo.ac.jp
www.mansell.com
http://nagasakipeace.jp
www.peace-museum.pref.okinawa.jp

285

Index

Note: illustrations are indicated by page numbers in **bold**.

Index

Index